A CAPITALISM
for the
PEOPLE

A CAPITALISM
for the
PEOPLE

Recapturing the Lost Genius
of American Prosperity

LUIGI ZINGALES

BASIC BOOKS
A MEMBER OF THE PERSEUS BOOKS GROUP
NEW YORK

Book design by Linda Mark
Text set in New Caledonia

Library of Congress Cataloging-in-Publication Data
Zingales, Luigi.
 A capitalism for the people : recapturing the lost genius of American
prosperity / by Luigi Zingales.
   p. cm.
 Includes bibliographical references and index.
 ISBN 978-0-465-02947-1 (hardcover : alk. paper)—
 ISBN 978-0-465-02952-5 (e-book) 1. United States—Economic
conditions—2009 2. Capitalism—United States. 3. Capitalism—
Moral and ethical aspects—United States. 4. United States—
Economic policy—2009-I. Title.
HC106.84.Z56 2012
330.12'20973—dc2
ISBN 978-0-465-08595-8 (paperback)
                                                    2012011557

10 9 8 7 6 5 4 3 2 1

To my parents, who raised me with a belief in a just world.
Their example and teaching gave me the strength
to fight to transform their dream into reality.

CONTENTS

vii

FOREWORD TO
THE PAPERBACK EDITION

I N THE LAST FEW YEARS THE ECONOMIC POLICY DEBATE IN Washington and the nation at large has been dominated by current events: the unemployment crisis, the Euro crisis, the partisan squabble over the debt ceiling in fall 2013. Much less attention has been dedicated to the fundamentals of the US economy. Does our system work? Does it provide enough incentives to enhance the prosperity of the American people? Does it generate opportunities for everyone?

Most Americans today are likely to respond negatively to all these questions and for good reason: the evidence supports their pessimistic view. Yet despite this generalized dissatisfaction, the mainstream political debate ignores these questions. The reason is simple: neither of the two main political parties can provide a satisfactory response. The traditional Left and Right division has lost much of its meaning. Is it a Right or a Left policy to tax heavily the young to protect the privileges of the old? Is it a Right or a Left policy to eliminate the subsidies to industry and farming? Is it a Right or a Left policy to reduce the obstacles to competition created by the heavy lobbying of large incumbent firms?

This book was written not only to expose what it is not working in America, but also to provide a new direction on how to fix it. It was written to change the nature of the political conversation in America from an excessive focus on partisan policies aimed at addressing short-term problems to proper attention to the fundamental choices that determine the future of America. Since the time this book was written, the need for such a change in the political discourse has only grown. The unique brand of American capitalism—which in the last sixty years has created tens of million jobs, lifted out of poverty millions of immigrants, and inspired the world over—seems to be losing its luster, slowly degenerating into a form of crony capitalism that undermines both our prosperity and our democracy.

Americans who are lucky enough to have been born in this country may fail to appreciate how different American capitalism has been from the various flavors of it prevailing in most of the world. At its best, American capitalism has been a fiercely competitive system, where the state ensured that the playing field remained level. It is a meritocratic system where everyone is offered an opportunity to succeed. It is a fully democratic system that guarantees that this engine of growth works for everyone's benefit. In the great words of Abraham Lincoln: "Nowhere in the world is presented a government of so much liberty and equality. To the humblest and poorest amongst us are held out the highest privileges and positions. The present moment finds me at the White House, yet there is as good a chance for your children as there was for my father's."[1]

I believe that only an immigrant like myself can fully appreciate how rare this brand of capitalism is. In much of the world the rule of the day is a dangerous marriage between an economic elite, made politically powerful by their wealth, and a political elite, made economically powerful by an overly intrusive government. This Faustian pact between powerful politicians and powerful businesspeople reshapes the playing field to the benefit of the incumbents, creating space for corruption and cronyism. It suffocates the creative spirit that generates growth. It denies to the have-nots a chance to succeed. It undermines the very values this great nation was built upon. If one wants to get a glimpse of where this policy leads, one has to look no further than my native country, where a spiral of low (even negative) growth and excessive debt are leading the country to a collapse.

The secret ingredient of this unique brand of "capitalism for the people" has been a balance between the redistributive tendencies of a democratic system and the plutocratic risks of an autocratic capitalism. By its very nature, a democratic system tends to redistribute wealth from the few to the many—even at the cost of violating property rights and thus possibly killing incentives to create wealth. By contrast, an autocratic capitalism tends to protect the interests of few incumbents at the expense of the hoi polloi, even at the cost of suffocating competition, which is the ultimate source of generalized prosperity. Unfortunately, once they begin, both these degenerations trigger a negative spiral from which it is difficult to emerge. Once a government has developed a reputation for expropriating its citizens there is little cost in living up to that reputation because the risk of it has been built into the expectations. So expropriation leads to more expropriation. Similarly, lack of competition leads to nepotism and cronyism because, in the absence of fierce competition, incumbent firms can afford to appoint their friends and still survive. Once an incompetent appointee finds himself in a powerful position, he tends to hire only subordinates of equal or lower quality, because talented people pose a threat to him. After a few years, a firm's human capital becomes so eroded that it is not able to compete without some form of protection. The more protection it gains from the government, the greater the possibility of cronyism, which in turn makes protection even more necessary.

For this reason, it is very important to stop this degeneration early on. As an immigrant from Italy, I have seen the tragic end to this devolution and am therefore sensitive to early signs. But the signs in the United States are becoming increasingly clear. More money is made on K Street than on Main Street. Young entrepreneurs develop a lobbying strategy before a business one. Even innovative Silicon Valley firms find the need to develop their lobbying department. Consequently, between the years 2000 and 2010 lobbying expenses more than doubled, rising from $1.56 billion to $3.55 billion.[2] In the meantime, the total cost of the presidential campaign, which was "only" $1.4 billion in 2000 rose to $2.6 billion in 2012, and the cost of all the congressional races leaped from $1.7 billion in 2000 to $3.7 billion in 2012.[3]

Lobbying does not involve political donations alone. As a report from the US House Committee on Oversight showed, infamous mortgage lender Countrywide offered cut-rate mortgages to elected officials as a lobbying tool. Congressional members, staffers, and even judges received fast loan processing and, most importantly, preferential terms. In exchange for what? Although the committee cannot prove any quid pro quo, these statistics suggest an obvious benefit: influence.[4]

Former Senator Chris Dodd, who was for many years the chairman of the Senate Banking Committee, received several discounted loans from Countrywide. Coincidentally, in June 2008 Dodd proposed a housing bailout program that would have helped lenders like Countrywide. Similar VIP treatment was given to Kent Conrad, chairman of the Senate Budget Committee.

From the industry's point of view, this was money well spent. The financial industry, the largest political fund contributor, survived untouched in the aftermath of the 2008 financial crisis. Although CEOs, corporate presidents, directors, and officers were prosecuted and convicted after the savings and loan crisis, they were not after the 2008 financial crisis. The Justice Department no longer keeps score of boardroom prosecutions because—as a commentator said—"it would be really embarrassing."[5]

Similarly, the pharmaceutical industry, the second largest political contributor, succeeded in obtaining what it wanted: preventing free trade in drugs. As recent revelations uncovered, President Obama, the same Obama who as a candidate denounced the excessive role played by the pharmaceutical industry in the 2003 Medicare Modernization Act, bought off the consensus of big pharmaceutical companies to his Affordable Care Act by suppressing free trade in the drug market. Far from being ashamed of this, many of his fellow Democrats saw in this alliance with big business a key strategy to win elections.[6] Unfortunately, the Republican Party has done even worse: defending indefensible farm subsidies to rich farmers while at the same time cutting food stamps for the poor in the name of budgetary considerations.

Not surprisingly, as capitalism becomes more cronyistic and corrupt, popular resentment against it rises; the economic pie does not grow fast enough and its division is perceived as increasingly unfair. Yet there is an additional element that contributes to the rising populism: the increasing tightness of the fiscal budget. Since World War II, Western democracies have maintained a high degree of consensus thanks to relatively high real GDP growth rates and little government budget constraint. When per capita GDP doubles every ten years, even a repressive regime like that in China can enjoy wide support. Western governments have maintained consensus as growth rates have slowed by borrowing against the future. These structural deficits, which shift the burden of repayment to future generations, are made possible by positive population growth and real GDP growth rates. Debt-financed deficits do not really burden future generations when future generations are richer and more numerous: they will hardly feel the burden. But when the population curve starts going negative and real GDP stalls, then the get-now-pay-later game ends. In fact, it sometimes starts to work in reverse when the current generation has to start repaying the debt past ones dumped on them.

Greece, Portugal, and Italy now find themselves in this situation, and most Western democracies (including Japan) will be there soon. In this context traditional Left-leaning policies lose their appeal: there is no money to spend. And if key social programs have to be preserved, the only solution is taxation, taxation, taxation. Facing this bleak prospect, voters are lured by dangerous forms of Left-leaning or Right-leaning populism. In the last Greek election 45 percent of voters supported radical extremist parties. In Italy a majority did, including the 25 percent of voters who were for a new anti-establishment party run by a professional stand-up comedian. These results are a clear sign of a crisis that is slowly affecting all Western European democracies and starting to show its ugly head in the States.

As these premises, which I make clear in the book, increasingly show themselves to be true, my main thesis becomes even more valid today than when the book was first published. Instead of rejecting these populist movements, we should understand them and so help to direct their destructive force toward the crony component of capitalism, not capitalism itself.

This book provides a road map for doing so. It does not lay out a platform for the next election, but rather a coherent set of policies for the next twenty years. I have to admit that in the current political environment most of my proposals have no chance of succeeding. The lack of immediate success, however, does not mean these policies are not useful. In fact, their small chance of success today almost proves their validity. In the current political environment proposals need a powerful interest group to advocate for them. The easiest way to obtain this support is to tilt a proposal so as to benefit one powerful group at the expense of everybody else. Proposals like mine, which try to distribute fairly both benefits and costs, stand the least chance of being adopted. Indeed, this political game is so well known that many economists already design their proposals with the aim of subtracting resources form the uninformed many to give to the informed few—thereby transforming themselves from impartial advisers to advocates of vested interests. Not I.

If my proposals are not easily implementable today, are they irrelevant? I do not think so. Rome wasn't built in a day, as the saying goes, and the radical transformation I propose cannot take place overnight either. Yet it is important to devise a plan to fix the perpetual problems we face. My plan, as originally laid out in *A Capitalism for the People*, may not be an easy path to recovery but it is a coherent one.

I am confident that in the long term good ideas prevail over entrenched interests, over the tyranny of the status quo, over less valid ideas. Only time will tell if the solutions I lay out in this book are able to solve all our problems. I certainly hope so. But I want my ideas to be evaluated on their merit, not on whether the current political environment deems them feasible. After all, if good ideas cannot be implemented in the current political environment, it is probably because the political environment needs to be changed, not the ideas.

I hope this book provides an inspiration on changing that environment.

PREFACE

MERICANS ARE ANGRY. THEY ARE ANGRY AT BANKERS, who contributed to the financial crisis but didn't pay for it. They are angry at the ineffectual political establishment, which blamed the bankers but deserved at least as much blame for failing to rein them in. They are angry at an economic system that makes the rich richer and leaves the poor behind. They are angry because the ideal of "a government of the people, by the people, for the people" is at risk of perishing from the earth.

This anger has surfaced in many spontaneous movements: the demonstrations in front of executives' houses, the activism of the Tea Party, the Occupy movement. Though these movements are united in their opposition to the status quo, one searches in vain among their writings and platforms for a workable alternative. While the Tea Party has successfully channeled the anger against government, it has failed to do so for the resentment against bankers. While the Occupy movement proclaims that it fights for the 99 percent, it has been unable to figure out *how* to conduct that fight.

What can I bring to this discussion? In theory, I am one of "them": a professor of finance at a leading university and fortunate enough to be in the top 1 percent of the income distribution. Yet I am angry, too, and scared. Angry because the idea of free markets has been increasingly taken over by entrenched business interests, fundamentally altering the equilibrium of American democracy. Scared that Americans, in their justifiable anger about the way things have gone, will choose a path that brings an end to American capitalism as we know it. For all its defects, that capitalist system offers the best hope for the most people. It is a model that defenders of freedom all over the world look to for guidance.

While my academic training gives me a special understanding of American capitalism (including what is wrong with it), it's another part of my experience that drove me to write this book. I am an immigrant to the United States. I came here in 1988 from Italy because I was trying to escape a system that was fundamentally unfair. Italy invented the term *nepotism* and perfected the concept of cronyism, and it still lives by both. You are promoted based on whom you know, not what you know. Americans were recently exposed to the corruption of the Italian system by Silvio Berlusconi, the tycoon-turned-politician who ran the country for nearly two decades. While Berlusconi represented an extreme, even by Italian standards, he was not an accident but the product of a degenerate system. I emigrated to the United States because I realized that it offered me an inestimably brighter future than my native country. And when I got to America in 1988, I wasn't disappointed; I experienced for the first time the inebriating feeling that any goal was within my reach. I had finally arrived in a country where the limits to my dreams were set only by my abilities, not by the people I knew.

Wherever you stand on the political spectrum, whether you're a conservative Republican or a liberal Democrat or somewhere in between, I would gently suggest that you have no idea what it's like to live in a country where there is virtually no meritocracy and competition is considered a sin. Even emergency-room doctors in Italy are promoted on the basis of political affiliation instead of ability. Young people, rather than being told to study, are urged to "carry the bag" (*fare il portaborse*) for powerful people, in the hope of getting back some favors. Mothers push their daughters into the arms of the rich and powerful, seeing it as the only avenue of social promotion. The talent selection process is so broken that you easily find very smart people employed in very menial jobs and very mediocre people in powerful positions. Until 1990, companies in Italy could openly and legally collude to defraud their customers; they still collude today, but they are less open about it. The best way to get rich is to be politically connected and receive a government contract.

The only protesters against this system came from the radical Left, which was less interested in changing the system than in replacing it with a socialist one. In a country full of privileges based on birth, the Left, instead of fighting for equality of starting points, fought to eliminate all selection mechanisms, viewing them as discriminatory against the have-nots. One consequence of this was that universities were not selective in admissions. Regardless of your grades, you could get into any college you wanted, forcing all colleges toward lower standards. The unintended consequence of this egalitarianism was that it produced an undifferentiated mass of mostly ignorant graduates. Companies seeking workers resorted to hiring on the basis of the only system that works in the absence of credible sorting: personal connections.

While in college in Italy, I developed an interest in economics and hoped to study it at the graduate level and to become an academic. For the average college graduate in the United States, such a goal might require practicing for the GREs and analyzing various rankings to figure out what the best graduate programs were. Not in Italy. Many people, including my father, told me that if I wanted to have a university career, I had to pay my dues to some local professor—to carry his bag—which meant essentially working for free not only on his academic projects but also on his consulting ones. I decided instead to apply to universities in the United States. But even that plan did not seem promising, because I was unable to secure a letter of recommendation from the most famous professor at my college. When I had asked him to supervise my undergraduate thesis, he had declined, saying that he lacked the time—despite my excellent grades, and despite the fact that he had found the time to supervise a classmate of mine, who had the support of an influential person. When I later approached this professor for a recommendation, his secretary told me that he wrote letters only for the people he had advised. Thus, I was out of luck. I studied extra hard for the admissions tests, however, and I made it into MIT. In spite of my less than positive experience, I considered returning to Italy upon receiving my PhD from MIT. At the very time the University of Chicago was hiring me, an Italian professor asked me to withdraw my application from national competition for Associate Professor in Italy. I knew it was a long shot, but if I made it in Chicago as an assistant could I at least try to compete for a position as an associate in Italy? The worst that could happen to me was that my application would be discarded, right? No. I was told that they would write a terrible report on me that would stay on my record forever. The real reason—I suspect—was that in spite of my young age I had a better record than the local candidate who had paid his dues (after all, my father was right). They did not want me in the race, so they resorted to not-so-veiled threats.

I realized Italy was not for me. After six years, I received tenure at the University of Chicago. In Italy, the process would have taken more than twice as long. I was able to build a career without needing to trade on family connections—or, worse, flattering people just because they had seniority. I owe more than my success to this country: I owe my life. I would not have survived the humiliations and frustrations of the Italian system.

And so, until the financial crisis of 2008, I was fairly disengaged from the American political debate. With all its defects, the US system looked so much better than the Italian one that I was not inclined to do much more than appreciate my good fortune. I felt that I could add more by being involved in the public square in my home country, where the problems are so much greater and the system hobbles the few competent people it hasn't driven away.

But it wasn't long after arriving in the United States that I began to notice things that felt more like home—as if I were watching a movie I'd seen before. The first case was the 1998 rescue of the largest hedge fund of the time: Long Term Capital Management (LTCM). Founded by genius "quants," the fund was actually playing fairly simple arbitrage strategies, but it had borrowed so heavily that when a few of those strategies went wrong, the fund blew up. At the time, Warren Buffett offered to rescue LTCM, though in a manner that would have cost its owners their entire investment. Instead of allowing that to happen, the Fed stepped in and coordinated a rescue effort that proved more generous to LTCM's investors and managers—a group that happened to include David Mullins, former vice chairman of the Fed. Unlike many to come, this Fed-brokered deal cost American taxpayers nothing. But the Fed had used moral suasion to alter the normal market rules—worse yet, for a friend. As the *Financial Times* wrote at the time, this was a case of crony capitalism, American-style.

Then came the ascent of George W. Bush, scion of a former president. Under him, the Republican Party moved away from the promarket principles espoused by Ronald Reagan and became increasingly pro–big business, placing a tariff on imported steel in 2002 to protect American manufacturers, for example, and offering corporations special rates to repatriate their profits. At the same time, Democrats were becoming cozier with big-business interests, launching "public-private partnerships," a way to suck money from the government while pretending to do good.

By the time the financial crisis hit in 2008, I felt I had something to contribute to the US public debate. As Austrian-born economist Friedrich Hayek put it in the introduction to his 1944 book *The Road to Serfdom:* "By moving from one country to another, one may sometimes twice watch similar phases of intellectual development." What I was watching was the transformation of American finance into an Italian-style crony-capitalist system. Indeed, in one way the American situation is worse, since Americans, unlike Italians, cannot place blame on one bad guy. Berlusconi is *us.* Through our retirement funds and stock investments, *we* are the owners of the very companies that lobby to grab our tax money and dominate our political life.

At stake is not just our money but our freedom. Cronyism represses freedom of speech, eliminates the incentive to study, and jeopardizes career opportunities. It has robbed my home country of much of its potential for economic growth. I do not want it to rob the United States as well.

This is neither an academic book nor a trendy summary of the latest economic findings. Rather, it is a description of the problems of the American economic system and a passionate call for change—a call coming from a strong believer in the free-market system, who loves America for what it has always stood for: freedom in the pursuit of happiness.

Fortunately, America has in its DNA the ability to reform itself. Unlike the citizens of most other countries, Americans share a strong belief in the power of competition. As I shall explain in this book, competition is an enormous source for good. To improve the economic system, we need more competition, not less. Unlike many other countries, where populism means demagogy and autocratic dictators, America has a positive populist tradition of protecting the powerless. As I shall explain, this populist vein has greatly contributed to making American capitalism better than all other forms of capitalism—and it can continue to do so. *Capitalism for the People* is not an oxymoron but a hope: the hope that by merging the best of America's populist tradition with its strong promarket orientation, we can fight the degeneration of our system.

INTRODUCTION

HAVE YOU EVER RECEIVED A DEATH THREAT? IN THE United States death threats are very uncommon, at least among the law-abiding. Yet a friend of mine actually received one. His transgression? He worked as a consultant for the now-infamous insurance giant American International Group before the 2008 financial crisis. AIG had been so pleased with his performance in devising a mathematical risk model that it offered him a noncompete contract: a sum of money meant to compensate him for agreeing not to move directly to another company or to start his own hedge fund. This is a standard corporate practice that allows companies to retain talent, but unfortunately for my friend, his payment under the agreement was to be made at the end of 2008—just after the biggest government bailout in financial history, with the US government lending $223 billion to AIG at favorable conditions to prevent it from failing. If you find it difficult to appreciate the magnitude of this bailout, consider that it was as if every household in the country had lent AIG $2,000. Thus, few were surprised by the public anger that exploded after the revelation that the insurer, despite its catastrophic performance, had paid $165 million in bonuses to its top executives.

My friend's noncompete contract was one of those bonuses. Even before the scandal, he had received several death threats when a newspaper mentioned that he had worked for the financial-products division of AIG. Now he was terrified that his name might appear in the paper as one of the recipients of the reviled bonuses. Though he had no legal obligation to do so, he returned the money to the company, hoping that the gesture might keep his name from being published. Fearing for the safety of his wife and his two teenaged daughters, he also began preparing an evacuation plan for them.

How do you feel about this story? In principle you doubtless think it's wrong to terrorize someone like this, no matter what he's done. But I would bet that, if you're like most Americans right now, at least part of you thinks my friend got what he deserved—especially when I tell you that he was in charge of calculating the risk underlying the credit-default swaps underwritten by AIG. Many of you would consider irrelevant the fact that his contract was not subject to performance clauses. After all, he was part of a company that wrought untold economic havoc on the country. The implications of this story—and of our feeling that the system is rigged—go well beyond the fortunes of any one man or company. Historically, respect for property rights, the sacredness of contracts, and faith in the free-market economy have greatly benefited America. They brought prosperity not only to the lucky people who were born in this country but also to the millions of immigrants who came here from all over the world, attracted by American freedom and opportunities.

But our faith in free markets is being eroded. In the past decade, the real income of the median family dropped by 7 percent.[1] The median male in his twenties makes 19 percent less (in real terms) today than his father made at the same age, even when he is lucky enough to be employed.[2] Today many more young people are unemployed. Looking at the statistics, we find that the chances of an ascent from rags to riches are shrinking, undermining the American Dream. In this context, many people are wondering whether the sacredness of contracts is just a fig leaf to protect the interests of the wealthy at the expense of taxpayers. After all, had the government not intervened, AIG would have defaulted, and those bonuses, like the claim of other AIG creditors, would have yielded only cents on the dollar. Why, then, should they be honored in full with our money? Heads they win, tail we lose. Is this what the free-market system is all about?

Since most of the government-lent money was eventually returned, one might have expected these problems to subside. Yet in the fall of 2011, three years after the bailout, thousands of protesters were camping in New York's Zuccotti Park (and many other parks around America) to express their anger. And though the protesters may not have been representative of society at large, they earned at least a degree of public support. According to a December 2011 Pew Research Center survey, more Americans agreed than disagreed with the concerns the protesters raised (by a 48 to 30 percent margin), though they did not approve of the ways the protest was being conducted. Some of the themes of the protest have even broader support. For instance, 61 percent of Americans now think "the economic system in this country unfairly favors the wealthy," and 77 percent believe that "a few rich people and corporations have too much power in this country."[3] For defenders of American-style capitalism, these are troubling numbers.

AMERICAN EXCEPTIONALISM

Most of the Italian economists I know who immigrated to this country—and there are many—came to the United States as extreme leftists, in some cases as active communists. They came here despite their dislike of the US system, because the best universities were here. And I've noticed that once they moved to the United States, they tended over time to become free-marketeers. In part, they "saw the light" thanks to the economic knowledge they accumulated. But even more important, I think, is their firsthand realization that many of the free-market benefits that they study in theory actually hold true in this country. Rewards are more likely to be allocated on the basis of merit here than on the basis of political connections. Competition provides people with better products at lower prices. And the low barriers to entry—on average it takes 4 days to start a business in the US, versus 26 in Japan, 62 in Italy, and 128 in Indonesia[4]—promote the emergence of new ideas and provide opportunities for social mobility.

As I discuss in the chapter that follows, a fortunate combination of historical, geographic, cultural, and institutional factors made American capitalism different from the versions of capitalism prevailing elsewhere in the world. For one thing, in America, democracy predated industrialization (at least in the form of the second industrial revolution, which brought us large and powerful corporations). Accordingly, when these corporations became dominant at the end of the nineteenth century, Americans had a good tradition to appeal to in order to limit their political influence. The Sherman Antitrust Act, passed in 1890, was more the result of a popular revolt against the political corruption perpetrated by large corporations than an attempt to reduce the economic distortion associated with monopolies, which is how it is often interpreted.

American capitalism also developed at a time when the government share of GDP was minuscule. As a result, entrepreneurs' only route to success was to win in the marketplace, because the penniless government had little to offer. This is very different from the situation faced by latecomer industrial powers, such as the Asian tigers (Hong Kong, Singapore, South Korea, and Taiwan), where capitalism was in significant part a creation of the state and where, from the very beginning, industrial policy favored the politically connected. A capitalism that lets people get rich through political connections, not through succeeding in the marketplace, is a capitalism that feels unfair and corrupt to many people.

Another distinguishing feature of American capitalism is that it arose relatively untouched by foreign influence. In France, Brazil, and even Canada, the fear of economic dominance by American firms created an excuse to grant privileges and protection to the local business elites—often in the name of patriotism. This, too, fostered cronyism.

Finally, the United States benefited from a Protestant ethic that saw wealth as a just reward for hard work, rather than as a gift of luck or even as a sin. In a study focusing on international comparisons, participants were asked to express their degree of relative support for the statement "We need larger income differences as incentives for individual effort" and its opposite, "Income should be made more equal." Protestants predominantly supported the first, while Catholics and especially Muslims supported the second.[5]

For all these reasons, the United States fostered a culture that believed in the possibility and promise of economic freedom and open competition. The much-contested notion that hard work will pay off is still an essential part of how most Americans think about life. This attitude has reduced antimarket pressures in the United States and helped to make capitalism popular and secure here. The diffused prosperity generated by American capitalism consolidated the popular support.

A CRISIS OF CONFIDENCE IN CAPITALISM

Over time, many of these factors have changed. The fraction of GDP controlled by the government increased more than sevenfold between 1900 and 2005, while government influence increased even more through ever-expanding regulation. Business has learned to work with this increased government presence in the economy and turn it to its own advantage. Business, for example, did not fight the 2009 stimulus package; it fought to grab the biggest share.

Indeed, the corporate world has become ever more skillful in milking money from the government. Only in the 1980s did Congress start to pick winners and losers by earmarking funds for specific business recipients. As we will see in Chapter 5, the growth in these earmarks, once it started, was enormous. Intensifying this growth has been the widely accepted—and misguided—view that public funds can promote private-sector growth in the form of "public-private partnerships." All of this has helped increase the power of business interests over the market. And as business started to control more of the political agenda, popular support for the free-market system began to decline.

That popular support had also been based, as noted above, on the diffused benefits associated with the system and the perception that it was fair. Regrettably, as Chapter 2 will show, these strengths, too, have started to fade. The slow growth and decreased mobility of the last decade have damaged the image of the free market as a creator of prosperity for everyone. The hundreds of millions of taxpayer dollars awarded for disastrous economic performance have in turn weakened the sense of the fairness of the system.

THE BETRAYAL OF THE ELITE

One of the greatest achievements of capitalism was to liberate writers from the yoke of political servitude. With a market for books, intellectuals could freely and profitably write for a large public, not just for their rich patrons. This process has worked well for generalist intellectuals but less so for more specialized ones: nuclear engineers rarely argue against nuclear plants—and financial economists rarely argue against financial derivatives. Part of the reason for specialists' partisanship toward their own discipline derives from a selection process in which only those who are passionate about a field, and are therefore likely to become its advocates, choose to specialize in it in the first place. But this tendency can also result from what economists call *natural capture due to specialization.* In this context, the term *capture* refers to any situation in which a person or an agency in charge of regulating or evaluating a group of firms ends up advancing the *firms'* interests. The more specialized my human capital is, the smaller the market for my ideas is. If I were a nuclear engineer I would find it difficult to make a living writing popular books about nuclear energy. The most profitable use of my talents would be to work for a nuclear power company. Thus, the value of my human capital would severely depreciate if I spoke against nuclear plants. Jeffrey Wigand, the former head of research and development at the Brown & Williamson Tobacco Corporation who exposed the practices of the tobacco industry, went from a $300,000 job to a $30,000 one.

The fewer potential employers are present in an area of expertise, the less free and independent the specialized technicians are. This phenomenon is well established in newspapers and magazines. The *Wall Street Journal* and the *New York Times* are more objective in giving mutual funds advice than more specialized magazines, because they rely on a broad set of advertisers, while specialized magazines are heavily dependent on a few that they cannot afford to alienate.[6] The problem, however, is not limited to magazines but is spread across every profession: the most competent are also the least objective, because the most competent tend to be the most specialized, with a small potential set of employers they are afraid to alienate. This problem creates a detachment between ordinary people and experts, which fuels mistrust.

Consciously or subconsciously, capture has always existed. Yet in recent years, several trends have contributed to make it much more severe. The first trend is increased specialization. At the beginning of the twentieth century a doctor could easily span the entire knowledge in medicine. Today she can barely keep up with the articles and the discoveries in a sub-subfield. This extreme specialization has increased the influence of business over ideas—so much so that, according to a former editor of the *British Medical Journal,* "in some medical specialties it is impossible to find anybody who does not have a conflict of interest."[7]

The second trend is an increased concentration of industry. For many years, Fannie Mae and Freddie Mac, the two mortgage giants, were able to capture, deprive of data, or cajole any researcher who tried to challenge their methods. They were so rich and influential that opposing them was extremely bruising. Similarly, large financial conglomerates can dominate the intellectual debate by capturing experts and dictate the political agenda by lobbying.

To appreciate how commanding their power can be, consider the reform effort that followed the 2008 financial crisis. From the beginning of the process, large banks made it clear that they wanted to be regulated by the Federal Reserve. The reason wasn't that the Fed had the best record in solving problems or that it was the most logical regulator (there is a potential conflict of interest between supervising banks for stability purposes and protecting consumers). Rather, it was that the Fed was already influenced by the large banks, which choose the board of the New York Fed and provide much of the information needed by the Fed to operate. Few objected to the proposal, perhaps because banking experts who want to consult or work in the banking world, whether on the private-sector side or the government side, have to deal with the large banks or the Fed (or both). Between the lobbyists and friends of the Fed and the lobbyists and friends of the large banks, the debate was ruled by the theme that the Fed, in spite of its major past regulatory mistakes (such as its failure to clamp down on mortgage lending standards before the crisis) was the best agency to supervise the banks. The 2010 Dodd-Frank Act—unsurprisingly, in my view—handed this responsibility to the Fed.

TIME FOR POPULISM

If one were to enumerate the key factors that are predictive of populist movements, income inequality, a struggling middle class, and distrust of elites would top the list. All these elements are present in today's America. The Tea Party and Occupy movements are just the beginning. Some form of populism is inevitable. The only question is: Which form?

Most populist movements have been characterized by some desire for wealth redistribution. Yet populism really becomes a threat to the survival of the free-enterprise system when markets lose legitimacy as a way of allocating rewards—in other words, when the system looks unfair to growing numbers of people. When 77 percent of Americans believe that there is too much power in the hands of a few rich people and large corporations, and when voters lose confidence in the economic system because they perceive it as corrupt, then the sanctity of private property becomes threatened as well. And when property rights are not protected, the survival of the free-market system itself is in doubt.

In response to the uncertainty stemming from today's populist backlash, companies have begun to demand special privileges and investment guarantees. Witness the Public-Private Investment Program announced in March 2009 by Treasury secretary Timothy Geithner, in which major private investors essentially received a subsidy of $2 for every dollar they put in. Such privileges and guarantees stoke the public anger that generated the populist backlash in the first place by confirming the sense that government and large-market players are cooperating at the expense of the taxpayers and the small investors. Then, to avoid being linked in the public mind with the companies they are trying to help, politicians encourage and even take part in the populist assault. No longer certain they can count on contracts and the rule of law, legitimate investors then grow scarce. This, in turn, leaves troubled businesses little recourse but to seek government assistance, thereby reinforcing crony capitalism. I saw this happen in Italy: a vicious cycle from which it is difficult to escape.

Yet even in the presence of strong populist tensions, this cycle is not inevitable. In the late nineteenth century, as Chapter 7 will describe, a reduction in transportation costs spurred a globalization process that is similar to the current one, leaving many middle-class Americans feeling squeezed and certain businesses disproportionately powerful. The goal of the muscular populist movement that emerged in response to these events, however, wasn't to destroy capitalism but to contain that disproportionate power. While the resulting Populist Party failed to achieve any major electoral victory, its platform and its requests greatly influenced a host of Theodore Roosevelt's reforms—from antitrust to accounting transparency, from antifraud to a less concentrated financial system—that helped establish a new balance of power allowing capitalism to work effectively in the United States. Can we now channel populist anger into fighting crony capitalism and corrupt elites instead of destroying the free-market system?

A CALL FOR CHANGE

The time to act is now, before the United States follows either the South European crony capitalism system or the South American one into long-term decline. What is necessary is nothing less than a rethinking of traditional political categories. Traditionally, America's political spectrum was divided between a probusiness side, which understood economic incentives and wanted to grow by playing on those incentives, and an antibusiness side, which, to quote Churchill, saw business as either a "predatory target to be shot" or a "cow to be milked."

As these ideological differences have begun to diminish, both sides have reached a new agreement about who is the cow to be milked: the taxpayers. Indeed, both sides are happy to endorse the marriage of business and government. The real divide is between those who have bought into this perverse union and those who have not. Among the latter, the vast majority come from the extreme Left, who continue to see business as a predator to be shot. Promarket politicians and intellectuals who are mindful of the excessive power that big business is gaining are rarer than they should be. Yet a majority of Americans recognize that big business and the free market are very different things. According to a survey conducted as part of the Chicago Booth/Kellogg School Trust Index, which I help direct, 53 percent of Americans agreed with the statement "The free market is the best system to generate wealth," whereas 28 percent were neutral and 19 percent disagreed. Similarly, 51 percent of Americans agreed with the statement "Big business distorts the functioning of markets to its own advantage," while 30 percent were neutral and 18 percent disagreed. In short, most Americans believe in the power of markets but are disturbed by the influence of big business.

It is for that majority that I have written this book. It is a mostly silent majority—one that seeks a promarket rather than probusiness agenda. I am also addressing two recent populist movements at the opposite ends of the political spectrum: the Tea Party and the Occupy movement. Paradoxically, these movements have much in common. Each is anti-elite, and each is fighting a Leviathan (the government in the Tea Party's case and bailout-addicted big business in the case of Occupy). Many people do not understand that these Leviathans are two faces of the same coin. The problem is not big business per se but monopolistic and politically powerful business; it is not government per se but intrusive and corrupt government. Is Fannie Mae inefficient because it is a large monopolistic company or because it is a state-sponsored enterprise? The answer is that it is both.

When the private sector fails, it is often because the government intervened with some subsidy or granted it some special monopoly power. When the government fails, it is often because private interests captured it. Does the blame lie with the government or with the private sector? Neither, as these failures are the fault of a bad system: a crony system.

A PROMARKET POPULIST AGENDA

The aim of this book, however, is not just to create awareness about the cancer of crony capitalism in America but to outline an agenda for fighting it before it metastasizes. It is an agenda that, while true to America's capitalist spirit, also incorporates the best of its populist tradition.

At the beginning of the twentieth century, the Progressive Era response to the insurgence of crony capitalism was to increase the regulatory power of the state. The agenda I develop in Chapters 8 to 15 fully recognizes that all too often the state is part of the problem rather than part of the solution. While I am not always against regulation (to function properly, markets need rules), I am fully aware that most of the time rules are designed to protect the incumbents and discourage entry, thus damaging competition.

My agenda instead focuses on the power of competition. It is only from competition among conflicting economic interests that we improve everybody's welfare. It is only from competition among opposing political interests that we gain intellectual freedom.

Lack of competition and the distortions created by government subsidies are the primary causes of all the problems we face in the economy today, including the declining real income of middle-class America. My proposals aim at harnessing the power of competition, not only in the economic sphere but also in the political, cultural, and legal spheres. It is from competition among greedy lawyers that powerless people are legally protected; it is from competition among academics and journalists in search of fame that political and economic powers become accountable.

For this competition to work its wonder in these areas, however, data need to be available. The twentieth century was characterized by ideologies. The twenty-first century will be characterized by data analysis. Paraphrasing legendary journalist Joseph Pulitzer I would say that when data are available there is no crime, no dodge, no swindle that can survive a good analysis.

Competition does not work, however, when legal protection is weak. When shareholders are not well protected, competition favors the most crooked managers, not the best ones. When investors are ignorant, competition favors the biggest swindlers, not the best money managers. When customers are poorly informed, competition induces firms to exploit this ignorance rather than to improve efficiency.

For this reason, I recognize the importance of rules. But I advocate few and simple rules, which have several advantages. They make it more difficult to target specific interests, reducing the incentives to lobby. They minimize the number of professionals dedicated to interpreting and manipulating the rules, improving the efficiency of the economic system. They are easier for voters to monitor, which prevents or at least minimizes capture by special interests and favors accountability. Last but not least, simple rules are necessarily rough, limiting their use to the cases where they are really necessary. As President Theodore Roosevelt used to say, "It is difficult to make our material condition better by the best law, but it is easy enough to ruin it by bad laws."

The law, however, is not the only solution. We need sound social norms that promote the long-term survival of the capitalist system. Opportunistic behavior undermines the viability of American capitalism. It is incumbent upon all of us who believe in free markets to support the norms that facilitate economic interaction and punish those who take advantage of the system.

PART ONE

THE PROBLEM

THE NIGHT I ARRIVED IN THE UNITED STATES OF AMERICA FOR the first time, I remember two distinct feelings. The first was the inebriating sense of feeling in control I described earlier—that any goal was within my reach. But with this power also came a certain fear. Living in a corrupt system, I could always blame the system for my own failures—even the ones that were my responsibility. Now, lacking any scapegoat, I could only blame myself, like an acrobat working without a safety net.

Privileged though my experience has been (I came by plane and my luggage was not made of cardboard), it mimics that of millions of immigrants who have come to the United States attracted by its unique appeal. What makes America so special is not just its size, beauty, and richness but—most important of all—its freedom.

When a few disgruntled British emigrants decided to find their own path to the pursuit of happiness, they set in motion the most successful social experiment in human history. The Founding Fathers not only established a government of the people, by the people, and for the people; in spite of all the government's limitations, they also created an economic system of the people, by the people, and for the people. In contrast to the rest of the world, where capitalism is too often the creature of a rich elite who saw an opportunity to become richer, America's brand of capitalism has survived and thrived because of a unique set of circumstances: a government attentive to the interests of ordinary people, a set of values that have made accumulation of wealth a moral responsibility rather than an end in itself, and a belief that the system provides opportunities for all. Small wonder that this land of opportunity has attracted hard-working and talented people from across the planet. For all its defects and limitations, American capitalism has been the gold standard against which the rest of the world is measured.

America's unique form of capitalism cannot be taken for granted, however. Only by understanding why it is so rare in the rest of the world can we appreciate how fortunate we are to have this system—and how necessary it is to preserve it.

1

THE AMERICAN EXCEPTION

For every migrant should well consider, that in a country like the United States of America, . . . where no princes and their corrupt courts represent the so-called "divine right of birth," in spite of merit and virtue—that in such a country the talents, energy and perseverance of a person must have a far greater opportunity for display, than in monarchies, where the evils above mentioned have existed for centuries, and with their sad effects exist still.

—F. W. Bogen, *The German in America* (Boston, 1851)

WHAT DETERMINES PUBLIC SUPPORT FOR CAPITALISM? A recent study shows that in any given country it is positively associated with the perception that hard work, not luck, determines success and negatively correlated with the perception of corruption.[1] These correlations go a long way toward explaining public backing for America's capitalist system. According to another recent study, only 40 percent of Americans think that luck rather than hard work plays a major role in income differences. Compare that with the 75 percent of Brazilians—or the 66 percent of Danes and 54 percent of Germans—who think that income disparities are mostly a matter of luck, and you begin to get a sense of why American attitudes toward the free-market system stand out.[2]

WHAT IS SO SPECIAL ABOUT THE UNITED STATES?

Some scholars argue that this public belief in capitalism's legitimacy is merely the result of a successful propaganda campaign for the American Dream—a myth embedded in American culture. And it's true that there is scant evidence that rates of social mobility are higher in the United States than in other developed countries. But while the difference in economic openness of the American system does not show up clearly in aggregate statistics, it is powerfully present at the top of the income distribution—which also shapes people's attitudes most extensively. Even before the Internet boom of the late 1990s gave us many young billionaires, one out of four billionaires in the United States could be described as "self-made"—compared to just one out of ten in Germany. In fact, in Europe self-made people are often referred to as *parvenus* (newcomers). This is a derogatory expression implying that such people are not as "classy" as those who have inherited money and did not have to work hard to earn it. In other words, in Europe wealth tends to be seen as a privilege, not a reward for effort.

Self-made billionaires also exist outside of the States, of course, but the way they have made their money is often quite different from the way America's very rich did. The wealthiest self-made American billionaires—from Bill Gates and Michael Dell to Warren Buffett and Mark Zuckerberg—have made their fortunes in competitive businesses, not much affected by government regulation, whereas in most other countries the wealthiest people frequently accumulate their fortunes in regulated businesses in which success often depends more on having the right government connections than on having initiative and enterprise. Think about the Russian oligarchs or Silvio Berlusconi in Italy and Carlos Slim in Mexico. They all got rich in businesses that are highly dependent on governmental concessions: energy, real estate, telecommunications, mining. In much of the world, in fact, the best way to make lots of money is not to come up with brilliant ideas and work hard at implementing them but, instead, to cultivate a government ally. Such cronyism is bound to shape public attitudes about a country's economic system. When asked in a recent study to name the most important determinants of financial success, Italian managers put "knowledge of influential people" in first place (80 percent considered it "important" or "very important").[3] "Competence and experience" ranked fifth, behind characteristics such as "loyalty and obedience." These divergent paths to prosperity reveal more than just a difference of perception. Capitalism in the United States is distinct from its counterparts in Europe and Asia for reasons that reach deep into history, geography, culture, and the institution of federalism.

Historical Factors

In America, unlike in much of the rest of the West, democracy predates industrialization. By the time of the second industrial revolution in the latter part of the nineteenth century, the United States had already enjoyed several decades of universal (male) suffrage and widespread education. These circumstances forged a public with high expectations—one unlikely to tolerate evident unfairness in economic policy. It is no coincidence that the very concept of antitrust law—a promarket but sometimes antibusiness idea—was articulated in the United States at the end of the nineteenth century and the beginning of the twentieth.

American capitalism also arose at a time when government involvement in the economy was quite weak. At the beginning of the twentieth century, when modern American capitalism was taking shape, US government spending was only 3 percent of gross domestic product.[4] After World War II, when modern capitalism took hold in Western European countries, government spending in those countries was, on average, 30 percent of GDP. Until World War I, the United States had a tiny federal government compared to national governments in other countries. This was partly due to the fact that the United States faced no significant military threat, so the government had to spend only a relatively small proportion of its budget on the military. The federalist nature of the American regime, by empowering states, also played a role in limiting the size of the national government.

When government is small and relatively weak, the most effective way to make money is to start a successful private-sector business. But the larger the size and scope of government spending, the easier it is to make money by diverting public resources. After all, starting a business is difficult and involves a lot of risk. Getting a government favor or contract is easier, at least if you have connections, and is a much safer bet. Thus, in nations with large and powerful governments, the state usually finds itself at the heart of the economic system, even if the system is relatively capitalist—an arrangement that confounds politics and economics, both in practice and in public perceptions: the larger the share of capitalists who acquire their wealth thanks to their political connections, the greater the perception that capitalism is unfair and corrupt.

Another distinguishing feature of American capitalism is that it evolved relatively untouched by foreign influence. Although European (and especially British) capital did play a role in America's nineteenth- and early-twentieth-century economic expansion, Europe's economies were not more advanced than America's—and thus while European capitalists could invest in or compete with American companies, they could not dominate the system. As a result, American capitalism developed more or less organically and, indeed, still shows the marks of those origins. The American bankruptcy code, for instance, exhibits significant prodebtor biases, because the United States was born and grew up as a nation of debtors.

Things are very different in nations that became capitalist economies after World War II. These countries—in non-Soviet-bloc continental Europe, parts of Asia, and much of Latin America—industrialized under the giant shadow of American power. Local elites felt threatened by the potential for economic colonization by American firms that were far more efficient and better capitalized than their own firms were. To protect domestic companies from foreign ownership, local establishments created various forms of indigenous cross-ownership (from the Japanese keiretsu to the Korean chaebol). These structures encouraged collusion and corruption. They have also proven resilient in the decades since: once economic and political systems are built to reward relationships instead of economic efficiency, it is extremely difficult to reform them, since the people in power are the ones who would ultimately lose the most.

Another explanation for the United States' openness to a promarket agenda instead of a probusiness agenda is that the nation was largely spared the direct influence of Marxism, though it is possible that the nature of American capitalism is the cause, as much as the effect, of the absence of strong Marxist movements in this country. Either way, this difference from other Western regimes significantly affected Americans' attitudes toward economics. In countries with prominent and influential Marxist parties, defenders of free markets were compelled to combine their forces with large businesses, even when they did not trust them. If one faces the prospect of nationalization (i.e., the control of resources by a small political elite), even *relationship capitalism*—which involves control of those resources by a small *business* elite—becomes an appealing alternative. At least in relationship capitalism there are private owners, who lose out as a result of inefficiency and thus have an incentive to stay competitive.

Because they could not afford to divide the opposition to Marxism, many of these countries could not develop a more competitive and open form of capitalism. And the free-market banner wound up completely appropriated by probusiness forces, which were better equipped and better fed. Even as the appeal of Marxist ideas faded, this confusion of promarket and probusiness forces remained in place. After decades of fighting side-by-side with and being financed by the large industrialists, the promarket forces could no longer separate themselves from the probusiness camp. Nowhere is this scenario more evident than in Italy, where the free-market movement is almost literally owned by one businessman, Silvio Berlusconi, who also happened to be prime minister for much of the nation's recent history. Until he had to resign from political office in 2011, Berlusconi had basically run the country in the interest of his own business.

Geographical Factors

Besides historical factors, geography and demography have also played significant roles in shaping America's unique form of capitalism. Initially, what drove Europe's colonization of much of the Americas was the quest for gold and silver. In Central and South America, the Spanish sent their nobles and viceroys to preside over the extraction of precious metals, transplanting European hierarchies and institutions in the process. North America was lucky that the Europeans did not find gold right away. At this point in its history, the continent offered relatively inhospitable plains and forests. What attracted colonies here was not the search for gold but the search for freedom. In coming to America, immigrants left behind not only their relatives but also oppressive institutions. They arrived here determined to build a better system of government.[5]

They were also helped in this goal by the fact that the United States was relatively underpopulated. In Old Europe the scarce factor was land. Those who controlled the land could enjoy an economic rent; in other words, they could live off it without adding any value. This is what enabled the European aristocracy to thrive and to control the state. European (especially Continental European) institutions were designed to enshrine the power of the aristocracy. The Europeans created not only governments of the landlords, by the landlords, and for the landlords but also an economic system of the landlords, by the landlords, and for the landlords. Even though European countries slowly moved toward more democratic institutions, they initially granted the vote only to landowners and made education accessible only to the children of the upper class.

What made the difference in America was *competition*. Even with their wonderful new institutions, the original thirteen colonies might have degenerated into a more rigid, European-style society if not for the openness of the American frontier. The frontier made it easy for people to move, fundamentally undermining the power of American governments vis-à-vis their citizens. Unlike Europeans, Americans were free to choose where to live. No American state enjoyed a monopoly over its citizens, since it faced the competition of other states. And so American states have always had to compete, in terms of improving institutions, to attract the best and the brightest, just as businesses must attract customers in order to survive and flourish. Universal franchise and universal education, it is worth noting, were introduced initially in the western states, which were eager to attract a workforce from the eastern ones. Thus, the United States became not just a government by the people but also a government for the people.

Such is the power of competition, which transforms even the political state—the Leviathan—into an instrument for the people. By contrast, monopoly can transform private enterprises into a destructive form of the Leviathan. A terrifying example is the Congo Free State at the end of the nineteenth century. When Belgium showed little interest in colonial expansion, its king, Leopold II, decided to pursue it on his own. The Congo Free State was not a colony of Belgium but, rather, a personal property of the king, who ran it as his own private company. After initial problems, the enterprise became extremely profitable, making Leopold II one of the richest monarchs in Europe. Unfortunately, this occurred at the expense of both the local people and the environment. In 1904, British consul Roger Casement published a report of all the atrocities that took place in the Congo Free State.[6] Eventually, international pressure forced Leopold II to surrender his private state to Belgium, leading to an improvement of the living conditions of the local population. Nevertheless, Congo's institutions still reflect their sad origin as tools for the most ruthless extraction of resources ever recorded. This unfortunate legacy continues to permeate the culture of Congo as well. Even after independence Congo continued to suffer under brutal dictatorships.

Cultural Factors

America's Declaration of Independence fittingly starts with "We, the People." Unlike the countries of Europe, whose various foundings depended on monarchs allegedly vested with power by God, the United States of America is vested with power arising from the people. This popular, if not populist, foundation shaped the prevailing American culture for the better.

In the United States, juries and elected judges have always helped to limit the power and influence of money. And the common-law system itself, with its appeal to commonly shared values such as fairness, has always been a limit to lobbying power. Special interests can often find it easy to corrupt the legislative process, but they cannot as easily change the notion of fairness applied by popularly elected judges. For the same reason, common law provides a better shield against legislative corruption than a code of law, the system prevailing outside Britain and the former British colonies. In a system where law is enshrined into a rigid code (like the Civil Code of France and all of Continental Europe), little discretion is left to the judge, whose role is simply to map codified legal norms onto real-world situations. This system creates a strong incentive for various interests to lobby legislators.[7] Whoever "captures" lawmakers can more readily dictate the outcomes in future contingencies, gaining great benefit. By contrast, in a common law system the legislature is supposed to provide only general principles, limiting the payoff that lobbyists can obtain.

Another manifestation of the American populist bent that tempers the power of big business is the institution of class action lawsuits. Though they can be and have been abused, such suits not only provide an incentive for lawyers to fight in defense of powerless people but they also create an alternative lobby. In countries with no tradition of class action suits—such as France and Italy—the legal profession, completely captured by moneyed interests, becomes an apologist for large and powerful corporations and individuals.

Finally, although Americans have historically avoided anticapitalist biases, they have nurtured something of a populist antifinance bias— that is, an opposition to excessive concentration of financial power. A healthy financial system is crucial to any working market economy. And widespread access to finance is essential to harnessing the best talents, allowing them to prosper and grow, drawing new entrants into the system, and fostering competition. But the financial system also has the ability to allocate power and profits. As the old saying goes, whoever has the gold makes the rules—and banks are where the gold is. More important is that the financial system, by influencing entry into the market, affects the profitability of the industrial sector.[8] Thus, if this system is not fair, there is little hope that the rest of the economy can be. And the potential for unfairness or abuse in the financial system is always great. Americans have long been sensitive to such abuse.

Throughout American history, the populist antifinance bias has led to many political decisions that were inefficient from an economic point of view. But this bias has also helped preserve the long-term health of America's democratic capitalism.

Institutional Factors

Yet another ingredient of good fortune that made the United States so special is the federal nature of its government. Federalism was crucial in two important respects: it made competition among states possible, as I noted earlier, and it kept the power of individual corporations at bay. In individual states the power of certain large corporations was unlimited. Coal mines controlled West Virginia, the tobacco industry controlled Kentucky and North Carolina, and so on. Still, it was difficult for any industry to control a majority of the states. The excesses that come with absolute power were tamed.

Consider the case of Jeff Wigand, who, as mentioned in the Introduction, worked for the Brown & Williamson Tobacco Corporation. Just as he was about to blow the whistle on the company's deliberate policy to make cigarettes more addictive, the firm obtained a restraining order from a Kentucky state judge prohibiting him from speaking about his experiences at Brown & Williamson. Such was the power of the tobacco industry in Kentucky, where the tobacco sectors once employed more than seventy-five thousand people. It was only because the attorney general of Mississippi, a nontobacco state, brought a suit against the major American tobacco companies that Wigand's testimony was eventually revealed.[9]

Indeed, it was often the rivalry—the competition—among states that kept companies at bay. Throughout much of American history, state bank regulations were driven by concerns about the power of New York banks over the rest of the country—and, more generally, by fears that big banks would drain deposits from the countryside in order to redirect them to the cities. To address these fears, states introduced a variety of restrictions such as unit banking (banks could have only one office), limits on intrastate branching (banks from northern Illinois could not open branches in southern Illinois), and limits on interstate branching (New York banks could not open branches in other states). From a purely economic point of view, these restrictions were completely misguided. They forced reinvestment of deposits in the same areas where they were collected, badly distorting the allocation of funds. And by preventing banks from expanding, they made banks less diversified and thus more prone to failure. Yet the new policies did have a positive side effect: splintering the banking sector, they reduced its political power and thereby created the preconditions for a vibrant securities market.

The separation between investment banking and commercial banking introduced by the New Deal's Glass-Steagall Act was a product of this long-standing American tradition. Unlike many other banking regulations, Glass-Steagall had an economic rationale: to prevent commercial banks from exploiting their depositors by dumping on them the bonds of firms that were unable to repay the money they had borrowed from banks. The Glass-Steagall Act's most significant consequence, though, was the fragmentation of the banking industry. This fragmentation created divergent interests in different parts of the financial sector, reducing its political power. Over the past three decades, these arrangements were overturned, starting with the progressive deregulation of the banking sector.

THE LUCKY OUTCOME

For all of these reasons, then, the United States constructed a system of capitalism that comes closer than any other to embodying the free-market ideal of economic liberty and open competition. The image many Americans have of capitalism therefore calls to mind Horatio Alger's rags-to-riches-via-hard-work stories, which have come to define the American Dream. In most of the rest of the world, by contrast, Horatio Alger is unknown—and the concept of social mobility is defined by Cinderella or Evita stories, in which success comes not from hard work but from luck. This goes a long way toward explaining why the level of support for capitalism in the United States is greater than in any other country and, in turn, why capitalism itself has always seemed on firmer footing in America.

The American system is far from perfect. It does not lack stories of corporate abuses and political corruption. The ITT Corporation, for instance, is famous for having influenced America's policy toward Latin America in the 1960s and 1970s, including support for atrocious regimes. On a more personal note, I live in Illinois—two former governors of which are currently in jail for corruption.

Yet the greatest feature of the United States is its system of checks and balances. The fact that my two former governors are in jail shows that justice can prevail. A president of the United States, Richard Nixon, was forced to resign. Even more to the point, the US government was able to break up major monopolies, such as Standard Oil in 1912 and AT&T in 1984. No other country has a comparable record.

2

WHO KILLED HORATIO ALGER?

The Best Poor Man's Country
—Title of an old American history book[1]

THE FUNDAMENTAL ROLE OF AN ECONOMIC SYSTEM, even an extremely primitive one, is to assign responsibility and reward. In most animal packs, the responsibility of leadership and the reward of mating opportunities are generally assigned to the strongest. In human societies, responsibility tends to take the form of employment, and the rewards are money and prestige. The dominant criterion in traditional society was birth: the king's first-born son was the next king; the landowner's first-born son, the next landowner; and the son of the company's owner, the next chief executive. Most modern societies, by contrast, try to select and reward according to merit. Indeed, surveys show that most people in developed countries agree with the idea that merit should be rewarded.

WHAT IS MERITORIOUS?

It isn't easy to decide what constitutes merit, of course. Consider an environment with which I'm familiar: American academia. Let's say you want to determine who the best professors are. How do you rank publications? Do you value the number of papers that someone has written, or their impact? How do you measure that impact—is it merely the number of times a paper has been cited, or should citations be weighted by the importance of the journal in which they appear? Do you value good citations ("This is a seminal paper") and bad citations ("This paper is fundamentally flawed") equally? What about teaching? How do you evaluate that? Should it be measured by students' satisfaction, or should other criteria come into the picture? If so, which? And what about other dimensions, such as collegiality and "service" to the school? Any system of determining merit must assign various weights to each of these dimensions, a process that is inevitably somewhat arbitrary; moreover, that arbitrariness can create the presumption of unfairness and favoritism.

As that example suggests, a system of measuring merit should be efficient and difficult to manipulate, and above all, it should be deemed fair, or at least not too unfair, by most of the people subject to it. We can now begin to understand why support for meritocracy tends to translate into support for the market system. Markets are far harder to manipulate than, say, a list of tenure requirements that an academic committee has created, or, to take a broader example, the decisions of statist regimes determining which lucky citizens get which consumer products. The market system has the reputation, too, of producing efficient results. Finally, if the market system does not deliver excessively unequal outcomes and does not acquire a reputation of rewarding luck rather than hard work, it will broadly conform with the notion of fairness most people have.

Naturally, not everyone embraces the market system. I suspect the reason that some intellectuals reject it is that it doesn't reward what they think is meritorious: Lady Gaga makes a lot more money than Nobel laureates do. But in America, people largely accept the system—not merely because they think that it will deliver a reasonably efficient outcome but also because they consider it mostly fair. As in Horatio Alger's stories, they believe, such virtues as honesty, frugality, and hard work will be rewarded.

THE TENSION BETWEEN DEMOCRACY
AND MERITOCRACY

But this rosy picture obscures a hard fact: meritocracy is a difficult principle to sustain in a democracy. Any system that allocates rewards on the basis of merit inevitably gives higher compensation to the few, leaving the majority of people potentially envious. In a democracy, the majority generally rules. Why should that majority agree to grant a minority disproportionate power and rewards?

A little more than a decade ago this dynamic played out neatly at the University of Chicago, an institution that still attracts market-oriented people, thanks to its association with the great free-market economist Milton Friedman. Who could be more promarket and promeritocracy than Master in Business Administration (MBA) students who attend such a school, investing tens of thousands of dollars and two years of their lives to reap the rewards of a meritocratic system? Nevertheless, in a move that contradicted the meritocratic spirit, University of Chicago MBA students voted in 2000 not to reveal their grades to recruiters. The reason was clear: allowing recruiters to distinguish among them on the basis of merit would benefit a minority of them at the expense of a majority. Even the most meritocratic people, then, can vote against meritocracy when it damages their own prospects. No wonder meritocracy is so politically fragile.

Nevertheless, two factors help sustain a meritocratic system in the face of this challenge: (a) a culture that considers it legitimate to reward effort with higher compensation and (b) benefits large enough, and spread widely enough through the system, to counter popular discontent with inequality. The cultural factor is easy to spot in America, which encouraged meritocracy from its inception. In the eighteenth century, the social order throughout the world was based on birthrights: nobles ruled Europe and Japan, the caste system prevailed in India, and even in England, where merchants were gaining economic and political strength, the aristocracy wielded most of the political power. The American Revolution was a revolt against aristocracy and the immobility of European society, but unlike the French Revolution, which emphasized the principle of equality, it championed the freedom to pursue happiness. In other words, the United States of America was founded on equality of opportunities, not of outcomes. The subsequent economic success of the new country cemented the belief in assigning rewards and responsibilities according to merit.

This historical heritage is reflected in American attitudes today. The income-inequality gap in the United States is among the largest in the developed world. Yet in a recent survey of twenty-seven developed countries by the Pew Charitable Trusts, only one-third of Americans agreed that it was the government's responsibility to reduce income inequality. (The country with the next-smallest proportion was Canada, with 44 percent, and the responses rose as high as Portugal's 89 percent.)[2] Americans do not want to redistribute income, but they do want the government to provide a level playing field: more than 70 percent of Americans said that the role of government was "to ensure everyone has a fair chance of improving their economic standing."

This belief in equality of opportunity is supported by another belief: that the system is actually fair. Sixty-nine percent of Americans in the same Pew survey agreed with the statement "People are rewarded for intelligence and skill"—a far larger percentage than in any other country. At the same time, only 19 percent of Americans thought that coming from a wealthy family was important for getting ahead; this compares with 39 percent in Chile, 53 percent in Spain, and a median response across all nations of 28 percent.

In America, the legitimacy of rewarding hard work is so pervasive that even undergraduates in perhaps the country's leftmost precinct, Berkeley, seem to endorse it. Economists have created an experiment called the "dictator game" in which a subject is given a sum of money and asked to divide it however he likes between himself and an anonymous player. After running the experiment thousands of times, the researchers have calculated that, on average, people give 20 percent of their money to the anonymous players, presumably out of altruism or compassion. Recently, economist Pamela Jakiela changed the conditions of the experiment. In one treatment, the subjects—Berkeley undergrads—were told that the anonymous players had worked hard; in another treatment, they were told that the players had done nothing. The students, it turned out, were much more willing to reward the hard workers than the slackers. In still another experiment, in which the subjects who were allocating the money had to work hard to gain it (by sorting beans, as it happened), they were much less willing to give it away than were those who had not worked hard. This goes a long way toward explaining the redistribution preferences of the so-called *gauche caviar*: trust-fund kids who have not earned their way and embrace socialism (*gauche* is French for "left") to attenuate their sense of guilt for their privileged lives.

Don't suppose that the culture of meritocracy is universal. When the same experiment was conducted in Kenya, it yielded opposite results, with the subjects more willing to reward luck than hard work. But in America, from Berkeley to Boston, people believe in greater reward for greater effort, and that belief helps protect meritocratic capitalism from the forces that threaten to undermine it.

A meritocracy can't survive on a supportive culture alone, however; it must also confer benefits large enough for people to recognize them. Meritocratic systems emerge when their potential benefits are the most acutely felt. At the national level, this tends to occur in wartime, especially when the country's survival is at stake. In 1793, when the French Revolution was threatened by the invading armies of other European powers, the Jacobin government started to promote talented soldiers rather than well-bred ones. This simple innovation allowed the Revolution to beat back Europe's better-armed and better-trained forces. A similar effect was demonstrated by a friend of mine who felt sick one day. His wife offered to call their doctor friend. "No, I'm *really* sick," he said. "I need a *real* doctor." When your life is in danger, there's an enormous benefit in choosing according to merit instead of loyalty.

Thus a meritocratic system, to engender a broad consensus, must confer benefits that are relatively sizable, even if they aren't quite as huge as saving a country from defeat. That isn't an easy task. In politics, for example—a field in which value is mostly redistributed rather than created—the benefits conferred by meritocracy are relatively small compared with the benefits conferred by cronyism. If I appoint my friends to office, even when they aren't terribly competent, I lose relatively little efficiency and gain quite a lot of power. Hence meritocracy is difficult to sustain in government.

The same is true when a firm enjoys a monopoly. Since the firm's market position isn't at risk, it doesn't benefit much from hiring the best people; instead, its executives focus on bureaucratic infighting, trying to grab an ever-larger share of the profits from each other—and, once again, hiring loyal workers pays more than hiring competent ones. Contrast that with what happens in a competitive market, in which firms find themselves constantly threatened by competitors. It doesn't pay to struggle for a larger slice of the pie if the pie is at risk of disappearing: a larger share of zero is still zero. Better to fight to preserve the pie, even at the cost of getting a smaller piece. This is another way in which meritocracy is intrinsically related to free markets. Without the threat that arises from economic competition, organizations have no reason to be efficient and thus no reason to be meritocratic.

Meritocracy can give rise to virtuous circles.[3] The more frequently citizens see that the principle of rewarding merit is consistently and fairly applied, the more willing they are to accept this principle. Their very acceptance means that the system will be applied more and more consistently and fairly, which in turn further increases support for it. But when a system is corrupt, it induces people to try to cheat. This makes the system even more unfair—a vicious circle.

These "circles" point to the existence of what economists call *multiple equilibria*—stable situations that are very hard to change. For example, a country that has developed a tradition of meritocracy will generally be able to sustain it, even under adverse conditions, whereas a country in which the meritocratic tradition has never developed will have great difficulty introducing it. In an equilibrium, small perturbations tend to have no effect. If the perturbation is sufficiently large, however, an economy can find itself in a different equilibrium—from which it will have difficulty moving away.

The good news for the United States is that it occupies a meritocratic equilibrium. But we have witnessed some big perturbations in recent years, such as the University of Illinois clout scandal, in which subpar applicants to the school received special considerations based on their connections to politicians and university trustees,[4] and, on a much broader scale, the financial bailout, in which bank CEOs walked away with hundreds of millions of dollars after destroying their banks. When the fairness of the rules grows questionable and the benefits of the system are distributed too unequally, the consensus for free-market meritocracy can collapse. Returning to a meritocratic consensus is next to impossible once a country reaches that point. Unfortunately, America is approaching it.

Several powerful forces are threatening to drive America away from a meritocratic equilibrium and toward a nonmeritocratic one. Recall that, in order to survive in a democratic country, a free-market meritocracy must offer large, widespread benefits to citizens and possess a welcoming culture. In the United States, both of these qualities are being challenged—the first by a reduction of the benefits that most people derive from markets and the second by a delegitimization of markets as a good method of rewarding the meritorious.

TIGER WOODS AND THE GREENSKEEPERS

People care not only about their absolute status but also about their status relative to others. Statistics on the income gap—the divergence between the income of the top 1 percent and that of the rest—abound. This divergence is often attributed to corporate greed. But unfortunately, the problem is much broader than that. I say "unfortunately" because if it were *just* the result of corporate greed it would be easier to fix.

To appreciate better the nature of this divergence, we may find it helpful to watch a golf tournament. Even on the links, far away from corporate high-rises, not everybody is paid the same. Tiger Woods and the greenskeepers receive very different compensations. This difference is what we economists call *skill premium*. (Historical data on tournaments' monetary prizes make it easy to measure the evolution of skill premium over time.[5] While data for greenskeepers are not easily available, I will assume that at any point in time they are being paid the minimum wage. If I were to cite the median or average wage, the picture that I'm about to draw would be no different.)

In 1948, the prize to win the most prestigious golf tournament, the Masters, was a meager $2,500. In 2008 dollars, that's a bit more than $22,000. In 2008, the same first prize was $1,350,000—sixty times the previous amount. Obviously, the economy has grown and so have real wages, so the more relevant ratio is that between the first prize and the annual salary of a greenskeeper. In 1948, the first prize was three times the annual salary of a greenskeeper; in 2008, it was 103 times. Interestingly, even the temporal pattern of the rise in the Masters prize follows closely that of CEO compensations, which did not increase much in real terms until the early 1980s and then skyrocketed.[6] What can explain this surge in the skill premium?

First of all, comparing the winning prize with the minimum or average wage ignores how difficult it is to get that prize. In 1948, Claude Harmon, that year's Masters winner, was a club professional who did not compete full time. Today, such an outcome would be unconceivable. In fact, no club professional after him has ever won a major golf championship.[7] When the Augusta National (as the Masters was originally known) started in 1934, it was a local competition and remained one for many years. In its first twenty years, every tournament was won by an American, while in the following twenty, only 14 percent of the winners were foreigners. After that, roughly 50 percent were foreigners.

The increase in the popularity of golf, too, means that it has become harder to win the Masters. Between 1948 and 2008, the number of golf courses in the United States quadrupled.[8] The number of golf courses in the world has increased by a factor of 8. If the number of golf players per course is roughly constant over time and if all the players are potential candidates (two big ifs), we can say that it is 8 times more difficult to win the Masters tournament today than it was in 1948. The tougher odds go a long way toward explaining the increase in the skill premium. Instead of 3 to 103, the actual ratio between the expected payoff of a golfer and that of the greenskeeper has increased from 3 to 13 times. Still, what accounts for that rise?

Note that the Masters started as a subsidized event.[9] As the founder of the Augusta National Golf Club remembers, initially the tournament's financial results were "a bit disastrous," inasmuch as "[t]he start-up cost exceeded the amounts raised to cover such outlays."[10] Were it not for monetary gifts from members, the club couldn't have paid the professionals in the field of the first tournament.[11] At that time (and until 1966), a spectator could walk up to the gate on the day of the event and purchase a ticket. Since 1972, however, there has been a waiting list—a list so long that the last time new names were accepted was in 2000. On the Internet, a $175 Masters badge, good for all tournament rounds, goes for between $1,500 and $5,000.[12] And since 1995, even practice tickets have been sold through a lottery because demand so extensively outstrips supply. Meanwhile, thanks to TV broadcasting, the competition has become a money-making machine. The competition's total revenues increased more than sixty times in the last sixty years, despite little effort on the part of the Augusta National Golf Club. All this helps us understand why the value of the prize has vastly increased: not only because it is more difficult to win but also because the value of the golf tournament has increased so much.

But even so, isn't it true that the prestige of the tournament and the nonmonetary prize (the famous green jacket that the winner receives) are sufficient to motivate the most famous golfers to participate? "As far as major championships are concerned, it doesn't matter if you're playing for five dollars or a million dollars," admitted James Furyk, one of the top ten golf players in the world. "Everyone is going to want to win the Masters."[13] So why did the Augusta National Golf Club increase the purse? Because the Masters is *competing with other tournaments*. If it consistently paid much less than the other major golf competitions in the world, such as the PGA Championship, the US Open, and the British Open, it would run the risk of losing its cachet. Should the Masters risk losing its reputation as the "most prestigious sporting event in America"[14] to save a few bucks? Doing so would be silly. It is no coincidence that the big increase in the prize occurred in the late 1980s and 1990s, when the four major championships took turns at being the most generous golf competition in the world.

The golf example is illuminating because the same two phenomena that are driving the rise in golf prizes—enhanced competition and the increased value of being at the top—have also occurred in the corporate world, roughly at the same time As the world market becomes integrated, it is more difficult for a company to survive. In turn, a lot of executives who would have earned a decent living running mediocre companies are wiped out.

At the same time, the most efficient firms can apply their advantage over the entire world market now. The value of being the best has increased disproportionately, and companies—just like the Augusta National Golf Club—are not going to run the risk of losing the jackpot to save a few dollars on the executives. Do these executives really make a difference? Superstar managers like Steve Jobs clearly do. For others, the answer is less obvious. When we look at changes in profitability that are due to changes in CEO, we find that CEOs in the top quartile of ability have a return of assets of 6 percentage points higher than CEOs in the lowest quartile.[15] When applied to larger and larger corporations, this difference is quite important. Even in situations where it is unclear whether CEOs add value, it is so costly for board members to experiment that they prefer to play it safe (as the Augusta National Golf Club does) and pay handsomely.

The explanation for this increase in wage inequality, both in sports and in business, can be summed up in one word: *globalization.* Globalization increases competition and the return on being the best, thereby also increasing inequality. It has certainly increased the size of the pie. More people now watch the Masters Tournament (and other US-based tournaments), more sponsored merchandise is sold around the world, and more international companies are willing to sponsor the TV broadcasting of the tournaments. These benefits, however, are distributed in a highly unequal fashion. Endorsements are even more unequally distributed. When he was at the top of his game Tiger Woods was making $12 million in winnings and $100 million in endorsements,[16] whereas the second-best male golfer, Phil Mickelson, was making $4 million in winnings and $47 million in endorsements and the third-best was making less than $15 million combined.

Globalization generates a further sense of disenfranchisement among local elites by making unaffordable some of the goods they once enjoyed. For instance, if the Masters were run for profit, tickets would easily cost more than $1,000 each, and many of the local amateur golfers, who used to be able to stroll over and buy a ticket for a few bucks, would grow resentful at being unable to afford the cost. (In the Masters this did not occur because the tournament was owned by the local golf association, which has other objectives.)

What has happened in sports is happening in the economy at large. While the net benefits of free trade are unquestionably positive, these gains are distributed in an extremely unequal way—and there are definitely losers. It is no consolation for the former top reporters at the *Buffalo Gazette,* who have had difficulty making a living after losing their jobs, to know that the most famous columnists of the *New York Times* have their work syndicated in dozens of countries, making them world superstars. Similarly, even as Facebook takes over the world, making billions for Mark Zuckerberg, ordinary software engineers are having a hard time competing with their Indian counterparts.

MANY GREENSKEEPERS LEFT BEHIND

It is painful to fall behind in relative terms, but if this occurs at a time of quickly rising absolute standards, it is tolerable. The income inequality between Tiger Woods and his caddy skyrocketed, yet his caddy ended up a rich man. Does he care if he became less rich in relative terms? Probably not.

Unfortunately, as the American increase in income inequality took place, the real wages of most Americans stagnated. Take a look at Figure 1. As economics graphs go, this one is pretty amazing.

The dashed line, which is more or less straight, represents the growth in productivity of the US economy (excluding agriculture) from 1946 to 2009. It tells us that productivity quadrupled over the last sixty-five years and that the increase has been roughly constant over this period, with a slow-down in the second half of the 1970s and a catch-up in the second part of the 1990s. The solid line represents the average real weekly wage of workers. Until the mid-1970s the lines moved together. But around 1973, productivity kept growing while real wages remained nearly flat; in fact, they ran a loss over time. The graph illustrates an increase in inequality and a shrinking middle class.

As I will explain in Chapter 8, part of this difference is a matter of perception, not reality. When it comes to political support for the free-market system, however, perceptions count. And unfortunately, not just perception is involved. Between 1989 and 2009, as the median national income increased by 3 percent, the real per-capita income of the poorest 20 percent of the population as computed by the US Census Bureau declined by 1 percent.

Figure 1. Productivity and Average Real Earnings

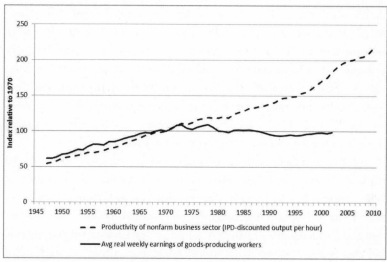

Source: US Bureau of Labor Statistics.

THE DEATH OF HORATIO ALGER

Horatio Alger was a rather mediocre writer. Yet his inspiring rags-to-riches novels have become inextricably linked with American capitalism. His tales recount their protagonists' journeys from poverty to respectability, celebrating American capitalism and suggesting that the American Dream is within everyone's reach. The novels were idealized, of course; even in America, virtue alone never guaranteed success, and American capitalism during Alger's time was far from perfect. Nevertheless, the stories were close enough to the truth that they became best sellers, while America became known as a land of opportunity—a place whose capitalist system benefited the hard-working and the virtuous.

For a long time, people believed, despite the obstacles they faced, that either they or their children would better their positions one day. Indeed, according to a recent survey conducted by the Pew Economic Mobility Project, 72 percent of Americans today think that their economic circumstances will be better in the next ten years and 62 percent think that their children will have a better standard of living than they have.[17]

Unfortunately, empirical evidence suggests that these outcomes are becoming less common. Start with *intragenerational mobility*, the likelihood that a person will move from one segment of the income distribution to another. Typically, about 30 percent of the people in each income quintile move up to the next quintile over ten years. But intragenerational mobility seems to be decreasing, most notably at the bottom of the income distribution. In the 1990s, according to the Economic Policy Institute, 36 percent of those who started in the second-poorest quintile of the income distribution stayed there, versus 32 percent in the 1980s and 28 percent in the 1970s.[18]

Another kind of mobility, *intergenerational mobility*, refers to the extent to which people move up or down the economic ladder relative to their parents. In situations where the children in low-income families have a low income themselves, intergenerational mobility is low. A recent and shocking study by the Organization for Economic Co-operation and Development showed that America was markedly *less* mobile in this way than other OECD countries.[19] Similarly, a study by researchers at the Federal Reserve Bank of Chicago reported that intergenerational mobility, though it increased between the 1950s and the 1980s, started dropping in the 1990s and fell even further in the following decade.[20]

CONCLUSIONS

It seems the benefits conferred by meritocratic capitalism are neither as great nor as widespread as they once were, and this change weakens political support for the market system. But what undermines the free-market system the most is the perception that the rules don't apply equally to everybody—that the system is rigged. When my children were small, they occasionally tried to play Monopoly. These attempts inevitably degenerated into arguments. My daughter, who is two years younger than my son, would claim that my son was cheating. My son, with the official instructions in hand, would protest his innocence. And he was right: he never invented any rule. But my daughter was right, too: my son was engaging in selective recollection of the rules, counting on my daughter's ignorance and bringing up only the rules that were in his favor. In spite of her youth, my daughter sensed a lack of fairness and employed the only response she had available: giving up.

Her frustration is similar to what many people are increasingly feeling about the US system overall: that the game seems rigged. Most people do not understand how it is rigged, much less how to fix it—and like my daughter, some, including the young people camping in Zuccotti Park and in squares around America, think the answer is to quit. They do not understand that by rejecting the whole system they make it more difficult to change it. In order to restore fairness to the system, they—indeed, all of us—need to understand what went wrong in the first place.

3

CRONY CAPITALISM AMERICAN STYLE

We have a saying here in this company that penetrates the whole company. It's a saying that our competitors are our friends. Our customers are the enemy.

—James Randall, former president of
Archer Daniels Midland

CAPITALISM BRINGS INCOME INEQUALITY WITH IT. THE public generally accepts this inequality as long as it is not excessive, is seen as part of a system that benefits everyone, and, most importantly, is justified by a principle that a large fraction of the population considers "fair." A competitive free-market system delivers all three of these things. Competition limits the possibility of earning extraordinary profits—and thus limits income inequality as well. Competition ensures that consumers enjoy the benefits of innovation. Competition creates a pressure toward efficiency and hence meritocracy, a system in which responsibilities are given to the people who can deliver the most and in which the rewards are then seen as the just prize.

Competition brings even more than this: it gives customers the freedom to choose. That customers can switch from one vendor to another not only protects them from companies that try to gouge them with high prices; it also ensures that their welfare is maximized. To keep their business, firms will offer customers the most favorable terms.

When a business gains excessive market power, so that it can increase prices indiscriminately, customers can seek protection through the political process. But when a business obtains both market and political power, escape becomes impossible. Under these circumstances, the system starts to resemble a socialist economy instead of a free market. In a socialist economy, the political system controls business; in a crony capitalist system of this kind, business controls the political process. The difference is slim: either way, competition is absent and freedom shrinks. Without competition, economic life becomes unfair, favoring the connected insider.

Competition is the magic ingredient that makes capitalism work for everyone. Most of the elegant results that economists have derived about the benefits of free markets are based on the assumption that markets operate competitively. But economists do not focus sufficiently on the goal of ensuring that the competitive condition is met in practice. The problem is not the temporary advantage that companies secure through innovation but, rather, the longer-lasting political power they can secure through their size and lobbying influence. When companies operate in a noncompetitive market and are run by managers accountable to nobody, we should stop thinking of them as parts of a free market and see them instead for what they really are: small, centrally planned economies.

The battle against crony capitalism is older than the nation itself. It started in Boston in 1773, when the American colonists rebelled against the abuses of British monopolies. In fact, these colonists, who threw overboard three shiploads of English tea, were revolting not against higher taxes but against a monopoly and British crony capitalism. The Tea Act of 1773 had *lowered* the taxes on American tea importers. But it also granted tax-free status to the East India Company, a firm so politically connected to the British government that the two were almost indistinguishable. The colonists despised this privilege and feared that government-created monopolies might extend to other goods as well. The American Revolution was a battle for political rights, yes. But it was also a battle for economic freedom against crony capitalism.

To many of today's readers, fighting to establish or maintain competition might seem unremarkable. In 1773, however, it was something radically new. Throughout history, economic competition had been regarded as an evil to avoid at all costs. The guilds of the Middle Ages, for instance, were designed to restrict competition within a trade. The first modern corporations (the Dutch and English East India Companies) were monopolies that the Crown had granted. The long-prevailing economic doctrine, mercantilism, held that the state should help create, promote, and defend monopolies, which were considered the best way to organize economic activity. Even today, if you search for the term *competition* on the Internet, you will find it mostly associated with negative adjectives such as *cutthroat, unfair,* and *hurtful.*

When Adam Smith published *The Wealth of Nations* in 1776, he started a revolution at least as important as the one the American colonies began in the same year. Smith's revolutionary idea was that competition was a force for good. Merriam-Webster's modern-day definition of *economic competition* partly reflects this idea: "the effort of two or more parties acting independently to secure the business of a third party by offering the most favorable terms." The notion that competition is welfare-improving was completely foreign before Smith. It turned out to be profoundly right, both in theory and in practice.

THE BENEFITS OF COMPETITION

Smith's idea that competition leads profit-motivated firms to produce the goods that people want at the lowest possible cost was initially just an intuition. After the publication of *The Wealth of Nations,* economists tried to figure out scientifically whether what Smith called the "invisible hand" indeed guided markets. Finally, in the middle of the last century, Kenneth Arrow and Gerard Debreu were able to prove, under very general assumptions, that Smith's intuition was indeed correct: competitive markets lead to an efficient allocation of resources (what economists call the *first welfare theorem*). The most important of those general assumptions is that economic agents are "price takers"; in other words, they act independently (i.e., they do not collude) and are sufficiently small in market size that they can ignore the impact of their actions on market prices. In most economic models, these conditions are just assumed. In reality, they need to be sustained, an important point I will return to momentarily.

Consumers are the major beneficiaries of competition. On January 1, 1984, when AT&T's local operations were split into seven independent regional holding companies and the market for long distance was opened to competition, the price of a one-minute call from New York to San Francisco (in 2011 dollars) was $1.90 and one from New York to Paris was $3.54.[1] Today, after you pay a small flat fee, domestic calls are free, while calls to Paris cost only 9 cents a minute.[2] Cell phones, formerly a luxury reserved for billionaires, are now common even in Brazilian favelas. Behind these enormous welfare improvements was no Samaritan, no benevolent central planner, no government subsidy. In fact, governments the world over raised billions of dollars auctioning off the radio frequency spectrum (thus saving taxpayers money).

Competition generates social benefits, too, by penalizing discrimination. In a competitive market, individuals who want to discriminate against others, refusing to trade with them, wind up worse off themselves.[3] For this reason, when the intensity of competition increases, discrimination diminishes. Recall that racial walls in America initially began crumbling in the highly competitive world of sports. Gender discrimination, too, has been reduced by competition. Between 1970 and 1995, as the banking sector became more competitive as a result of deregulation, the wage gap between men and women in that industry closed significantly, while the share of women in managerial positions increased by about 10 percent more than it did in other industries.[4]

Last but not least, competition gives people broader freedoms. I am reminded of a young colleague who recently went walking in the rain with a senior one. The latter, born in Europe, said jokingly (though certain jokes are not funny when stated from a position of power): "In Europe, the young assistant professors carry the umbrella for the senior ones." My younger colleague quickly responded: "Why don't *you* go to

Europe?" What gave him the power and freedom to speak his mind was competition—in this case, among universities, since my colleagues and I at the University of Chicago had competed aggressively with many other schools to hire him. As a consequence, even as a young assistant professor, he was more "powerful" in some ways than the older one.

Competition may be a customer's best friend, but firms like it much less. Companies do their best to hamper competition, because that makes it easier to make money. When I teach entrepreneurial finance, I tell students that in establishing a new firm, they would need to think about how to create barriers to entry for new competitors. Without any such barriers, a firm would operate in a perfectly competitive market: profits would be nonexistent. So it is only natural that entrepreneurs and businesspeople try to block competitors. If kept within acceptable limits, this is economically healthy. Without the hope of gaining *some* market power in the future, entrepreneurs would have little motivation to devote their lives to the success of their enterprises, and customers would be deprived of great new products.

Yet it is not easy to decide what constitutes "acceptable limits." Developing a reputation for high quality, for instance, is one way of building a barrier to new entrants; it does not hurt customers and might even benefit them. Creating bugs in an operating system to prevent full compatibility with the application software of one's competitors is another way, one that doesn't benefit consumers. The most debilitating barriers to entry, though, are those that the law creates. The state has the ultimate monopoly: the monopoly on the legitimate use of violence. Accordingly, any other monopolies that the state protects are the most difficult to overcome.

To understand just how powerful and dangerous monopolies can be when government sanctions and amplifies their power, consider the East India Company—the firm against which American colonists revolted and at which Adam Smith leveled his cutting remarks.

THE EAST INDIA COMPANY

Adam Smith's views were shaped by witnessing the corruption of the corporations of his time, in particular the East India Company (EIC), perhaps best known today in its fictionalized form in the *Pirates of the Caribbean* series. The *Pirates* movies make no claims to historical accuracy, but they are broadly accurate in their portrayal of the company's efforts to control the export and import trade among the islands.

Founded in 1600, the EIC immediately received from the Crown a monopoly on trade with all countries east of the Cape of Good Hope and west of the Straits of Magellan (an area that includes the Caribbean). Initially, this monopoly right was granted for fifteen years. But thanks to its political influence (and the bribes it offered), the EIC was able to get the monopoly renewed until 1694. That year, the English Parliament, under pressure from other merchants, liberalized trade with India and a short time later granted a charter to one rival company: the English Company Trading to the East Indies.

In the presence of a politically and economically powerful incumbent, it is not easy to introduce competition. An incumbent monopolist, strong in terms of financial resources and political connections, can easily buy out a single new competitor. It is only when market entry is completely free—and when there are therefore many competitors—that this approach becomes too expensive. Thus, we should not be surprised that the British Parliament's bid to introduce competition for the EIC, by giving a charter to one other competitor, failed to work. Absent any antitrust law, some EIC stockholders bought enough shares of the one rival and forced it into a merger, thereby regaining the monopoly position. To seal the deal and prevent future competitive challenges, the EIC extended a £3.2 million loan to the Treasury, which, in exchange, again granted the monopoly of trade, allegedly only for three years. But repeatedly, when the monopoly expired, the EIC would lobby and pay bribes and get it extended—until 1813 for most goods and until 1833 for tea.[5] That a fifteen-year monopoly right lasted 233 years is a harsh reminder of how dangerous the commingling of economic and political power can be.

Owing to geographical distance (at the time, a voyage from England to India and back took roughly two years) and the impossibility of long-distance communication, the East India Company's managers were pretty much free to rule at their own discretion.[6] In fact, it quickly became common practice to give the captains of EIC vessels up to twenty feet of deck space for their private cargos, so that they could do some trading on the side.[7] Similarly, EIC employees, though paid little, could enrich themselves via "commissions" on the EIC's procurements. This system of legalized bribes became the norm, contributing greatly to the culture of corruption that still plagues the Indian subcontinent.

It is difficult to imagine anything more distant from the invisible hand of markets. The outcome was predictably awful for all the parties involved, with the notable exception of some EIC managers and employees. Consumers back in England had to pay much more for tea and other spices than they would have in a competitive market, and EIC employees, despite their commissions, had to work for a deeply corrupt company. Adam Smith himself lamented the inefficiency of the EIC and similar organizations, observing that "they have, accordingly, very seldom succeeded without an exclusive privilege, and frequently have not succeeded with one. Without an exclusive privilege they have commonly mismanaged the trade. With an exclusive privilege they have both mismanaged and confined it."[8] This confinement meant that other merchants were prevented from operating or forced to conduct business illegally (and therefore inefficiently).

The EIC's political power damaged British citizens even more. The EIC and the state became so thoroughly entwined that the interests of the British Empire were subjected to EIC interests. Even the American Revolution partly resulted from the EIC's influence on British parliamentary decisions.

Worst of all, however, was the experience of the Indians, who endured ruthless and brutal treatment from the EIC. Probably the most nightmarish episode was the 1770 famine in the Indian territory of Bengal. By 1764, the EIC had become the de facto ruler of Bengal, where it established a monopoly in grain trading and prohibited local traders and dealers from "hoarding" rice (i.e., keeping reserves to shield the population from crop fluctuation). A year after drought struck in 1769, the EIC raised its already heavy tax on the land. The result was that one out of three Bengalis (more than 10 million people) died of starvation.[9]

Another of the EIC's claims to shame involved opium. Having lost its monopoly of trade with India (except for tea) in 1813, the EIC aggressively promoted its export of Bengali opium to China. Despite

Chinese authorities' efforts to keep it out, by 1820 the EIC was exporting nine hundred tons of opium to China every year. To defend the EIC's right to sell opium to China, the British Empire would wage two wars.

As the awful history of the EIC demonstrates, the profit goal by itself does not make private business superior to state ownership. A privately owned monopoly like the EIC can be even more destructive than a publicly owned one when it captures state power. While much of the history of European colonization is far from pretty, probably the two worst chapters were written by two private companies: the EIC and Leopold II's Congo Free State, which I mentioned in Chapter 1. Both of these private monopolies were eventually broken up in response to the international uproar over the cruel conditions in which they kept local populations. If *business* remains a bad word in those parts of the world, much of the responsibility falls on these two monopolies.

THE TRADITIONAL VIEW OF MONOPOLIES

The most visible effect of a monopoly is higher prices. Competition drives companies to offer their products at a price close to their production cost. In a perfect and stable monopoly, this pressure is gone. When selling its tea in England, for example, the EIC could set the price that was most convenient to itself, realizing that lower prices would induce higher demand but that higher prices would yield a higher profit per unit. In deciding the optimal price level, a monopolist like the EIC will generally settle on a number that is above the competitive price. One might therefore think of monopoly as a tax that producers impose on consumers. But that conception isn't always accurate. Imagine that the profit-maximizing price at which a hypothetical EIC sells tea is $10 per pound, when its cost of production and transportation is only $3. There are probably many people who are unwilling (or unable) to buy the tea at $10 but would be delighted to buy it at $5. Since 5 is bigger than 3, the company would be happy to sell to these customers at $5, if only it weren't simultaneously lowering the price paid by rich customers. Many monopolists resolve the problem by segmenting the market and discriminating among customers. If they are unable to do so, however, they are forced to give up selling to thriftier consumers in order to preserve the high profit they get from higher-spending consumers. Notice that the profit lost on the nonbuying customers is not a transfer from consumer to producer, as we had just imagined, but a loss both for the consumers, who were willing to buy at $5, and for the producer, which could have sold at $5 what cost $3 to produce. This is an example of what economists call *deadweight loss*. Who should capture the difference between the $10 that the company charges and the $3 cost of production depends upon your view of who is most "deserving." But the lost customers certainly represent a pure loss for society as a whole—a loss that, for example, patent law should try to minimize. This is the main reason why patent life is finite: the monopoly it creates (while necessary to motivate innovation) is inefficient, and there is a strong economic reason for it not to continue indefinitely.

The loss described above is not unique to monopolies. It occurs, albeit in a milder form, every time barriers to competition exist and firms have some market power over their customers. To address this problem, the United States developed antitrust legislation.

THE BENEFITS OF ANTITRUST LAW

Starting with the 1890 Sherman Antitrust Act, antitrust (or competition) law was introduced to oppose the coming together of entities—such as monopolies, cartels, or trusts—that could potentially harm competition. As is often the case, the motivation behind the act was suspect. Three months after proposing the law, Senator John Sherman sponsored the William McKinley Tariff, which restricted foreign trade and penalized consumers through higher prices. Some critics claimed that the Sherman Act was merely a scam to trick voters and introduce tariffs that severely penalized consumers. Regardless of the original intent, over the years the act and subsequent antitrust legislation have been used to reduce monopoly power and curtail business practices that set up detrimental barriers to entry. As the US Supreme Court has explained, "The purpose of the [Sherman] Act is not to protect businesses from the working of the market; it is to protect the public from the failure of the market. The law directs itself not against conduct which is competitive, even severely so, but against conduct which unfairly tends to destroy competition itself."[10]

One of the main targets of antitrust actions has been mergers between competitors. There are several arguments in favor of mergers, including the fact that they improve efficiency by introducing economies of scale; this efficiency can be passed along to customers. Mergers also allow superior companies offering superior products to expand throughout the country. Consider Starbucks, which, in its expansion, bought out local coffee shops, presumably at least some of which had inferior fare or took too long to get customers in and out during rush hour. Without being able to acquire existing coffee shops, Starbucks would not have found it convenient to expand into markets too small to support multiple coffee shops. Old coffee shops, shielded from competition, would have had little reason to improve. The customers would have lost out.

To justify mergers, firms usually push the economies-of-scale argument. But economies of scale are no panacea—if they were, the Soviet Union would have had the most productive economy on the planet. The idea of a static trade-off between greater competition and greater economies of scale misses the gains that competition generates over time. The genius of capitalism is the continuous trial-and-error process it encourages. Without trial and error, it is exceedingly difficult to produce innovation and growth.

Accordingly, the purpose of an antitrust law is to prevent excessive consolidation, which deprives consumers of the benefits of innovation. But if antitrust enforcement helps keep an industry competitive, it also has two significant costs. The first is squelching some economies of scale. The second and more important one is massive government intrusion into the private sector—an intrusion that can be exploited for political reasons.

For this reason, antitrust law and its enforcement remain controversial among economists. Former Fed chairman Alan Greenspan has argued that consolidation will always benefit customers and that antitrust law is a waste of resources. In a 1962 pamphlet, he wrote: "The entire structure of antitrust statutes in this country is a jumble of economic irrationality and ignorance."[11] He arrived at these extreme conclusions having started from the reasonable assumption that any monopoly that the government leaves unprotected is subject to the threat of competition from new businesses. In Greenspan's view, the threat alone is sufficient to ensure that customers get most of the benefits of competition, even in the absence of actual competition.

Yet this argument is valid only under very special circumstances.[12] If Greenspan were right, companies would be unable to sustain prices above the competitive level even if they had made secret agreements with one another (also known as cartels). Sadly, we know that this is not always true. A good example, well known thanks to the movie *The Informant*, is the price-fixing scheme perpetrated by Archer Daniels Midland (and foreign competitors) in the market for lysine, an amino acid used in animal feed. ADM, a food processing conglomerate, was not new to price-fixing allegations. Between 1965 and 1998 it was accused of price fixing five times in markets ranging from bakery flour to monosodium glutamate (MSG).[13] What makes the lysine case so striking is that, thanks to the informant who wiretapped the secret meetings, we can actually listen in as ADM conspires with four foreign competitors to raise the price of lysine from below 80 cents a pound to $1.20. "You're my friend," we hear ADM Corn Processing Division president Terry Wilson tell the foreign lysine makers in a secret meeting. "I want to be closer to you than I am to any customer 'cause you can make us money."[14] We also hear ADM president James Randall tell the group: "We have a saying here in this company that penetrates the whole company. It's a saying that our competitors are our friends. Our customers are the enemy." The price fixing lasted three years and—contrary to Greenspan's claim—the threat of entry did not push prices to their competitive level. This is evidence of the benefit of antitrust enforcement.

Yet the most powerful argument in favor of antitrust law is one that is rarely made: antitrust law reduces the political power of firms. Most economists (including Greenspan) agree with the statement that the worst and most enduring form of monopoly is the one sanctioned by state power. The ability to obtain this state reinforcement, however, is directly proportional to the size of a firm (or a cartel)—the larger the firm, the easier for it to overcome the fixed cost of lobbying, and the higher the returns will be. The bigger the firm, too, the more likely it will be able to wield the power of the state to its own advantage. For all of these reasons, the monopoly costs traditionally cited are neither the only ones nor the most important.

OTHER PEOPLE'S MONEY

Writing in 1776, Adam Smith had the theft and graft of the East India Company fixed vividly in his mind. For him, this corruption was an indictment not just of monopolies but of all corporations that separated ownership from control. While his conclusion was too pessimistic—the corporate form has been extremely successful over the last two hundred years—his concerns were legitimate and remain valid today.

In the late 1990s, many Russian oligarchs enriched themselves by siphoning money from the companies they were running. For oil oligarchs, one of the most popular schemes was to sell oil at below-market prices to foreign trading companies that they themselves owned. To get a sense of the potential magnitude of this manipulation in transfer pricing, we can consult a report showing that in 2000, one Russian firm was selling oil to a foreign trading partner at just $2.20 per barrel, considerably below the average export price (net of export costs and excise taxes) of $13.50.[15] The opportunity to channel profits toward a trading partner that the oil company's managers personally owned, as was likely the case here, was enhanced by the opacity of Russian firms' ownership structures.

Such episodes are not limited to foreign countries, of course, as the example of Enron can attest. Enron became infamous for its accounting fraud, which it perpetrated through a complex web of companies that did business solely with Enron. Enron's chief financial officer, Andrew Fastow, who designed this web, had a financial stake in the companies, either directly or through a partner. He personally profited from many trades.

Nevertheless, despite some egregious examples, outright theft of this kind is fairly rare in the United States. But when competition is limited, the managerial corruption that Adam Smith feared can easily occur. In a competitive market, managers are unable to divert significant resources or pay themselves excessive salaries. Doing so, after all, would jeopardize the firm's survival. By contrast, a firm with market power can earn more than it needs to compensate its workers and remunerate the capital invested. This extra return provides a cushion that top managers can easily exploit.

Consider the case of Ray Irani, the CEO of Occidental Petroleum. In 2010, he earned $76 million. His total compensation over the 2000–2010 period was a whopping $857 million. In these ten years, the company performed very well, but this performance largely resulted from a global surge in oil prices. The unhappiness of Occidental Petroleum's shareholders about this compensation level was evident at the 2010 annual shareholders' meeting. In a rare sign of lack of confidence, 54 percent of the shareholders voted against Occidental's pay program. Yet it wound up going forward, because Securities and Exchange Commission (SEC) regulations ensure that these shareholder votes are only *perfunctory*—that is, inconsequential.

These kinds of massive salaries resemble those that the top officers of the East India Company were paying themselves. After the victory at Plassey, Sir Robert Clive, an officer of the EIC, awarded himself £234,000—a staggeringly high sum at the time. So a lack of competition penalizes ordinary citizens twice. It leads to higher prices and lower availability of a service or product, and it generates unjustified (and thus excessive) incomes, undermining consensus for the economic system as a whole.

CRONYISM

Raised as I was in Italy, I know a few things about nepotism. In its origins, the term is a euphemism: historically, the "nephews" receiving favors were in fact natural children of a pope (Alexander VI), who—being a Catholic pope—was not supposed to have children.

It is no surprise that nepotism was born in Rome, in the Catholic Church. Historically, the Church enjoyed tremendous market power. When that power was not won through the superiority of the Church's message, it was obtained through the use of force. Repression, intolerance against heretics, and, ultimately, the Inquisition—all were aimed at preventing competition. It was precisely these barriers to entry that allowed the popes (and other members of the Catholic hierarchy) to wield—and often abuse—enormous power, including that of placing their children and cronies in positions of influence, regardless of merit.

This problem has not existed for Protestant churches, which are smaller and tend to compete with one another aggressively; thus they have little scope for favoritism. In these churches, appointing the wrong minister or the wrong treasurer can easily result in the disappearance of a congregation: room for error is scant. The same holds true for business. In a truly competitive market there is no room for cronies. The "room" arises when there is slack—that is, when a company can dominate a market. Cronyism, then, is another major cost of monopoly.

Unfortunately, it's a cost that compounds over time. Once an incompetent "nephew" or stupid crony finds himself in a position of importance in a company, he tends to hire only subordinates of equal or lower quality, since he will feel threatened by people smarter or more talented than he is. After a few years of such cronyism, there is no easy way back. The human capital of the firm will become so eroded that it won't be able to compete in the marketplace without some form of protection. Faced with any future threats to its own survival, should they somehow arise, the firm will then resort to lobbying, since it has forgotten how to compete. The more protection it is able to gain from government, however, the greater the available scope to continue the nepotism, which in turn makes protection even more necessary. A vicious circle is created that, once in motion, will drag down even the most successful economy.

THE POLITICIZATION OF DECISIONS INSIDE FIRMS

Firms and markets operate differently. Let's say there's a manager who wants to have a simple task done—photocopying, for instance. In a market transaction, the only information needed is the market price of this service. If the price is less than his assessment of how much the copies are worth, he will have the copies made; otherwise, he will not. He does not need to know the value of the possible alternative uses of the employees who work at the copy center, or the cost of the wear and tear on the photocopying machine. A single price saves him a lot of thinking. This is one of the great advantages of a market-based economy.

Consider now the same transaction *within* a firm. If the manager asks an assistant to make copies, the assistant will do the task (or risk getting fired). Within firms there is no contractual freedom: employees follow orders. There are also no prices involved. On the one hand, this makes things simpler: there is no need to haggle over how much any single task costs. On the other hand, the manager's decision becomes tremendously more complicated. Not knowing the price, he must think about the alternative use of the assistant's time and the alternative use of the copy machine. This can be done only within the context of an overall plan in which time is allocated to tasks and each task is given a value. In short, firms are small command-and-control economies, small socialist economies. What makes them so efficient (and keeps the capitalist economy vibrant) is the fact that they operate in a competitive environment. Once they acquire market power, however, they increasingly resemble their socialist cousins.

Conglomerates tend to be more socialist still. Before it merged with Exxon in 1998, Mobil Oil was not just an oil company; it was a large conglomerate. When oil prices plummeted in the mid-1980s, Mobil cut investments in all its divisions—not only in oil explorations (a decision that made sense, given the reduced price of oil) but also in its Montgomery Ward department-store business (quite unrelated to oil). Mobil even reduced its investment in its petrochemical divisions, the investment prospects of which should have benefited when oil prices fell, since they use oil as an input.[16]

This is an example of a well-documented fact: investment behavior within conglomerates deviates significantly from what similar firms that aren't conglomerates but that are in the same line of business do. One could argue that such deviation is understandable, since the reason conglomerates are created in the first place is precisely to manage resources in a way that is different from what markets do. For example, a conglomerate may provide financing to information-sensitive projects, which cannot raise the necessary funds in the marketplace without revealing their valuable secrets. Interestingly, though, the more the investment behavior of a conglomerate differs from that of the market, the less valuable the conglomerate becomes.[17] The same seems to be true of salaries. A student of mine, having looked at the patterns of salaries in conglomerates and compared them with the salaries for similar jobs in single-segment firms, has found that when one division in a conglomerate is in a sector that pays high salaries, all of the other divisions receive higher salaries, too.[18]

These tendencies are a manifestation of the conflict (which I discussed in Chapter 2) between efficiency and redistribution. To maintain consensus, companies and conglomerates tend to redistribute resources from the haves to the have-nots. By "taxing" the winning divisions and employees in order to subsidize the losers, this redistribution tends to reduce the incentive to work hard. Furthermore, it gives workers an incentive to lobby the managers, who have the power to affect redistribution, so as to grab a larger share of the existing pie.

Economists call such lobbying *rent seeking* to distinguish it from profit-seeking behavior. In seeking profits, companies or individuals engage in mutually beneficial transactions. In seeking rents, they spend resources trying to influence the division of a given pie. This behavior not only fails to create value (it basically steals from Peter to give to Paul) but actually *destroys* value, since time and effort are wasted in the process. Rent seeking is one of the greatest costs of bureaucracies, with talented individuals diverting large portions of their working day to efforts to influence the decision-making process in their favor.

Most economists distrust government because government enterprises are the ultimate form of monopoly and, as such, extremely inefficient. But as all these examples show, private companies untrammeled by the need to compete are also highly inefficient. Firms are socialist islands in a free-market ocean. The smaller the market power of these islands, the more the system conforms to Adam Smith's ideal; the larger it is, the more it resembles its socialist alternative. If one big firm controlled the entire economy, would a capitalist system differ from a socialist one?

MODERN-DAY EAST INDIA COMPANIES

For the invisible hand to work best, firms must be small enough that they cannot manipulate prices. Even when they do, free markets work pretty well as long as the firms' market power is limited. The larger their market power, the larger the distortion. The worst outcome is a scenario in which firms' market power transcends the industry they operate in and becomes political power. The state, as noted earlier in this chapter, has the ultimate monopoly—the one on the legitimate use of force. When the power arising from this monopoly merges with the market power arising from the economic dominance of a sector, the results are invariably disastrous—whether a government-owned firm is given market power (as with Fannie Mae and Freddie Mac) or a private monopoly takes over government power (as with the East India Company).

A modern-day version of an EIC and its negative consequences on a country are represented by Silvio Berlusconi. He won multiple electoral campaigns on his promise to run the government like a business. Unfortunately, he ended up running the government as his *own* business. Even when he did not bend the rules in his own favor, competitors bowed out for fear of government retaliation. Not since the East India Company has such a corrupt intermingling between government and business been seen. Berlusconi was prime minister for eight of the ten years between 2001 and 2011, during which time the Italian per-capita GDP dropped 4 percent, the debt-to-GDP ratio increased from 109 percent to 120 percent, and taxes increased from 41.2 percent to 43.4 percent of GDP. During the same period, Italy's score in the Heritage Foundation's Index of Economic Freedom fell from 63 to 60.3 and in the World Economic Forum Index of Competitiveness from 4.9 to 4.37. By capturing (or, more precisely, purchasing) the free-market flag the way one might acquire a business brand, Berlusconi has likely destroyed the appeal of the free-market ideal in Italy for a generation.

Unfortunately, Berlusconi is not the only example of a modern-day EIC. Under the Andreas family's reign, ADM was another. In addition to its participation in price-fixing scandals, ADM has been the most prominent recipient of corporate welfare in recent US history.[19] The libertarian *Cato Institute Policy Analysis* estimates that in 1995 at least 43 percent of ADM's annual profits were tied to products heavily subsidized or protected by the American government.[20] Between ethanol subsidies and a cane-sugar tariff protecting its high-fructose syrup, ADM has made billions of dollars over the years in subsidized profits at the expense of customers and taxpayers.

The government favors derive from the Andreas family's political connections. In addition to contributing millions of dollars to both political parties, Dwayne Andreas, the family patriarch, has provided personal assistance to politicians. He bought Jimmy Carter's peanut warehouse for $1.2 million[21] and sold Bob Dole and his wife an apartment at the Sea View Hotel in Bal Harbour, Florida.[22] He was not shy about his political influence. As he declared to a journalist: "There isn't one grain of anything in the world that is sold in a free market. Not one! The only place you see a free market is in the speeches of politicians. People who are not in the Midwest do not understand that this is a socialist country."[23] As the *Cato Institute Policy Analysis* correctly points out, "Andreas has exerted his influence in Washington to ensure that the U.S. form of 'socialism' resembles 1930s' Italian corporate statism: the government plunders the citizenry for the benefit of politically connected corporations."[24] The conservative *National Review* labeled him a modern robber baron.[25]

ADM bought support through the media as well. For a company that does not sell consumer products, it has wielded a massive TV advertising budget. Its ads in the past have inundated political talk shows. From January 1994 to April 1995, ADM spent $4.7 million on NBC's *Meet the Press,* $4.3 million on CBS's *Face the Nation,* and $6.8 million on PBS's *MacNeil-Lehrer Newshour,* and it was the primary sponsor of ABC's *This Week with David Brinkley.*[26]

Fannie Mae and Freddie Mac are likewise modern-day EICs. The conservative press has often described them as government entities pressured by politicians to make bad loans. A better characterization is private monopolies, which use their political connections to make money at the expense of taxpayers. Their operations are so massive that one could describe them as a state within the state. They have become so crucial to the US economy that they cannot be allowed to fail. They are so politically influential that reform becomes a Herculean task.

The political might of large financial institutions is not much smaller. Consider Citigroup's effort to change the Glass-Steagall Act, which severed the economic ties between investment banking and commercial banking. In 1998, Citigroup acquired Travelers (an insurance company), even though the law prohibited banks from merging with insurance companies. At the time of the merger, Travelers' CEO, Sandy Weill, explained why the companies were moving forward in spite of an apparent conflict with the law: "we have had enough discussions [with the Fed and the Treasury] to believe this will not be a problem."[27]

At that time, the head of the Treasury was Robert Rubin, who worked very hard to convince his fellow Democrats to change the law. Rubin left the Treasury in July 1999, the day after the House passed its version of the bill by a bipartisan vote of 343 to 86. Three months later, on October 18, 1999, Rubin was hired at Citigroup at a salary of $15 million a year, without any operating responsibility. It is hard not to see a connection between these two events.

Both Citigroup and Rubin acted within the law. But so did Berlusconi when he had the law changed to benefit himself and his own businesses. The legality of such commingling of business and government does not make it right. In a healthier state of affairs, one can use the resources created by private business to resist the grasping hand of the government or use the power of the state to restrain the abuses of private monopolies. But when private monopoly controls the power of the state, remedies vanish.

CONCLUSIONS

In the Introduction to this book, I mentioned that 51 percent of Americans agree with the statement "Big business distorts the functioning of markets to its own advantage." This conviction is shared not only by those who distrust free markets but also by those who agree that "the free market is the best system to generate wealth." The distinction between a promarket agenda and a probusiness one has not escaped the attention of a majority of Americans. While the two agendas sometimes coincide—as in the case of protecting property rights—they're often at odds. A probusiness agenda aims at maximizing the profits of existing firms; a promarket agenda, by contrast, aims at encouraging the best business conditions for everyone.

Adam Smith was promarket rather than probusiness, as all economists who believe in his principles should be. Free and competitive markets are the creators of the greatest wealth ever seen in human history. But for markets to work their magic, the playing field must be kept level and open to new entrants. When these conditions fail, free markets degenerate into inefficient monopolies—and when these monopolies extend their power to the political arena, we enter the realm of crony capitalism. Unfortunately, as the Citibank example suggests, one industry in which crony capitalism has gained a tremendous amount of influence in the last decade is finance, which deserves a separate analysis.

4

CRONY FINANCE

*I sincerely believe, with you, that banking establish-
ments are more dangerous than standing armies.*

—Thomas Jefferson

FINANCE IS AN ESSENTIAL INGREDIENT IN INJECTING competition into an economic system. Widespread access to it is crucial for drawing new entrepreneurs into the system and giving them the chance to prosper and grow. Finance is also a big equalizer: when the financial system works the way it's supposed to, ideas matter more than money, which means that talented people can compete head-to-head with anyone, regardless of individual wealth. Without that access to funds, the talented cannot strike out on their own, and often they end up working for the wealthy, just making the rich richer. Finance can turn the American Dream into a reality.

Recently, however, instead of greasing the wheels of economic growth, finance has been more like sand in its gears. From the burst Internet bubble to the Enron and WorldCom scandals, from the subprime mortgage crisis to Bernard Madoff's ruinous fraud, finance seems at the heart of many of our contemporary woes. Furthermore, it appears to be contributing to extremely unequal economic outcomes, not an equalizing of starting points. Countrywide CEO Angelo Mozillo—who had pioneered and pushed the subprime mortgages that caused so much havoc in the US and world economies, and who was ranked by the magazine *Condé Nast Portfolio* as the second-worst CEO of all time[1]—walked away with $470 million when he resigned.[2]

It is hard to blame this situation on lack of competition, since in many areas of finance, competition is intense, often cutthroat. Finance is also meritocratic, with talent highly compensated. Gone are the days when blue-blooded Ivy League executives closed the doors of the temples of finance to Italian Americans, Jews, and other minorities. Mozillo was the son of a Bronx butcher and has a bachelor's degree from Fordham University.

The problem, or at least a significant part of it, is the rising political hegemony of the financial sector. In this chapter, I will discuss how the fairness of the rules governing finance and of the process that determines those rules is crucial to making capitalism work for everyone. I will also explain how, thanks to its resources and cleverness, the financial sector has increasingly been able to rig the rules to its own advantage. This has damaged not only the economy but the financial sector itself.

Historically, the United States, through a combination of sound principles and serendipitous decisions, kept the financial sector in check. But as the financial system gained strength, it also gained political influence. In the last decade, our financial sector has become too concentrated and too powerful for its own good.

HOW DID IT HAPPEN?

Whoever controls the money spigot controls the life and death of businesses. In the venture-capital world, for instance, even contracts written to protect early investors are worthless when a start-up is running out of cash and needs new financing; whoever has the money to invest can dictate the terms of the transaction. This advantage enables finance to determine the extent to which new companies enter a sector and existing companies exit, thus affecting the allocation of profit in the economy.

Too much entry into a particular sector means too much competition and too few profits, as we saw in the previous chapter; too little entry, however, means that incumbent firms can sometimes make a fortune at the expense of consumers.

Americans have long been sensitive to such abuses and have nurtured something of a populist antifinance tradition. This tradition has led to many political decisions throughout American history that were inefficient from an economic point of view but helped preserve the long-term health of America's democratic capitalism. In 1832, President Andrew Jackson had to consider a bill that would extend the charter of the Second Bank of the United States (SBUS). Though it was a private company, the SBUS was functioning as a clearinghouse and as an early bank regulator, in ways similar to those of the modern Fed.[3] The bank, which greatly benefited from being the depository of the federal government's revenues, had become the mightiest organization in the country. Its loose lending policy fueled widespread land speculation, fraud, and eventually a bubble.[4] (Sound familiar?) Worried about the Second Bank's role, Jackson ordered an investigation that established "beyond question that this great and powerful institution had been actively engaged in attempting to influence the elections of the public officers by means of its money."[5] From an economic point of view, Jackson's decision—to veto a renewal of the charter—was hard to defend. It removed a valuable centralized clearinghouse that would have helped smooth individual state bank shocks, one of which snowballed into a panic in 1837. Yet by busting up the bank, Jackson successfully reduced the financial sector's sway over US policy.

As I noted in Chapter 1, American states have long feared the power of New York banks and restricted the industry using various methods, such as limiting banks to one office apiece and forbidding banks in one state to open branches in other states. In 1933, the Glass-Steagall Act continued this tradition by erecting a wall between two ways that banks could help customers borrow money. No longer could commercial banks (which make direct loans using depositors' money) engage in investment banking (helping customers, mostly companies, borrow by issuing debt securities on their behalf). The idea was to keep commercial banks from exploiting their depositors—who, legislators feared, might get saddled with the bonds of firms that could not repay the money they owed.[6] One beneficial side effect of the Glass-Steagall Act, as with most of the other banking regulations, was to fragment the banking sector and reduce the financial industry's political power. The act also fostered healthy competition between commercial banks and investment banks.

Starting in the 1970s, all these restrictions to banking were progressively removed. The first to go were the state restrictions on branching. Highly inefficient to begin with, the restrictions became untenable because of technological advances. What good does it do to restrict branching when, for example, banks can set up ATMs throughout the country?[7] The deregulation unquestionably increased the efficiency of the banking sector and fostered economic growth.[8] But with this growth came financial concentration. In 1980, there were 14,434 banks in the United States, about the same number as in 1934. By 1990, this number had dropped to 12,347; and by 2000, to 8,315. In 2009, the number was below 7,100 and continued to fall. Most important was that the concentration of deposits and lending increased significantly. In 1984, the top five US banks controlled only 9 percent of the total deposits in the banking sector. By 2001, that figure had increased to 21 percent, and by the end of 2008, to nearly 40 percent.

The apex of this process of deregulation and consolidation was the 1999 passage of the Gramm-Leach-Bliley Act, which completely removed Glass-Steagall's separation between commercial banks and investment banks. Gramm-Leach-Bliley has been wrongly accused of playing a major role in the 2008 financial crisis; in fact, it had almost nothing to do with it. The major institutions that failed or were bailed out during the crisis were either pure investment banks that did not take advantage of the repeal of Glass-Steagall (e.g., Lehman Brothers, Bear Stearns, and Merrill Lynch) or purely commercial banks (e.g., Wachovia and Washington Mutual). The only exception was Citigroup, which had merged its commercial and investment operations even before the Gramm-Leach-Bliley Act, betting that the law would be changed.

The real effect of Gramm-Leach-Bliley was political, not economic, at least directly. Under the old regime, commercial banks, investment banks, and insurance companies had different agendas, so their lobbying efforts tended to offset one another. But after the restrictions ended, the interests of all the major players in the financial industry aligned. This alignment gave the industry disproportionate power in shaping the nation's political agenda. The concentration of the banking industry amplified this power—which the banking industry was not shy about using, as the example of the 2005 bankruptcy reform shows.

TOO MUCH POWER

After more than ten years of discussions in Congress, on April 20, 2005, President George W. Bush signed into law the Bankruptcy Abuse Prevention and Consumer Protection Act, which reformed the rules overseeing bankruptcy, especially personal bankruptcy. Historically, the United States has been a prodebtor country. At its inception, the nation had to borrow heavily from England, and thus the protection of debtors was in the national interest.[9] Consider the unconditional discharge of debt introduced in the Bankruptcy Act of 1898: "When an honest man is hopelessly down financially, nothing is gained for the public by keeping him down, but, on the contrary, the public good will be promoted by having his assets distributed ratably as far as they will go among his creditors and letting him start anew."[10]

Partly because of this prodebtor bias, which has made defaulting on credit-card debt relatively painless, the percentage of Americans filing for personal bankruptcy has been high even during economic expansions. In 2003, for example, the percentage of adults filing for bankruptcy in the United States was ten times higher than that in the United Kingdom.[11] The laudable goal of the 2005 reform was to discourage opportunistic filings by debtors who used bankruptcy strategically to wipe out their debt even when they could afford to repay at least part of it. A reduction in opportunistic filings, it was thought, would lower the cost of credit for all Americans.

Bankruptcy law must strike a difficult balance between preventing opportunistic filings (also known as strategic default) and showing leniency toward people who, through no fault of their own, cannot pay their debts. In a competitive credit market, the benefit of reducing the number of strategic defaults will be enjoyed by all debtors in the form of cheaper and more widely available credit. If a reduction in strategic defaults is achieved by making all defaults (including nonstrategic ones) more painful, however, it might have negative implications for human welfare. Though jailing debtors who fail to repay their debt is a good way to ensure that they do not default strategically, it is an undesirable option for both humanitarian and economic reasons. If an entrepreneur knows that she will end up behind bars if she is unlucky and cannot repay a loan, she will hesitate to take any risk at all, and economic growth will suffer.

In determining where to strike this difficult balance, it helps to have a debate in which various viewpoints are presented. This took place in previous bankruptcy reforms, in which diverse professional organizations, such as the National Conference of Bankruptcy Judges, participated energetically.[12] By contrast, the debate over the 2005 reform was completely dominated by the credit lobby and organized by the National Consumer Bankruptcy Coalition. In the words of one legal scholar: "Never before in our history has such a well-organized, well-orchestrated, and well-financed campaign been run to change the balance of power between creditors and debtors."[13]

Prior to the repeal of the Glass-Steagall Act, an important barrier kept creditors from pooling together to lobby: they often had different interests. Consider a borrower who has both a car loan and credit-card debt. The holder of the car loan wants that debt to be paid out first and fast, whereas the holder of the credit-card debt has no interest in expediting the car payment, since doing so would leave the borrower with less money to pay down the credit-card debt. In the past, different kinds of lending were often carried out by different types of institutions, which, when it came to lobbying, found it difficult to speak with one voice. Following the major consolidation that took place in the banking sector, though, a smaller number of entities performed all of these lending functions—and for them, a consensus was easier.[14] As a legislative assistant to a member of the Senate Judiciary Committee commented, "The bankruptcy bill is a poster child for what should not happen in Congress. Maybe when there are two opposing powerful [interest groups], you get a wash, but in the bankruptcy bill, there is a real imbalance."[15] The result was a law that shifted the above-mentioned "balance of power" entirely in favor of creditors.

The idea behind the reform was legitimate: to reduce abuses in the system. But armed with this worthy goal, the credit lobby was so strong that it managed to take over the legislative agenda and ostracize all its opponents. Henry Hyde, the Republican chairman of the House Judiciary Committee, felt compelled to defend his fellow committee members: "I am as capitalist as anybody, I am as conservative as anybody, but it does not seem to me when there is a bill that is truly tilted towards creditors, that giving a little flexibility for living standards for people who are bankrupt is a violation of one's credentials as a conservative."[16]

Never has the expression "be careful what you wish for" been more appropriate, however. Only eight months after the law was signed, house prices plateaued and then started to drop, straining the financial situation of many homeowners. In the pre-bankruptcy-reform world, distressed homeowners would have filed for personal bankruptcy, which would have allowed them to discharge their credit-card debt, making it easier to hold on to their houses. Under the new law, this option was no longer open. According to calculations based on a recent study, the 2005 reform increased the number of people defaulting on their mortgages by almost half a million; and when a mortgage holder defaults and the house is auctioned off, on average it loses 27 percent in value.[17] If we apply this loss to the average price of a house sold in 2005 ($290,000), we can estimate that the financial industry lost $39 billion as a result of bankruptcy reform.

Yet the reform's strongest negative effect on the financial industry resulted from an arcane section of the bill that was little noticed at the time. The section strengthened the rights of derivatives owners in bankruptcy cases. Derivatives are contracts that shift the risk of a certain event—say, an increase in oil price—to a counterparty. Imagine that Southwest Airlines wants to lock in the current oil price. Through derivatives, it could pay today's price to receive oil at a set date in the future—ensuring that if the price of oil rises between now and then, it won't have to pay the higher price. Southwest can do so, though, only if another party—a financial institution like Lehman Brothers, say—is willing to take the other side. If oil prices do go down, Southwest will owe Lehman the difference between the earlier price and the new market price. If oil prices go up, Lehman will owe

Southwest the difference between the two. But suppose oil prices rise and Lehman goes bankrupt. What happens to the debt that Lehman owes Southwest?

One reasonable answer is that Southwest should be treated like all Lehman's other creditors, who would share the assets of the bankrupt firm. A more favorable treatment for Southwest would consider the derivative holder *senior*, meaning that it would be paid first out of the pool of assets available. The 2005 reform went further. Rather than paying derivative holders back as much as possible with the bankrupt company's assets, it allowed them to pretend that nothing had happened at all. So in our example, instead of receiving the difference between the market price of oil and the older price, Southwest would have the right to receive a contract *identical* to the one it had signed with Lehman, but now with a different counterparty. Lehman would have to shoulder the transaction cost of the new contract, which typically ranges between 0.1 and 0.2 percent of the contract's total value.

If this transaction cost seems insignificant, just look at what happened in Lehman's case. At the time it went bankrupt, Lehman had derivative contracts with a notional value (face value) of $35 trillion. At an average transaction cost of .15 percent, reintegrating those contracts amounts to $52.5 billion of extra cost! In other words, in addition to repaying its debt to derivative holders before anybody else was paid, the Lehman bankruptcy estate had to spend another $52.5 billion on new contracts.[18] This rule reduced the payoff of all the other creditors by $52.5 billion. In fact, it is part of the reason why Lehman's bonds, which were AA-rated until the day before it went bankrupt, paid only 8.625 cents on the dollar.[19]

This hugely important change was so overlooked that later, a major hedge-fund manager admitted to me that he had no idea what the rules were until the Lehman bankruptcy occurred. He then asked his lawyers to brief him and was shocked at what he heard.

TOO BIG TO FAIL

Another reason that large banks are politically influential is that their demise can create a catastrophic disruption in the economy—or so, at least, policy makers believe. Whether or not they are right is irrelevant. Suppose a large asteroid is hurtling toward Earth—as in the movie *Armageddon*—and has a 5 percent chance of hitting the planet, creating $10 trillion worth of physical damage to the United States. And let's say you're the president. Should you authorize a $700 billion mission to destroy the asteroid and stave off disaster? If you reason in purely statistical terms, the expected cost of failing to act ($0.05 \times$ $10,000 billion = $500 billion) is much less than the cost of acting.

But if you do spend the money to stop the asteroid, nobody will know whether it would indeed have hit the Earth, had you neglected to act—so you can go down in history as the president who saved the planet. By contrast, if you do nothing, you have a 5 percent chance of going down in history as the president who knowingly failed to avoid catastrophe. Doesn't the Operation Armageddon to destroy the asteroid suddenly look much more appealing? And, after all, the aerospace industry would be delighted to be paid to work on the mission. It pressures you to act—and begins a campaign to scare the public. Who can really tell with any degree of certainty, industry representatives warn, that the probability of disaster is only 5 percent? Perhaps because all of the experts would, directly or indirectly, benefit from the proposed mission, you start hearing that the chances of disaster are really 10 to 20 percent. With those odds, Operation Armageddon would make all the sense in the world, both politically and statistically. There is nothing like self-interest to help you believe in something.

The circumstances that make policy makers succumb to the "too big to fail" doctrine are similar to those in the Armageddon scenario. An important difference, however, is that a Fed chairman's resolve to bail out banks actually increases the likelihood of disaster, since his implicit promise to intervene has a perverse influence on the banks' willingness to take risk. To understand the nature of this influence, let's consider a place where gambling is commonplace: a roulette table in Las Vegas. Roulette is designed to ensure that the payout when someone wins is inversely related to the odds of winning, so that every bet's *expected* payoff—that is, the probability of winning times the payoff of winning—is the same. If you bet $100 on red and you win, the croupier will pay you 1 to 1 and hand you a total of $200. Since you have an 18 out of 38 chance of winning (American roulette includes a double zero), your *expected* payoff is $94.73. A winning bet on any single number will pay you 35 to 1. Though the probability of winning is much lower (1 out of 38), your expected payoff is the same: $94.73.

Now imagine that instead of playing in person, you hire an agent to wager $100 on your behalf. To motivate this agent to play well, you promise him 20 percent of your winnings. How would he play? If he bets on red and wins, the net gain (the payout minus the money invested) is only $100, of which he will get $20. Given the odds of red, his expected payoff is $9.47 (i.e., 18/38 × 20). If he bets on a number and wins, the net gain is $3,500, of which the agent will get $700. Given these odds, his expected payoff is almost twice as much: $18.42 (i.e., 1/38 × 700). If the roulette game is designed so that the expected gain of all the bets is the same, why does the agent gain more from the riskier bet?

The answer is simpler than one might think. The agent gets 20 percent of the gain—*but he pays nothing for the loss.* Unless he is highly risk averse, an individual who has a share of the upside and none of the downside has a strong incentive to take on a lot of risk. This structure of incentives is typical of Wall Street, and it explains why managers take excessive risks.

True, if the principal (i.e., the person hiring the agent to place bets for her) is smart, she can minimize the problem by limiting the types of bet that the agent has permission to take. For example, many hedge-fund managers are contractually restricted to invest only in certain asset classes. Suppose now that the principal herself had borrowed the money being bet. In that case, she will not be overly concerned about making restrictions for her agent. If the agent is lucky and wins, the principal will profit from the gain; if the agent is unlucky and loses, the *lender*, not the principal, loses out. Obviously, the incentive to set restrictions on risk has now shifted to the creditors, which is why the typical lender imposes extremely strict rules on what kind of investment a borrower can make.

When large banks borrow, however, their lenders don't impose those rules. That's because they know that the government considers the banks "too big to fail." The lenders therefore know that they will always be paid back, either by the bank or by the taxpayer. But without restrictions, the bank's managers and shareholders alike are free to take on all the risk they want. This is the infamous moral-hazard problem that bank bailouts cause. Moral hazard cannot be fought by strengthening the control that banks' shareholders have over their managers, because both parties have the same perverse incentive. The only way to fix the problem is to make creditors face some losses when the bets do not pay off. But that requires letting some big banks fail, something that politicians increasingly have refused to do. In 1998, the Fed coordinated the private bailout of Long Term Capital Management, a hedge fund that had such complex entwinement with financial markets that its failure was deemed potentially disastrous. In that instance, which some see as beginning the "too big to fail" moral-hazard problem in finance, the only expense the Fed incurred was the cost of the (bad) coffee and doughnuts offered at the meeting to hash out the bailout deal.

The cost would grow astronomically. Rational lenders now understood that, when push came to shove, the government would probably intervene with help if a big or extensively interconnected financial firm was set to collapse. This proved glaringly true during the financial meltdown, when the government bailed out Bear Stearns (creditors did not lose a dime), and it did the same for all the other failing institutions except for Lehman Brothers and Washington Mutual. Both of these exceptions occurred during the same week in September 2008—and the market was so surprised that panic ensued. "Too big to fail" had become a self-fulfilling prophecy. If the belief becomes sufficiently entrenched in the marketplace, the cost, when policy makers surprise the market by *not* bailing out a big bank, grows even greater. Shortsighted policy makers will always prefer the cost of a bailout to the cost of upsetting the market. As a consequence, the problem continues and expands. In 2008, the government had to intervene with $700 billion. What will the bill be in 2018?

Anticipating government bailouts in case of emergency, lenders are willing to lend to large financial institutions very cheaply and without restrictions. Offered cheap credit, the managers of these financial institutions find it attractive to borrow a lot and to take wildly risky gambles, because they can maximize their profits in doing so. Unfortunately, the risky bets also maximize the probability that the government *will* have to intervene, as well as the cost that the government will pay when it does. The value of this implicit government subsidy to banks considered "too big to fail" is estimated to be half of a percentage point of interest.[20] Multiplied by the debt of the top eighteen bank holding companies, it corresponds to a $34.1 billion subsidy per year.

By reducing the cost of credit for large banks deemed "too big to fail," this subsidy also distorts competition, hampering small banks' ability to compete. The result, naturally, is an increase in the number of big banks—banks that may need to be rescued in the future.

TOO BIG TO MANAGE

Shortly after the Enron and WorldCom scandals, I started researching the actors who bring corporate fraud to light.[21] In principle, the people with the strongest incentives to detect fraud should be the shareholders, who pay the cost of fraud. But shareholders are dispersed and need to delegate the task. To whom? Not the board members of corporations, for starters: they rely on external auditors to detect fraud. A good friend of mine who sits on the board of a large company once asked the firm's head of purchasing what prevented him from overpaying for an item and having part of the difference rebated to a secret Swiss bank account. A lawyer on the board interrupted him, arguing that board members were responsible for making sure that procedures existed, not ensuring that they were effective!

The investment bankers who underwrite firms also rely on external auditors to detect fraud, even if those bankers also charge hefty fees to lend their own credibility to the firms. But the external auditors do not view fraud detection as their responsibility. In fact, analysis of the standard reference for the US auditing profession during the twentieth century demonstrates that, over the years, accountants deemphasized fraud detection and instead placed their emphasis on adherence to formal procedures.[22] The reason for this trend toward merely formal controls is, as a recent study put it, the "attempt [by auditors] to shift the blame for any fraud to management, who must have failed to maintain effective internal controls."[23] A study that I conducted with two colleagues found external auditors responsible for just 10 percent of fraud detection and investment banks for none.[24]

Unfortunately, a similar emphasis rules at the Securities and Exchange Commission. When I presented our findings at a seminar there, I got the same kind of response that my friend did: it is not the SEC's job to detect fraud. Our work confirms this: the SEC accounts for only 7 percent of fraud detection.

Who, then, brings fraud to light? The answer: an unlikely combination of people who have other roles in the organization. In 17 percent of the cases we studied, a single employee had blown the whistle, often at high personal cost. In 13 percent of the cases, non-financial-market regulators, such as the Federal Energy Regulation Commission and the Federal Aviation Commission, had happened to spot wrongdoing. The media had uncovered another 13 percent of the cases.[25] And the remainder were accounted for by analysts (14 percent), short-sellers (15 percent), competitors (5 percent), law firms (3 percent), equity holders (3 percent), external auditors (10 percent), and the SEC (7 percent, mentioned earlier).

I finally got it: it was *nobody's* job to detect fraud. Most fraud was detected serendipitously. If this remains the case, which is likely, the chances are that much fraud continues to go undetected. Using various methods, my colleagues and I estimate that every year fraud occurs in 5 to 10 percent of publicly traded companies, with a median cost of 41 percent of the prefraud enterprise value of the firm.[26]

Of course, detecting fraud is expensive, so it is not feasible to eradicate it at all costs. Yet the incompetence and lack of control in this area seem endemic. One can get a sense of this in the testimony of Robert Rubin, former chairman of Citigroup (and former secretary of the Treasury), to the government's Financial Crisis Inquiry Commission. He admitted that until the fall of 2007, he was unaware of some of the risk that Citigroup was assuming—investments that eventually cost Citigroup $30 billion.[27] If top executives cannot even monitor major risk like this, how can they prevent fraud? More recently, UBS has lost $2 billion in unauthorized derivatives-trading bets done by a rogue trader—and this was *after* billions were lost in the 2008 crisis and *after* the company imposed new risk controls! If UBS is unable to prevent a

$2 billion loss even after its best attempt to rein in risk, has it become (and the same could be said of other mega-banks) too big to manage?

When organizations become very large, it is inevitable that they will rely on delegation. But delegating should not be a way for companies to wash their hands of responsibility for exposing fraud perpetrated within their walls. As former Fed chairman Alan Greenspan has honestly admitted: "Those of us who have looked to the self-interest of lending institutions to protect shareholders' equity—myself especially—are in a state of shocked disbelief."[28]

All this evidence suggests that some financial institutions have grown beyond the point where they can efficiently monitor themselves. How, you might ask, could this happen in a free market? Isn't it in the banks' best interest to detect expensive fraud? Here again, the answer may implicate the "too big to fail" mentality. That is, the political benefit that banks receive by being so big—and also their ability to influence legislation, such as bankruptcy reform—is so significant that it offsets the inefficiencies, such as fraud, that arise from their enormous size. Citizens, meanwhile, pay twice: once for the subsidy they provide, and a second time for the distortions and inefficiencies they have to bear, in the form of biased bankruptcy reform, inefficiently large institutions, and so on.

TOO "SMART" TO MANAGE

Physics in the early half of the twentieth century performed an exciting intellectual journey from Albert Einstein's idea of mass-energy equivalence in 1905 to the first controlled nuclear reaction in 1942. The development of financial economics in the second part of the twentieth century has some of the same elements of excitement. From the abstract theoretical work on market equilibrium done mid-century by Nobel Prize–winning economists Kenneth Arrow and Gerard Debreu to the emergence of the financial derivatives markets at the end of the century, the ride has been thrilling. Despite their terrible reputation, financial derivatives can be useful instruments for managing risk, reducing the cost of capital, and thus favoring investment and growth—just as nuclear power can be useful as a cheap source of energy. In evaluating both nuclear power and financial derivatives, we need to think about risks as well as rewards. In the case of nuclear power, the risks include accidents, hidden costs (nuclear waste and government-subsidized catastrophe insurance), and the chance that the technology might fall into the wrong hands. In the case of derivatives, there is the risk of massive mistakes (such as the one in January 2008 that led to a $7 billion loss in three days at Société Générale), the implicit government subsidy, and the chance that they might be intentionally misused by companies and countries trying to mislead regulators or defraud investors. These risks increase as these products become ever more complex.

The town of Baschi in central Italy has only 2,800 inhabitants.[29] In 2004, to manage its €2 million debt better, the town decided to transform some of its fixed-interest loans into variable-rate loans, hoping to benefit if interest rates fell. In principle, this is done by swapping loan payments with another borrower, one who has too much variable-interest debt and wants to transform it into fixed-rate loans. More often, a bank acts as a counterparty, taking opposite positions in many such swaps and netting the risk. By now, such contracts are pretty standard.

In 2006, however, an investment bank convinced Baschi to transform its swap into a more complicated contract, with the due date of the loan extended to the year 2034 and the town receiving an up-front payment of €25,000. In 2010, the town found that it owed the banks an extra €90,000, despite a decline in interest rates. The contract was so complicated that the town still doesn't understand what happened. It alleges that it was swindled. Similarly, in Germany, local municipalities claim they unwittingly ended up insuring some of the infamous collateralized debt obligations involved in the financial crisis.[30]

Sure, a little town like Baschi may have no business getting into complicated derivatives. But was the fault entirely the buyer's, or were the experienced sellers partly to blame? The fear that smarter or better-informed bankers could take advantage of their clients was at the root of the Glass-Steagall Act's separation of investment and commercial banking. Modern research suggests that the fear was then probably unfounded; in the 1930s, worry about earning a bad reputation might have been strong enough to keep banks from abusing their power.[31] But today, that outcome cannot be taken for granted. Recent Italian history is full of stories about banks that loaded their clients' portfolios with bonds of companies about to go bankrupt. Even more recently, during the financial crisis, Italian banks stuffed their depositors' portfolios with their own, highly risky bonds. The less financially sophisticated the depositors were, the more they were cheated.[32]

TOO OLIGOPOLISTIC

When we compare financial systems, either historically or across countries, the most relevant distinction is not between banks and markets but between *relationship-based* and *arm's-length* financing.[33] As the term suggests, relationship-based systems are based on repeated interactions. These favor cooperation, which allows the system to work even when decent legal protection is lacking. To sustain itself, however, a relationship-based system requires market concentration, because long-lasting relationships are difficult to sustain in a fragmented and competitive market. Precisely because it thrives in noncompetitive markets, relationship financing is prone to collusion and can easily degenerate into crony capitalism. In fact, the term *crony capitalism* first became popular when it was used to describe the entangled relations of East Asian banks at the time of the 1997 Asian financial crisis.[34]

By contrast, arm's-length financing is based on one-time transactions, generally in anonymous or quasi-anonymous securities markets. Individual investors bidding for Google shares at its initial public offering are a good example. To work well, these markets need to be competitive and regulated. They must be competitive because only then will small investors be protected against the risk of receiving an unfair price. And they must be regulated because, in anonymous markets, reputation cannot restrain fraud and abusive practices. When these conditions are in place, arm's-length securities markets are better than relationship-based markets at aggregating information and providing cheap financing. But if the conditions don't hold and the risk of fraud becomes high, the markets will freeze.

The relative importance of the two modes of financing has changed over time. Before World War I, arm's-length financing was as widespread in Europe and Japan as it was in the United States.[35] It was the response to the Great Depression that created a divide. In Europe and Japan, the dominance of a few large banks facilitated the formation of a political coalition between more interventionist governments and the banking system. As a result, the legal infrastructure needed to support arm's-length markets was never fully fleshed out, and the regulatory framework tilted toward large banks. By contrast, the United States entered the Great Depression with a fragmented banking sector. Rather than favoring consolidation, New Deal legislation introduced regulation that created the infrastructure in which securities markets could work. The consequence of these fortuitous circumstances was strong securities markets until the end of the twentieth century.

The recent process of bank consolidation, however, jeopardizes the development of other organized exchanges. Options and futures, which arrived on the scene before the consolidation, did get organized in regulated markets. Other derivatives, however, started to be traded mostly in unregulated, over-the-counter markets, dominated by a few big banks. According to a European Central Bank study, in 2009, the five largest credit-default swap dealers were party to almost half of the total outstanding notional amounts, while the ten largest accounted for 72 percent of the trades.[36] The markets for other derivatives are similarly tilted.

When the vast majority of trades go through a few intermediaries, the market becomes distorted in several ways. First, when they transact among themselves, large players do not insist on an adequate amount of collateral; rather, they rely on the counterparty's general creditworthiness (and on the implicit guarantees that governments provide to large firms). This distortion not only severely undermines the ability of small firms to compete but also contributes to systemic instability of the type that we experienced in 2008, thus increasing the likelihood that taxpayers will have to step in with bailouts. Meanwhile, the beneficent risk-spreading role of derivatives dissipates, because the bulk of the risk, after all, is borne by just a few players.

Over-the-counter trading also increases the opacity of derivatives markets. In organized exchanges, the exchange records all transactions and thus can keep track of whether any single player is overexposed, helping to monitor systemic risk. Furthermore, in organized exchanges, transaction prices are revealed to all parties involved, increasing transparency and competition. By contrast, in over-the-counter trading, transaction prices between two parties are not necessarily known to others, which reduces competition. The combined yearly revenues of the key players in this derivatives market total $60 billion—a massive tax on the real economy.

Finally, over-the-counter markets increase the instability of the system because their trading takes place through a few very large banks. Air travelers know how heavy snow at a large airline hub like Chicago's can cause havoc throughout the country. The same is true for over-the-counter markets: if a large hub like Lehman is taken down by bankruptcy, the entire system is severely affected.[37] This importance only increases the power of the big banks, as the government sees it. Even if they are not "too big to fail" from a financing standpoint, they are certainly "too big to fail" from a market-stability standpoint.

THE MODERN TEAMSTERS

In 1860, the share of GDP represented by financial services was 1.6 percent. Almost a century later, in 1950, it was still only 2.9 percent.[38] Since then, it has skyrocketed. In 1980 it reached 4.7 percent, and by 2007, 8 percent. Why did the financial sector grow so large? To answer this question consider another type of intermediation familiar to anyone who has bought or sold a property: real estate agents.

Before the Internet made shopping for properties easy, American real estate agents possessed a huge source of market power: the Multiple Listing Service (MLS), a central repository of all properties available for purchase. All real estate agents who used the MLS abided by a type of contract that made it extremely difficult for buyers and sellers to compete on price.[39] This system de facto guarantees real estate agents a commission of 6 percent of the property's purchase price. This market power, however, does not translate necessarily into a higher average compensation for the real estate agents. Because it is relatively simple and inexpensive to become a licensed real estate agent (i.e., the market is characterized by "free entry," as economists call it), the higher potential earnings attract more agents into the market. The result is a bloated and less productive real estate industry.[40] The same is true in finance.

What drove the increase in GDP share in the financial sector was a rapid increase not only in profits, but also in wages. In 1980, the wage of a worker in the financial sector was roughly comparable to the wages of workers with the same qualifications in other sectors. By 2006, a person in the financial sector was making 70 percent more.[41] It's true that the skills required of a worker in the financial sector have gone up; for example, the proportion of finance workers with more than a high school degree increased from 13 percent in 1980 to 20 percent in 2006. Nevertheless, every attempt to explain this gap using differences in abilities, or the inherent demands of the work, falls short. Even when you take these factors into account, people working in finance are still making from 30 to 50 percent more than equally qualified people working in a different sector.

How can we explain this difference? In a free-market economy, higher wages signal higher productivity. But in a regulated or subsidized sector, this is not necessarily the case. In an industry that is protected from competition and receives rent money—such as finance—the labor force captures part of the rent.

The clearest example of this rent sharing can be found in the trucking industry. From 1935 to the mid-1970s, interstate trucking was tightly regulated by the Interstate Commerce Commission, which restricted entry by requiring an ICC license to operate a truck and prevented price competition by denying the license to those who were offering lower prices. This regulation raised trucking rates and handed high profits to the trucking firms.[42] In the late 1970s, the industry was deregulated, culminating in the 1980 Motor Carrier Act. The data show that unionized truckers, such as the Teamsters, subsequently saw their wages decline 14 percent in relative terms.[43] Using this figure and an aggregate estimate of the overall rent that regulation had granted to the trucking industry, we can conclude that the unionized truckers had captured as much as 75 percent of the rent from regulation.

Can the abnormal wages in the finance industry be explained by the government subsidies that large financial firms receive? We have seen that the subsidy implicit in the "too big to fail" policy is roughly $30 billion a year. In 2006 the number of people (including secretaries and janitors) working in the top twelve investment and commercial banks was 1,100,000.[44] At an average compensation of roughly $200,000 each, the total wage bill was $220 billion. Had these workers been paid as much as workers with the same qualifications in the other sectors, the wage bill would have been only $170 billion. Thus, the "too big to fail" subsidy could explain 60 percent of that difference. I am not saying that the wage differential is necessarily due to the government subsidy. The point of this back-of-the envelope exercise is merely to show the plausibility of the speculation that some of the extra wages in the finance industry are due to the government subsidy.

While the rents paid to truckers did not have a major impact on the allocation of talent in the US economy, the same cannot be said of their financial counterparts. Among the men who graduated from Harvard around 1970, 22 percent were in finance or management fifteen years later.[45] Among those who graduated around 1990, the figure was 38 percent. The proportion of male graduates working in finance alone increased from 5 percent to 15 percent during the same period. An additional survey conducted in 2007 by Harvard's newspaper, the *Harvard Crimson*, found that 58 percent of the graduating men were headed for finance or consulting and more than 20 percent were headed for investment banks.[46] Similar trends hold at Yale. The percentage of graduates working in finance increased from 8 percent in 1975 to 20 percent in 2007, while the percentage of those going into medicine dropped from 16 percent in 1970 to 5 percent in 2007.[47]

The ability of the financial sector to attract the best talents has implications that extend beyond finance and deep into government. Thirty years ago, the brightest undergraduates went into science, technology, law, and business; for the last twenty years, they have gone disproportionately into finance. Having devoted themselves to this sector, these talented individuals inevitably end up working to advance its interests. A specialist in derivative trading is likely to be extremely concerned about the importance and value of derivatives, just as a nuclear engineer is likely to think that nuclear power can solve all the world's problems. By implication, if most of the political elite were chosen from among nuclear engineers, the country would soon fill with nuclear plants. In fact, precisely this scenario exists in France, where, for complicated cultural reasons, an unusually large proportion of the political elite is trained in engineering at the École Polytechnique. France derives more of its energy from nuclear power than any other nation: 80 percent.

An extraordinary proportion of people with training and experience in finance have worked at the highest levels of every recent presidential administration. Four of the last six secretaries of the Treasury fit this description. In fact, all four were directly or indirectly connected to one firm: Goldman Sachs. This is hardly the historical norm: of the previous six Treasury secretaries, only one had a finance background. And finance-trained executives staff not only the Treasury but many senior White House posts and key positions in other departments. President Barack Obama's former chief of staff, Rahm Emanuel, once worked for an investment bank, as did his predecessor under President George W. Bush, Joshua Bolten.

There is nothing intrinsically bad about this trend. It is only natural that a government in search of the brightest people will end up poaching from the financial world, to which the best and brightest have flocked. The problem is that people who have spent their entire lives in finance have an understandable tendency to think that the interests of their industry and the interests of the country always coincide. When Treasury Secretary Henry Paulson went to Congress in the fall of 2008 arguing that the world as we knew it would end if Congress did not approve the $700 billion bailout, he was serious. And to an extent he was right: *his* world—the world he lived and worked in—would have ended had there not been a bailout. Goldman Sachs would have gone bankrupt, and the repercussions for everyone he knew would have been enormous. But Henry Paulson's world is not the world most Americans live in or even the world in which our economy as a whole exists. Whether that world would have ended without Congress's bailout was a far more debatable proposition—and unfortunately, that debate never took place.

Compounding the problem is the fact that people in government tend to rely on networks of trusted friends for information "from the outside." If everyone in those networks is drawn from the same milieu, the information and ideas that flow to policy makers will be severely limited. A revealing anecdote comes from a Bush Treasury official who noted that in the heat of the financial crisis, the message was the same every time a phone call came through from Manhattan's 212 area code: "Buy the toxic assets." Such uniformity of advice makes it difficult for even the most intelligent or well-meaning policy makers to arrive at the right decisions. This problem pervades our political and economic life. It generates mistrust in government and institutions, and it feeds the worst kind of populism.

5

BAILOUT NATION

I get elected by voters, I get financed by contributors.
Voters don't care about this, contributors do.

—Unnamed US representative[1]

N FEBRUARY 2009, DURING ONE OF THE DARKEST PERIODS following the 2008 financial crisis, I was approached by two young entrepreneurs who wanted to pitch an idea for a startup. The idea was to bypass banks in the lending process. One of the problems facing the economy in the aftermath of the crisis was a lack of loans, especially for individuals and small firms. To make such loans, you need both specific expertise and capital. But the majority of banks, though they retained most of their expertise, were lacking capital following their large losses in real estate lending. The entrepreneurs wanted to hire credit specialists from banks and then fund loans to creditworthy individuals with money raised through a mutual fund rather than through deposits.

As I started to study the details of the entrepreneurs' plan, I happened to ask why they had approached me. It turned out that they had read a series of op-eds I had written following the financial crisis, arguing against the bailouts of large banks and in favor of facilitating the entry of new ones. They also knew that the new Obama administration had brought a bunch of economics professors to Washington. As we talked, it became clear that they thought I could help them connect with the administration and thus gain access to some of the Troubled Assets Relief Program's money, which they would funnel into their initiative. They wanted a lobbyist!

I was disappointed twice over—first, because I thought I had made it sufficiently clear in my op-eds that I detested government subsidies and would never lobby in favor of more; second (and more important), because I saw the entrepreneurs' plan as a sign of how America was changing. When the Pilgrims planned their trip, they did not ask the government for money; they asked for private investors. When Abraham Lincoln's family left Kentucky in search of new pastures in Illinois, they did not ask the government for money. When more than 300,000 people rushed to California in search of gold, they were not subsidized by the government.

When the primary concern of a startup is to devise a strategy to milk money from taxpayers—indeed, when a new company refines its lobbying strategy even before it defines its market strategy—it means that crony capitalism has corrupted American society. A subsidy-driven market selects not the firms most efficient at producing but those most efficient at sucking up public resources. How did the land of opportunity become the land of rent seekers?

THE GROWING LEVIATHAN

The first and most obvious reason for firms to lobby government is the growing reward for lobbying.[2] The bigger the government, the larger the pie, and thus the larger the incentive for businesses to try to grab a slice. In 1900, federal nondefense spending represented just 1.8 percent of GDP, while defense-related spending represented another 1 percent. In 2005, even before the recent surge in government spending due to the Great Recession, nondefense spending represented 16 percent of GDP and defense-related spending another 4 percent.[3] In one century, the government share of GDP has increased sevenfold.

The actual amount that government spends has exploded even more. In 1900, it spent only $8 billion (in 2005 dollars) on things other than defense, compared with $1,977 billion in 2005.[4] Some of this money was spent on education and on government employees, so private companies could not easily get access to it. But plenty was up for grabs. Of those $1,977 billion, $90 billion went toward subsidized loans, research, marketing support, and cash payments to businesses—activities that are often (accurately) defined as "corporate welfare."[5]

In part, this type of spending represents failed attempts by the government to develop a Japanese-style industrial policy. But the idea that governments can identify growth opportunities better than markets can is preposterous. As the Austrian economist and Nobel Prize winner Friedrich August von Hayek pointed out long ago, information is diffuse. The merchant noticing that, say, his supply of broccoli is running low while his supply of potatoes piles up will be the first to recognize a shift in demand between the two vegetables. Whether this is a local phenomenon or a general one will depend on the observations of thousands of other food merchants. Each merchant has an incentive to raise the prices of goods that sell fast and to lower those of goods that remain unsold. If the shift in demand is merely local, this price change will lead wholesalers to reshuffle the quantities of broccoli and potatoes supplied to the various local markets. But if the shift is widespread, the wholesalers, finding their supply of broccoli running low, will start bidding up the price they pay farmers for broccoli. Responding to the higher price, farmers will then plant more broccoli and fewer potatoes. In other words, in a free-market system, prices provide valuable signals of what should and should not be produced. In a centrally planned economy, by contrast, bureaucrats and statisticians must gather information from local managers in order to make decisions about production. These local managers often have an incentive to distort their reports in ways that benefit them. Part of the genius of the free-market system is that it's in the interest of all individual agents to transmit price signals truthfully. The wholesalers who bid up the price of the broccoli are not aware that they're sending a signal to the farmer; they're simply trying to maximize their profit.

If markets hold this advantage over bureaucrats in a field as relatively simple as vegetables, imagine how much more efficient markets are at making production and investment decisions in advanced economies. Nevertheless, Washington politicians love playing industrial policy because it allows them to benefit their cronies. After the Clinton administration gave $1.5 billion to US automakers for hybrid cars,[6] the Bush administration spent $1.2 billion over the next five years on hydrogen-car research. About a decade ago, the federal government gave $1.1 billion in loan guarantees to a company called American Classic Voyages to buy two cruise ships to be built in Senator Trent Lott's hometown.[7] Before the ships were completed, the company went bankrupt, leaving federal taxpayers with a $200 million tab. Examples of such deals are legion.

The sector in which the government share of the economy has ballooned the most is health care. At the beginning of the twentieth century, the US government spent little on health care, and until 1960, the amount remained a bit less than 1 percent of GDP. By the beginning of the 1970s, that share had doubled to 2 percent, and it doubled again by 1991. In 2009, health-care spending reached 8.4 percent of GDP.[8] This flood of government cash into the health-care sector has created an enormous monetary return for lobbying. Consider the 2003 Medicare Modernization Act, which added a prescription-drug benefit to Medicare at a cost of about $1 trillion over a decade. Thanks to heavy lobbying, the pharmaceutical industry was able to eliminate a requirement that Medicare negotiate bulk pricing for the most widely used drugs. According to reliable estimates, this legislative achievement netted the industry $24 billion a year.[9]

Rising spending isn't the only way that government has given businesses an incentive to lobby. An increasing amount of regulation has likewise swollen government's economic role and encouraged the private sector to ask for favors. Later in this book I will discuss which regulations I consider useful and which are deleterious to consumers. Yet we must remember that all regulation affects firm profitability: most of the time, it increases the profits of the incumbents at the expense of new entrants. Do you remember the real estate example in the previous chapter? After the introduction of the Internet, as they started to face the competition from Virtual Office Websites (VOW), real estate agents responded by lobbying state governments for minimum-service requirements. Why were they suddenly concerned about the way their customers were treated? To undermine the competition of the Virtual Office Websites. By forcing all agents to provide services that sometimes customers do not want, regulation reduces the comparative advantage of VOWs. It is as if we required all cars to have the safety standard of a Volvo. Thirteen states now have minimum service requirements. I fear that more will follow.

Before 1887, there were no federal government agencies, and regulation (aside from tariffs) was minimal. In 1900, there was only the Interstate Commerce Commission, followed by the Food and Drug Administration six years later. By the early 1990s, Congress had set up more than a hundred federal regulatory agencies in fields as wide-ranging as trade, communications, nuclear energy, product safety, medicine, and employment opportunity.

Since the early eighties, the growth of lobbying has been concentrated in a few industries: telecommunications, the pharmaceutical industry, financial services, utilities, and high tech. Detailed analysis suggests that lobbying initially tends to be reactive (for example, trying to fight a proposed regulation that would hurt an industry) but then starts taking the initiative (for example, trying to create economic advantage for the industry through further regulations).[10] Between 1981 and 1996, the lobbying presence of pharmaceutical firms in Washington increased fourfold—an increase that was especially sharp in 1993 and 1994, in response to the threat of government regulation and above all President Clinton's 1993 health-care reform effort. But after the plan failed, the pharmaceutical lobbying presence remained. Industry lobbyists would eventually push for the approval of the 2003 Medicare Modernization Act, which has been wildly profitable for drug companies.

Similarly, the number of registered lobbyists in financial services rose from 50 in 1981 to 240 in 1999. Many of them were fighting for the repeal of Depression-era banking regulations, most notably the separation between investment banking and commercial banking. This objective, as we saw earlier, was fully achieved in 1999 with the approval of the Gramm-Leach-Bliley Act. After that, though, the number of registered lobbyists for the financial industry remained stable.

TULLOCK'S PARADOX

Many people think that campaign financing and lobbying are excessive these days. But Gordon Tullock—one of the founders of *public-choice economics*, which applies modern economics tools to explain political choices—had the audacity to ask why these activities involve so *little* money, given the size of the prize. Tullock first raised this question in 1972, but his argument is even more relevant today, when government spending is far greater.

The paradox runs as follows. In 2008, total federal spending equaled $5 trillion. If we subtract pensions and interest payments, which aren't discretionary, we're left with $4 trillion, which the party in power gets to control for at least two years, bringing the total to $8 trillion. If we imagine the political system as a big lottery, with candidates buying tickets in the form of campaign spending, we would expect the total amount paid for the tickets—the total amount of campaign spending—to be no less than the size of the prize; otherwise, a single individual would find it sensible to buy all the tickets, win for sure, and enjoy a handsome profit. The problem is that the total amount spent in electoral campaigning isn't remotely close to the size of the prize. In 2008, the sum of all the money spent in the presidential, senatorial, and congressional campaigns was $5.3 billion.[11] That $5.3 *billion* bought the right to control $8 *trillion*, so the size of the prize is more than 1,000 times the total price of the tickets.

One could object that the actual size of the prize is much less than $8 trillion, since not all government expenses are pure transfers. But no matter how you cut it, the federal government spends *far* more than $5.3 billion in two years. One could also object that, since nobody can buy every election in the country and thus control all federal spending, the paradox is purely theoretical. But Tullock's paradox applies on a smaller scale as well. Consider agricultural subsidies, which have negative effects on developing countries and on the diet of Americans, too. In 1985, a series of amendments to the Farm Bill proposed cutting the subsidies for sugar, tobacco, dairy, peanuts, and wheat. After farm groups mobilized to fight the measure, the final vote in the House of Representatives was 146 in favor and 246 against—so the subsidies survived. According to figures based on one economist's calculations, the sugar lobby spent just $212,000 to defeat the measure. Contrast that with the annual transfer from consumers to sugar producers and processors, which has been estimated at $1.1 billion a year, and you'll see, once again, that too little money seems to be invested in politics.

A partial explanation of this puzzle is that companies can provide not only money but also votes. Read this statement by former senator Dennis DeConcini:

> I get a contribution from, say, Allied-Signal, a big defense contractor, and they have raised money for me. And then they come in and say: "Senator, we need legislation that would extend some rule of contracting that is good for us." They lay out the case. My staff goes over it. I'm trying to help them. Why am I trying to help them? The cynic can say: Well, it's because they gave you 5,000 bucks. And if you ran again, they'll give you another 5,000 bucks. Or is it because they have 15,000 jobs in Arizona and this will help keep those jobs in Arizona? Now to me, the far greater motivation is those jobs, because those are the people that are going to vote for me. But I can't ignore the fact that they have given me money.[12]

As the statement suggests, votes can matter even more than money to politicians. So when we consider the $11 billion in agricultural subsidies that the US Department of Agriculture spent each year, on average, between 1995 and 2004, we can't conclude that they were obtained with just $3.3 million in annual political contributions. Besides the contributions, the agricultural lobby offers the potential support of 2 million farmers, who will hear about which candidates favor their interests and which do not. Fortunately, economists have also estimated the value of a vote in dollar terms, by looking at how much a candidate has to spend to get one. The value is roughly $400.[13] Once you correct for the value of the votes brought by the agricultural lobby, the return of an extra dollar of political contributions drops from $3,333 to $12—

significantly reducing the size of the paradox but not eliminating it. Even at 12 to 1, the rate of return of political contributions is 1,100 percent, far exceeding that of all other investments.

So again: why is there so *little* money in politics? One reason may involve an imbalance between interest groups resulting from a phenomenon that economists call "free riding." Each year, in theory, taxpayers should be prepared to pay up to $11 billion in political contributions and organizing costs to avoid being taxed to pay for agricultural subsidies. But as each rational voter consciously or unconsciously realizes, the probability that his own action will make a difference is very slim, so nobody organizes to fight the subsidies. (When Congress discussed the sugar subsidy, there was no record of any lobbying on the anti-subsidy side.) Farmers, by contrast, get a huge benefit from the subsidies. It pays for them to get organized—and once they are, when it comes to buying votes, they are pretty much uncontested. That's why they spend so little. You can afford to fight with one arm behind your back if your opponent is fighting with both arms cut off.

According to this interpretation, the rate of return on political investment is simply the other side of taxpayers' impotence: the larger that rate is, the more we can assure ourselves that taxpayers have been taken advantage of. The theory explains why the return on political investments is so high, but not why companies don't do more of it. With such attractive returns, investment in politics should dominate all other forms of investment. Why do companies spend *only* $3.5 billion in lobbying and $2.5 billion in political contributions?

One potential answer here is chilling. It may be that companies spend so little because they are still in their learning phase. We have already seen evidence of this in the cost of political campaigns, which has risen dramatically from $200 million in 1972 to $5 billion in 2008. In constant dollar terms, this represents an almost fivefold increase. The lobbying effort has also skyrocketed. In 1981, according to the Washington Representatives Directory, S&P 500 corporations retained 1,475 inhouse lobbyists and outside consultants. By 2005, that number had almost doubled to 2,765.[14] This phenomenon is not limited to the S&P 500 corporations. The total number of domestic companies listed in the Washington Representatives Directory nearly doubled between 1981 and 2006 (from 2,120 to 4,144).[15] Total lobbying expenses doubled in the last decade.[16] The conclusion that companies are slowly learning about the benefits of lobbying is supported by the opinion of the lobbyists themselves: "When [the company in question] started, they thought government relations was something else. They thought it was to manage public relations crises, hearings and inquiries. My boss told me: You've taught us to do things we didn't know could ever be done."[17]

Lobbying has all the characteristics of an acquired skill the return of which increases with experience. Companies new to the game spend less and have more doubts about the return on their investment, but they rarely stop once they've started. A company that lobbies one year has a 94 percent probability of lobbying the next.[18] In part, this persistence is the result of inertia in organizations: when they start doing something, it is tough for them to stop. But it also shows that the lobbyist quoted above is correct: companies learn from the lobbyists what they can do and keep doing more of it.

Further evidence of the learning curve is the frequently observed move from defensive to offensive lobbying. In a recent survey that asked lobbyists to rate the reasons for retaining a lobbyist, "Need to improve ability to compete by seeking favorable changes in government policy" received 5.7 out of 7 points, just behind "Need to protect against changes in government policy" at 6.2 points.[19] This shift of lobbying from defensive to offensive owes much to the evolution of *earmarks*— that is, expenditures for a specific purpose added to a larger bill.

THE PROBLEM WITH PORK

When in 2008 John McCain aggressively campaigned against pork-barrel projects, I thought his emphasis was excessive. While unfair and inefficient, all these special projects together in 2006 amounted to only $27 billion[20]—a small fraction of US government spending.

What I didn't consider was that pork had become the currency through which Congress was bought. At the beginning of the twentieth century, a muckraking journalist wrote: "Strictly speaking we had no Senate; we had only a chamber of butlers for industrialists and financiers."[21] At that time, senators were appointed, not elected, and actual corruption was rampant. Today, cases of *illegal* corruption are virtually nonexistent—everything is done in a perfectly lawful way—yet senators and representatives are nevertheless becoming "butlers" again for well-connected big businesses. Before being sentenced to jail, Jack Abramoff confided to his friends: "I was participating in a system of legalized bribery"—though in his case, laws were broken.[22] And the mechanism that enables this system of legalized bribes is pork-barrel projects.

True, pillaging the federal coffers to "bring home the bacon" is a long-standing tradition in American politics. Only in the 1980s, however, did Congress start to pick winners and losers by earmarking funds for specific recipients. Once the earmarking started, lawmakers embraced it enthusiastically. The number of earmarks in federal highway bills, for instance, exploded, rising from 10 in 1982 to 4,128 in 2005.[23] Earmarks became the currency with which the passage of key pieces of legislation was ensured. Rather than convince representatives of the merit of a proposal, congressional leaders would buy their consensus by offering dedicated earmarks, which made it easier for the representatives to secure campaign contributions and hence win reelection. According to the nonprofit group Citizens Against Government Waste, the passage of the aforementioned Medicare prescription-drug benefit was secured through the dispensation of pork. The prescription-drug benefit increased Medicare's unfunded liabilities by 50 percent.

The most outrageous form of pork is material added to conference reports during the reconciliation phase, after a bill has been approved in different versions by the House and the Senate. Since each chamber has already passed its own version, the earmarks are included behind closed doors, with zero accountability. The rank-and-file members of each chamber then face an up-or-down decision on the entire bill. If they want to oppose the earmark, they may have to vote against an important piece of legislation that they otherwise support. This strategy was pioneered in 1978 by Gerald Cassidy, who lobbied to insert $27 million into a Department of Agriculture appropriations bill in order to build and operate a nutrition center at Tufts University.[24] His success led other schools, including Georgetown and Columbia, to seek his services. Then came private businesses. By 2006, Cassidy & Associates was making $26 million in revenues; the pork-barrel projects he helped pass through Congress have cost taxpayers tens of billions of dollars.[25]

THE DEMISE OF THE ANTIBUSINESS IDEOLOGY

A well-conceived idea or concept can greatly amplify the power of a lobbyist's campaign. Take the idea of expanding homeownership. Who could oppose that? Democrats see it as a way to help minorities and the poor achieve the American Dream. Republicans think that if everyone can become a homeowner, everyone will become conservative.[26] Accordingly, any lobbying effort that presents itself as aimed at expanding homeownership becomes difficult to resist. Fannie Mae and Freddie Mac would have been much less powerful had they been, say, tobacco manufacturers.

If ideas are useful lobbying tools, they can also be an effective lobbying deterrent. During the 1960s and 1970s, *business* was a four-letter word in Washington. Democrats, largely financed by unions, shied away from heavy fund-raising in the business community for ideological reasons: they saw outreach to business as a betrayal of their core principles. Republicans, too, were cautious, for fear of being seen as overly probusiness. Even Republican presidents, such as Richard Nixon, believed that government should interfere with business (for example, with price and wage controls). While deeply misguided from the standpoint of economic efficiency, this hostility to business did have a silver lining: in the pattern we've seen before, it helped keep big business's power in check.

With the Reagan revolution in the 1980s, *business* stopped being a bad word. In fact, one of the cornerstones of that revolution was the liberation of business from the shackles of regulation. But the more you eat, as an Italian saying goes, the hungrier you become. In the post-Reagan era, the success of business's attack against excessive government regulation opened a new opportunity: using political influence not just to reduce government interference but to mold it to companies' advantage.

When business was unpopular, it would have been easy for the Democrats to stigmatize this strategy. The resurgence of business's popularity, however, made it untenable for the Democratic Party's leadership to maintain a radical antibusiness attitude. And as the Democrats became more open to business, business realized the advantages of working with them. Partnerships with business, the Democrats began to reason, could help them achieve their social goals while avoiding accusations of building up big government. And thus the so-called private-public partnership developed, involving initiatives in which the government and the private sector collaborate toward a common goal.

THE PROTOTYPICAL PRIVATE-PUBLIC PARTNERSHIP

In principle, the term *private-public partnership* seems to capture the best of both worlds: the efficiency of the private sector combined with the social goals of the public sector. Republicans often like such partnerships because they reduce the direct role of government. Democrats like them because, through such partnerships, they are able to advertise their social goals without antagonizing business—and can sometimes do so with its support. Business loves them because the easiest way to make money is to suck it from taxpayers, and the best way to suck it from taxpayers is to do it behind the fig leaf of a noble goal.

The problem with many public-private partnerships is best captured by a comment that George Bernard Shaw once made to a beautiful ballerina. She had proposed that they have a child together so that the child could possess his brain and her beauty; Shaw replied that he feared the child would have *her* brain and *his* beauty. Similarly, public-private partnerships often wind up with the social goals of the private sector and the efficiency of the public one. In these partnerships, Republican and Democratic politicians and businesspeople frequently cooperate toward just one goal: their own profit.

The prototypical private-public partnership is Fannie Mae. Set up in 1934 by President Roosevelt to help Americans get long-term mortgages to purchase their houses, Fannie was initially a government agency. In 1968, however, to avoid consolidating its debt with that of the US Treasury, the Johnson administration decided to transform it into a privately owned company. Yet it differed from ordinary private companies, since the government retained some regulatory power and the right to appoint three board members. It was then labeled a GSE, or government-sponsored enterprise.

Thanks to its hybrid nature, Fannie Mae enjoyed the best of both worlds. On the one hand, like other government entities, it did not have to register securities with the SEC, and it was exempted from corporate income taxes in the District of Columbia, where its headquarters are located. On the other hand, its status as a private company allowed it to avoid the transparency demanded from government agencies. For example, it was not subject to the Freedom of Information Act, which forces government entities to release confidential data.

Yet Fannie's most important privilege was its ability to borrow with an implicit government guarantee. This amounted to a subsidy estimated at $6.1 billion in 2000 and $13.6 billion in 2003.[27] Only two-thirds of this subsidy was rebated to the borrowing public in the form of lower rates; Fannie Mae's shareholders and management captured the rest.

Even a company as large and powerful as Fannie Mae could not have retained these privileges without an allegedly noble cause. This is where James Johnson came into play. A political-consultant-turned-lobbyist-turned-corporate-executive, Johnson became chairman and CEO of Fannie Mae in 1991. He soon mastered the idea of using social goals to enhance private profits. The goal he championed was that of providing a house to every American—too noble an objective to resist. Armed with this cover, he raised lobbying to a new level. Not only did he play heavily with the standard lobbying and political contributions; he worked hard to create a glowing image for Fannie, so that no one in Washington would dare attack it. Despite the fact that Fannie did not need a national network, Johnson created regional offices in major cities to promote Fannie's image. The offices were staffed with relatives of politicians to enhance Fannie's connections.[28]

By using its privileges to guard internal data closely, Fannie was able to prevent most independent researchers from assessing its performance. As a result, most of the research available on Fannie was research that Fannie authorized or paid for. Fannie's influence in academia, however, was not limited to the occasional paid-for paper. In a textbook example of how economists can be "captured" just as regulators can, Fannie Mae financially backed the two leading academic journals in housing research, *Housing Policy Debate* and the *Journal of Housing Research*. Not surprisingly, the articles in these journals were not terribly critical of Fannie Mae.[29] The extent of this intellectual capture is illustrated by an episode reported in Gretchen Morgenson and Joshua Rosner's book *Reckless Endangerment*. A bank lobbyist trying to hire a housing expert to take on Fannie Mae admitted: "I tried to find academics that would do research on these issues and Fannie had bought off all the academics in housing. I had people say to me are you going to give me stipends for the next 20 years like Fannie will?"[30]

In spite of Johnson's alleged social goals, Fannie Mae was not shy about using the most aggressive for-profit strategies. For example, it used its privileges to avoid disclosing detailed data on its mortgage pools. Knowing more about the composition of these mortgages than the rest of the market did, Fannie Mae exploited that information in trading. Since Fannie insures all the mortgages it securitizes against default, the main risk an investor faces (besides a change in interest rates) is the so-called prepayment risk—that is, the risk that mortgage holders will refinance, reducing the value of the mortgage pool. Knowing in greater detail the characteristics of borrowers, Fannie can buy mortgage pools with low refinancing risk and sell those with high refinancing risk. This is tantamount to legalized insider trading. Since the market is aware of what's going on, it demands an extra yield to compensate for the losses that uninformed traders bear—and this cost is, of course, passed along to mortgage holders. So much for Fannie's social goals.

During his eight years as CEO, Johnson made more than $100 million for himself, while his successor, Franklin Raines, made over $90 million in just five years. Johnson ended up not only rich but socially respected. After stepping down from Fannie, he became chairman of the John F. Kennedy Center for the Performing Arts and a chairman of the Brookings Institution. Less lucky were the taxpayers, who had to bail out Fannie Mae to the tune of more than $180 billion.[31]

RUBIN'S BAILOUT DOCTRINE

Bailouts, in fact, are another example of the danger of using government money to try to do good. A bailout is a subsidy (often in the form of a below-market loan) that helps a firm or a country avoid insolvency. As with the goal of giving a house to every American, it is hard to contend with the objective of saving countries or companies from disaster. Financial distress and bankruptcy destroy value. Even the most conservative estimates put the costs of financial distress at 15 percent of a firm's value.[32] If we were to apply these figures to large companies or even entire countries, there is more than enough value to justify an intervention.

Yet while financial bailouts can have good short-term effects, they have bad long-term consequences. To appreciate these consequences, imagine that every time you try to discipline your kids for bad behavior, the kids' grandparents intervene and "rescue" them in order to maintain family harmony. In the short term, these interventions seem beneficial, since the children are happier and family harmony is preserved. In the long run, however, you end up with spoiled kids and unhappy parents.

Grandparents have an incentive to spoil their grandchildren, since they benefit from the grandchildren's gratitude and from the momentary peace—but they are unlikely to suffer the long-term consequences of the kids' bad behavior (partly because they aren't around as much, and partly because they die sooner). In much the same way, policy makers are happy to bail out firms and countries because they benefit from the momentary improvement in the economy and from the gratitude of saved businessmen—but they're unlikely to suffer the long-term consequences because they will be out of office by the time the perverse results occur.

As with the punishment of children, the costs of financial distress have an important incentive effect. Eliminate it, and you have the moral-hazard problem that I discussed earlier. The system of capitalism is based on the principle that individuals should take the consequences of their mistakes. Without this feedback mechanism, they cannot learn, and there is no chance that the allocation of credit will be efficient. But lenders like bailouts, regarding them as a convenient way to get indemnified of their losses. In bailouts, lenders generally receive 100 cents on the dollar for their loans. So in addition to their negative long-term incentive effects, bailouts have the disadvantage of redistributing money from taxpayers to lenders.[33]

Like political contributions by lobbyists, bailouts are a kind of drug—one that, in this case, financial markets grew addicted to. If you stop giving it to them, they start panicking from withdrawal. If you give it to them, you pacify them for a short while, but soon they want more. The escalation eventually leads to the point where even the strongest government cannot bail out the financial sector.

The person who may have done the most to make bailouts the prevailing doctrine in the United States is Robert Rubin. A former Goldman Sachs co-chairman of the board, Rubin became Bill Clinton's economic adviser and, later, his secretary of the Treasury. In these positions Rubin made financial bailouts the practice, if not the law, of the land.

His approach was first implemented during the 1994 Mexican crisis, when the collapse of the peso jeopardized the Mexican government's ability to pay its debt. Mexico would most likely have defaulted if an international rescue coordinated by the US government had not lent it $50 billion. At first glance, this decision seems to have been a win-win. Goldman Sachs and Citigroup, which, respectively, had lent $5.2 billion and $2.9 billion to Mexico, got repaid in full.[34] The Treasury turned a profit of $500 million in interest on its loan.[35] Mexico avoided the cost of a default. But this move also eliminated fear among lenders, and fear is an essential element in financial markets: it disciplines financial decisions. When a small part of the brain called the amygdala, which is associated with the emotion of fear, is damaged in an accident or removed for medical reasons, subjects tend to exhibit aggressive risk-taking behaviors.[36] The implicit promise of a bailout acts like the removal of the amygdala: an inducement not just for Mexico but for all big banks to take more risk.

After the Mexico crisis, Rubin's doctrine would be consistently applied in one international financial crisis after the other with the help of the International Monetary Fund. In 1997, South Korea received $55 billion; Thailand, $21 billion; and Indonesia, $23 billion. In 1998, Brazil received $41 billion. These countries benefited from the bailouts, but American banks benefited even more. Over the three days when the International Monetary Fund announced the rescue package for Brazil, the exposed banks exhibited a 7.7 percent return in excess of the market, while nonexposed banks exhibited none.[37] This return amounted to a gain of $17.8 billion—a massive reward that encouraged banks to take risk, knowing that there was no downside for them, since the taxpayers would intervene if things went badly. The more the Rubin doctrine was applied, the more countries took it for granted. And the banks, certain that any losses would be covered, engaged in increasingly risky lending to foreign countries.

Given Rubin's great contribution to the well-being of bankers, it's not surprising that he received several high-level offers from banks after leaving the Treasury in 1999, passing the baton to his deputy secretary and protégé Larry Summers. Even less surprising is the fact that the most attractive offer came from Citigroup, a bank that greatly benefited from Rubin's policies and would benefit even more from his connections. Three months after stepping down as secretary of the Treasury, Rubin became a board member and chairman of the executive committee of Citigroup's board. Although his position had CEO-level pay (during his eight years, he received $126 million in cash and stocks), it had, as noted earlier, no clear responsibilities.

Rubin continued his role as bailout advocate even in the private sector. In 2001, following revelations of accounting irregularities, Enron verged on collapse, which meant that Citigroup, a major lender, would lose a significant amount of money. Fulfilling a request made by Michael Carpenter, head of Citigroup's investment banking unit, Rubin called Peter R. Fisher, then undersecretary of the Treasury, and asked him to consider advising the bond-rating agencies against an immediate downgrade of Enron's debt.[38] In other words, Rubin (a Democrat) lobbied Fisher (a Republican) to help bail out Enron. (So much for Washington's ideological divide.) What Rubin did was technically legal, as *The Economist* explained, only because Bill Clinton, in his last days as president, had canceled an executive order that barred top officials from lobbying their old departments for five years after leaving office.[39]

More important was that, according to the *Wall Street Journal*, "Rubin was reportedly critical to securing the latest federal bailout of Citi" in the fall of 2008.[40] At the time, the risky investment strategy encouraged by Rubin, involving aggressive investments in bundles of toxic mortgages, also known as collateralized debt obligations, had brought

Citigroup to the verge of collapse. Yet Citi survived, thanks to two rounds of federal bailouts: first a $25 billion equity infusion provided by the Troubled Asset Relief Program, and then a specially designed package from which Citigroup received a $20 billion additional equity infusion and a taxpayers' guarantee on most of the risk in a $306 billion portfolio of dodgy assets.

THE GREENSPAN PUT

Rubin was not alone in providing implicit guarantees to the financial sector, inducing it to gamble more. His partner was none other than Federal Reserve Chairman Alan Greenspan. Greenspan's approach developed as a result of two personal experiences. As a freshly appointed Fed chairman, he had to confront the 1987 stock market crash. While a stock market correction was probably due, the magnitude of the crash (a drop of 23 percent in a single day) was, as we now know, caused by a breakdown in the liquidity of the market generated by new portfolio insurance trading strategies.[41] At the time, however, the cause was unknown. In the face of tremendous uncertainty, Greenspan flooded the market with liquidity, preventing the panic from spreading. The economy was completely unaffected by the crash, and Greenspan emerged as a hero (and rightly so). Successes are seductive, and it is difficult, even for a person of Greenspan's intelligence, to realize that a strategy that works well once won't necessarily work well all the time.

Though flooding the market with liquidity won Greenspan a lot of popularity, trying to dry up that liquidity caused him a lot of grief. In a 1996 speech, he dared to question whether some "irrational exuberance" had taken the stock market too high. The Shiller price-earnings ratio, based on the average of earnings of the previous ten years, was at 25 when Greenspan delivered that speech. It rose 77 percent—to 44.2 at the end of 1999—before it started to drop.[42] During those three years, many commentators ridiculed Greenspan's warning.

The lesson Greenspan learned was how politically costly it was to lean against the wind. He dutifully applied that lesson when real estate prices rose. In fact, he elevated the lesson to a principle—the Greenspan Doctrine—which held that it wasn't the responsibility of a central banker to try to resist the formation of potential bubbles. In academia, the staunchest supporter of this new approach was a Princeton University macroeconomist little known in the political world at the time: Ben Bernanke. In a 1999 article with fellow economist Mark Gertler, Bernanke analyzed the impact of monetary policy when prices moved up and away from fundamentals. Their conclusion: that the Fed should not intervene, both because it's difficult to identify bubbles and because "our reading of history is that asset price crashes have done sustained damage to the economy only in cases when monetary policy remained unresponsive or actively reinforced deflationary pressures."[43]

Academic articles rarely become instant hits. When they do, it is generally for the wrong reason: because they provide intellectual cover for a vested interest too ugly to be stated openly. This was the case with Bernanke and Gertler's article. Wall Street had no desire for the Fed to intervene in preventing possible asset bubbles. It loved Greenspan's practice of supporting asset prices during downturns with an accommodating monetary policy—what became known as the "Greenspan put." This "put" limited the size of the potential losses that Wall Street had to bear. But the financial industry did not like the possibility of a cap on the profits it could make during a boom, which would have been the effective result of a monetary tightening at a time when the market was becoming "irrationally exuberant." Bernanke and Gertler presented the theoretical justification and implicit assurance that the Fed would pick up the damage when the party was over. What more could Wall Street hope for?

BAILOUT NATION

The bipartisan consensus to help support business with taxpayers' money reached its zenith during the 2007–2008 financial crisis. In the years leading up to the crisis, thanks to Rubin's bailout doctrine, earlier federal bailouts, and Greenspan's put, the financial system had loaded up on risk, and by the summer of 2007, it was on the brink of collapse. During the period from August 2007, when the first serious crack in the system appeared, to the financial crisis's peak in September 2008, both the government and the Fed had plenty of ways to intervene. But nobody followed the example set in 1991, during a previous recession, by William Taylor, head of the Fed's supervision and regulation unit. Taylor had forced Citibank to stop its dividend to conserve cash. In 2007–2008, nobody at the Fed had the courage to do something comparable. The nine largest banks, which received $125 billion from TARP, were collectively paying dividends of more than $25 billion a year.[44]

The government not only took no action to reduce the risk of a crisis but contributed to precipitating it via inconsistent policy choices: bailing out creditors but not shareholders in Bear Stearns, Fannie Mae, and Freddie Mac; wiping out both creditors and shareholders in Lehman Brothers and Washington Mutual; and bailing out both in AIG. In the words of the legendary Yale endowment manager David Swensen, "they've [acted] with an extraordinary degree of inconsistency. You almost have to be trying to do things in an incoherent and inconsistent way to have ended up with the huge range of ways that they have come up with to address these problems."[45]

By the time the Troubled Assets Relief Program had been proposed, on September 19, 2008, the government had little choice but to intervene. The severe drop in the stock market caused what economists would call "a spike in risk aversion"—panic, in a simple word.[46] A direct consequence of the panic was the desire to flee from risky assets. Not all investors can sell at the same time. When most try, prices plummet. In short, the panic unleashed a self-fulfilling downward spiral, intensified by the high leverage of financial institutions.

I am not opposed to the idea of a government intervention in such extreme circumstances, but I do object to the way it was done. When a drug addict is undergoing a withdrawal crisis, one certainly should not stand by and do nothing—but one also should not give the addict a full year's supply of drugs, which is roughly equivalent to what the US government opted for with TARP. The program was a pillage of defenseless taxpayers that benefited powerful lobbies: not just the triumph of Wall Street over Main Street, but the triumph of K Street over the rest of America.

To justify their interventions, most policy makers and many economists use the metaphor of a house on fire: first you extinguish the flames, and then you catch the arsonists. What they miss is that if you put out the fire in a way that makes it impossible to catch the arsonists, you will almost certainly have many more fires to put out later. All of the interventions implemented during the fall of 2008, such as the equity infusion under TARP and the second bailout of Citigroup, were unnecessarily generous to the banks and their creditors. The Treasury secretary at the time justified this gift by arguing that there was no way to penalize the creditors without triggering a collapse of the system. In his view, the transfer from the taxpayers (who lost $32 billion in the equity infusion) to the unsecured debt holders (who gained $120 billion) was a necessary evil.[47] A simple tax, however—assessed on the unsecured bank debt that was rescued—would have done the trick, avoiding the transfer and maintaining for the future the incentives of a careful credit analysis.

Yet the worst long-term effect of TARP was not the burden it imposed on taxpayers but the distortions to incentives that it generated. The way the bailout was conducted undermined Americans' faith in both the financial system and the government. In the first wave of the Chicago Booth/Kellogg School Trust Index Survey, which I co-direct and which was conducted in December 2008, 80 percent of the respondents stated that government intervention made them less confident about investing in the financial market.

The bailout also entrenched the view that large financial institutions cannot fail and their creditors cannot lose. This expectation leads money-market fund managers and corporate CFOs to invest their funds in banks that are the most politically connected instead of those that are the most financially sound—a trend that, in turn, leads to the death of credit risk analysis and the rise of political analysis. Worse, it kills any residual incentive to prudence, substituting the incentive to be politically connected. A bailout nation lives on lobbying. Not surprisingly, seven out of the ten richest counties in the United States now are in the suburbs of Washington, DC.[48]

CONCLUSIONS

At the top of the Grand Canyon there is a sign that reads, in large print, "Please do not feed the wild animals." In smaller type, it explains that feeding the animals will make them lose their ability to search for food on their own, jeopardizing their ability to survive in the wild. Human beings put up the sign. If the matter had been left to the animals, most of them would probably have preferred no sign: they are better off taking advantage of tourists' generosity, and they don't care enough about the survival of their species to forgo free lunches.

Much the same is true for business. Individually, businesses are better off with the free lunches offered by the government. This is why they spend so much money lobbying Washington. The overall free-market system, however, is worse off as a result. Just as it would be dangerous to let the animals determine the rules of the national parks, it is dangerous to allow businesspeople to dictate the rules of doing business, since they do not consider how bailouts weaken the functioning of the market. Like feeding wild animals, helping a large firm or a country avoid financial distress seems charitable but in the long run hurts the recipient. A country that protects wild animals from the corruption of free food should likewise protect businesses from the corruption of subsidies.

6

THE RESPONSIBILITIES OF THE INTELLECTUALS

War is much too serious a matter to entrust to military men.

—Georges Clemenceau,
French prime minister during World War I

"**W**HY DID NOBODY NOTICE IT?" QUEEN ELIZABETH II innocently asked a gathering of London School of Economics professors in 2008. "It," of course, was the financial crisis. "At every stage, someone was relying on somebody else and everyone thought they were doing the right thing," one of the professors answered.[1] But then why didn't economists notice the risk that this chain of delegation might lead to such a gigantic disaster? In defense of the field, one can certainly point to plenty of theoretical papers that highlighted the possible instability of financial markets. But they were merely theoretical. Worried economists remained quietly inside the ivory tower, rather than trumpeting their worries in the public square. Many of my colleagues will object that such trumpeting is not our job—that we are scientists who should stay above the fray. But the fact is that most economists consult, sit on boards, fill important policy roles, testify in Congress, and opine in newspapers. Nevertheless, the economics profession had remarkably seldom warned the public about the risks at hand.

Take the housing bubble. Figure 2 shows an index of real house prices from 1905 to the peak of the housing bubble in the first quarter of 2006.[2] It does not take an economist to notice the spike. Yet one would be hard-pressed to find any article in the main economic journals pointing out the danger that this picture posed to the economy. In fact, one article published in 2005 dismissed the possibility of a bubble. "As of the end of 2004, our analysis reveals little evidence of a housing bubble," read the article. "Recent price growth is supported by basic economic factors."[3] This benign view was quickly broadcast in the financial press.

Of course, there are notable exceptions. Yale economist Robert Shiller had long talked about the existence of a real-estate bubble, and a chart similar to this one was published in the 2005 edition of his book

Figure 2. Real Home Price Index

Source: Robert Shiller; see http://www.econ.yale.edu/~shiller/books.htm.

Irrational Exuberance.[4] Yet his academic paper on the topic never appeared in any major journal; more important, his views were apparently ignored by the Federal Reserve. As the minutes of the Federal Open Market Committee meetings show, the Federal Reserve Board was not concerned about the housing situation even in 2006. "We think the fundamentals of the expansion going forward still look good, with strong household income growth," declared vice chairman Timothy Geithner in a December 12, 2006, meeting. "Regarding housing, we know we have terrible price data," added another governor. "So the past data on housing may not be too useful."[5]

A similar point can be made about the government-sponsored enterprises Fannie Mae and Freddie Mac. Few noticed that their equity capital was too thin until 2008, when we all found out the hard way. Indeed, many economists dismissed the problem. In 2002, Fannie Mae commissioned a reassuring paper written by Nobel Prize winner Joseph Stiglitz; Peter Orszag, later President Obama's budget director and vice chairman of global banking for Citigroup; and his brother Jon Orszag, an economic consultant. "This analysis shows that, based on historical data, the probability of a shock as severe as embodied in the risk-based capital standard is substantially less than one in 500,000—and may be smaller than one in three million," wrote the authors. In plain language, the very limited equity capital of Fannie Mae was more than adequate.[6]

Where was I? I could try to defend myself by saying that my research, at least until then, was not in housing or in banking. Still, I feel responsible. We economists have witnessed a failure of our profession, a failure that needs to be analyzed and fixed.

One view, most famously put forward by the documentary film *Inside Job,* is that economists are corrupt, the peons of powerful business interests. I do not believe that. Having spent the better part of my life among economists, I can testify that they are generally honest people whose passion for research has induced them not to take more lucrative jobs. Our intellectual honesty, however, does not necessarily protect us from potential biases. Collectively, we may be biased in ways that are not apparent to many, including ourselves. To appreciate how this might come about, economists might refer to a theory that we ourselves apply to regulators. We do not think that regulators are dishonest or corrupt people. Nevertheless, a widely espoused theory in economics is that regulators' decisions often become biased in favor of the industries they regulate; to use economic jargon, they become *captured.*

The reason that regulatory capture is a persuasive hypothesis is that economic incentives encourage even the best-intentioned regulators to cater to the interests of the businesses they regulate. To begin with, regulators depend upon the regulated for much of the information they need to do their jobs properly. This dependency creates an incentive to be friendly to the information providers. Also, regulators' human capital is highly industry-specific, and their best future jobs are likely to be with the regulated; hence, their desire to preserve future career options makes it difficult not to cater to those they regulate. Finally, the regulated are the only real audience of the regulators, since taxpayers seldom care about regulatory findings; hence the regulators will naturally define their on-the-job performance with the regulated in mind, a process that will again incentivize them to sympathize with the interests of the regulated.

If regulators can be captured, why couldn't economists (and especially economists like me, who work in business schools and have business ties) sometimes be captured as well—that is, defend the interests of business over those of free and competitive markets? Just as it is for regulators, this issue is problematic for business professors like me. Interacting with business is an integral part of the job. It enriches our knowledge and our teaching. Yet, it can also bias our views.

Let's start with information needs. Like regulators, researchers need data, and a proprietary data set from a business can make a researcher's career. What are the incentives for a business to share those data? Generally, its first concern is to avoid damaging itself in any way, so it will protect itself with some right of refusal, in case the researchers' conclusions prove negative for it. Anticipating that controversial evidence might prevent their work from being published, researchers will feel pressure to focus either on noncontroversial topics or on topics in which the results are likely to cast the company that provided the data in a good light.

It's important to note that a bias might occur even if the researcher is totally resistant to pressure because businesses can be selective about who exactly receives their data. A colleague of mine, for example, was offered the opportunity to conduct a field study with a payday-loan company. I do not think it is an accident that the privilege was granted to her, as she had already written a paper with a positive view of payday loans. Knowing her and her research integrity, I can vouch that she will never bend her results to please anybody. Yet, the access to those data allowed her to write a better paper, which became a leading article in a major finance journal. The bias thus does not lie within the individual but in the aggregate outcome.

If the overwhelming majority of published papers find, for example, positive results for the payday-loan industry, that doesn't necessarily mean that the industry is great. It could simply mean that access to proprietary data increases the chances of a paper getting published at all, and that the industry can selectively provide those data only to the type of studies expected to report reassuringly.

The fact that regulated companies can provide regulators with future employment also finds a parallel in academia. The companies we study today may offer us jobs tomorrow, a prospect that can influence research in many subtle ways. Taking a critical position on the level of executive compensation, for example, does not improve the marketability of an academic economist, while justifying that compensation as economically efficient will increase the likelihood of being offered consulting work or even a spot on a corporate board. Neither consulting nor board membership is bad (I myself sit on the board of Telecom Italia), but ignoring how the pursuit of these activities can potentially distort our opinions is naive.

Most economists do not leave academia and are not appointed to any board. They are much likelier, however, to work as expert witnesses for various firms, which again provides an incentive for them to cater to business interests. One might think that the adversarial nature of the litigation process guarantees against bias: for every plaintiff, there is a defendant, so shouldn't expert-witness positions offer opportunities on both sides of every issue?

The answer is only if both sides of the argument have a roughly similar ability to pay. This balance is not always there. In Italy, for example, where until recently there was no legal mechanism to organize a class action suit, there is a huge imbalance between the management and investor sides. Management can hire the best lawyers (and charge their hefty fees to their shareholders), while minority investors generally cannot afford any major expense. Not surprisingly, all the best lawyers opine that management is never responsible for any wrongdoing. As a result, unlike American managers, Italian managers are never charged with "violation of the duty of care," except in rare cases when the company goes bankrupt.

Even in the United States, where the existence of class actions helps level the playing field, there is often an imbalance between plaintiffs and defendants. Plaintiffs, more often than not, operate on a contingency basis and must bear the cost of suing. As a result, they tend to be much more cautious in their expenses (such as hiring expert witnesses) than defendants, who have a lot to lose and are consequently more willing to spend money—especially because the fees are paid not by the managers but by the shareholders. The hope of working as an expert witness probably won't induce an academic to skew his opinions, but it does give him an incentive not to introduce too much nuance into his work. Lawyers like consistency from the experts they use, since it minimizes the chances of a damaging cross-examination; thus, academics who want to play actively in this market have an interest in sticking to a very clear position in all their writing, including their academic writing, which is often read by the opposing counsel.

Industry pressure also works through the peer-review process. Unlike law journals, which are edited by students, major economics and finance journals are peer-reviewed. Hence, an economist's ability to publish is mostly determined by editors and referees. Editors probably have the greatest power in deciding whether to publish a paper: they choose two or three referees, who are generally predictable in their taste; they reserve the right to overrule the referees; and their power is further increased by the prohibition against submitting the same paper to multiple outlets simultaneously and the relatively long review time. Editors certainly receive no direct pressure to publish probusiness articles. Yet it proved, when I examined the mastheads of the three primary finance journals, that 49 percent of their editors had outside consulting activities and that 30 percent sat on corporate boards.[7] For the three primary economic journals, the intermingling of interests was less intense: only 10 percent of the editors appeared to consult, and only 10 percent appeared to sit on corporate boards.

Industry contacts are not a sin—again, I have them myself—and they do not necessarily affect editors' opinions. Is it even the case that people who sit on corporate boards have a disproportionately pro-management attitude about, say, executive compensation? To answer that question, I looked at a new survey created by the University of Chicago Initiative on Global Markets (IGM), of which I am a director. The IGM asks a panel of expert economists—"senior faculty at the most elite research universities in the United States," as we say on our website, chosen "to be geographically diverse, and to include Democrats, Republicans and Independents as well as older and younger scholars"—two policy-related questions each week. (Since I am one of those experts, I omit my own responses to avoid contaminating the results.) It turned out that experts who served on a corporate board were four times more likely than those who didn't to disagree with the statement "The typical chief executive officer of a publicly traded corporation in the U.S. is paid more than his or her marginal contribution to the firm's value." Experts who served on a corporate board were also four times more likely than those who didn't to disagree with the statement "Mandating that U.S. publicly listed corporations must allow shareholders to cast a non-binding vote on executive compensation was a good idea."

Clearly, this correlation does not prove causation. It is possible, for instance, that the people who sit on corporate boards understand these issues better and are therefore likelier to disagree with both statements. But the survey also asks people to state their confidence in their responses, and board members claimed no greater confidence than the rest of the sample—as they should have if they had superior knowledge.

Another possibility is that the direction of causality is reversed: it is not that joining corporate boards influences people's opinions, but that people with business-friendly views are likelier to be asked to join boards in the first place. Yet this wouldn't absolve a regulator in an economist's eyes! If an economist were confronted with evidence that regulators with more pro-management beliefs had better career opportunities, she would conclude that "on the margin," regulators had an incentive to tilt their beliefs in favor of management. Why should the conclusion be any different if the subject is an academic economist?

Finally, economists claim that regulators can be captured because regulated companies are their primary audience. If the companies complain bitterly, the regulator's life can be negatively affected, and he might even lose his job. There is a big difference here between academics and regulators: academics can earn tenure, after which they have virtually no risk of being fired and should be less subject to influence by industry.[8] Nevertheless, *on the margin,* career concerns and monetary rewards should matter. Even if economists are completely insensitive to monetary rewards and motivated only by fame and desire to influence the world, they can find themselves captured by vested interests. It is enough for these interests to offer more influence and fame, which they can easily do.

Let's consider an example. Suppose banks need to be regulated to curb the too-big-to-fail problem. There are two proposed methods, one that solves the problem completely but is costly for banks and another that provides only a partial solution but is much less costly. Which approach would be advocated by an economist who has no interest in money but is solely motivated by the desire to be famous? If she advocated the first one, she would be considered "out of touch with reality." She would not be invited to major conferences sponsored by banks or by regulators who were sympathetic with banks, and her papers would probably be rejected by major economic journals, whose referees, economists more attuned to industry needs, would publish more "realistic" schemes instead. When the inferior scheme was approved, the academic economists who first proposed it would receive fame and glory, while the advocate of the better scheme would be ignored. When the scheme, many years later, showed its shortcomings, blame would be assigned to the politicians who implemented it wrongly, and its academic supporters would still enjoy the reputation of "having done something."

The pursuit of "a quiet life" can also cause an academic economist to cater to an industry's interest. Articles portraying (directly or indirectly) companies in a positive light make the authors many friends. Articles criticizing companies or identifying problems with them create many enemies, exposing the authors to harassment and even potential lawsuits.

Many years ago, a young assistant professor of finance wrote a paper about anomalies in the way stock trades were executed across exchanges. Relative to the best quotes, orders sent to the NYSE traded about 5 cents inside the spread. Orders sent to the regional exchanges traded only 2 cents inside the spread (i.e., execution quality was 3 cents per share worse). This was an "issue" because some market makers were paying a penny a share to brokers to route orders to them. A senior colleague called the young researcher into his office, where he was confronted by a large market maker who berated him for his (allegedly) misleading results. Shaken, the young assistant professor abandoned that line of research.

The market maker berating him was none other than Bernard Madoff, who became inmate number 61727–054 at a federal correctional institution in North Carolina, convicted for the largest financial fraud ever.

Not all stories are so dramatic—but many are really unpleasant. A couple of years ago, three young researchers in finance noticed a strange feature in a database containing financial analysts' recommendations: as time passed, some analysts' recommendations disappeared from the data set.[9] Suspiciously, the missing recommendations were less accurate than the average recommendation in the sample. After several failed attempts to get an explanation from the provider of the data, the researchers wrote an article describing the problem. As soon as their working paper hit the Internet, they received an angry phone call from the legal counsel of the data provider threatening a libel suit if they did not withdraw the paper from the Internet immediately. They had to hire their own attorneys to find out that their case was strong, but they still risked spending a small fortune in litigation. Fortunately, their academic institutions promised to pay their legal fees, a commitment that softened up the data provider: now it was a fight not just against some young scholars but against powerful academic institutions. The provider was nevertheless able to get the researchers to strip from the paper any speculation about why the data had been changed. In spite of the relatively happy ending, one wonders what would have happened if their academic institutions hadn't backed them up.

I have spoken about economists because economics is the field I know best. But the problem exists in other fields. In 1998, an article in the *New England Journal of Medicine* examined the financial conflicts of interest of the authors of seventy-five pieces on calcium channel antagonists published in prominent medical journals.[10] The authors of this study asked the authors of the articles whether they had received reimbursement for attending a symposium, fees for speaking, fees for organizing education, funds for research, funds for a staff member, or fees for consulting from pharmaceutical companies. They also asked about the ownership of stocks and shares in companies. Of the sixty-nine authors who responded, forty-five had these conflicts of interest, even though they had disclosed them—a uniform requirement for all authors submitting articles to medical journals since 1993—in only two of the seventy-five pieces. The articles were then classified as critical of the drugs, supportive, or neutral. Ninety-six percent of the supportive authors had financial relationships with manufacturers, compared with 60 percent of neutral authors and 37 percent of critical authors.

Similarly, an important study from the *Journal of the American Medical Association* looked at what characteristics determined the conclusions of review articles on secondhand smoke. The authors identified 106 reviews, with 37 percent concluding that secondhand smoke was not harmful and the rest concluding that it was. The study found that 75 percent of the first group had been written by authors affiliated with the tobacco industry. Again, only a minority of the articles—23 percent—had disclosed the sources of funding for their research.[11]

It would be wrong to infer that the researchers who found that secondhand smoke was not harmful were paid off. The more likely hypothesis is that the tobacco lobby chose to fund the authors whose research is more compatible with its interest. But it's easier to find funding for a study proving a drug works wonders than to find funding for a study proving it's harmful. Given that incentives do matter to people, it is hard to believe that the entire process does not bias a study's outcome.

BEWARE OF EXPERTS

The LSE professor's answer to the queen, mentioned at the beginning of this chapter, had an element of truth. Modern, complex societies need to rely on experts. The more complex an organization or a society becomes, the more specialized its members must be, and the more everybody has to rely on others for technical expertise. Think of a bank. In Frank Capra's movie *It's a Wonderful Life,* Mr. Bailey is a jack-of-all-trades at his bank—taking deposits, granting loans, keeping the accounts, and managing the cash balances. Today, the person in charge of mortgage-backed securities is a specialist very different from the one deciding consumer loans. The derivatives expert is separate from the foreign-currency trader, and the accountant's expertise is completely different from that of the treasurer who manages the balances. This specialization has delivered great improvements in productivity.

But can we trust all these experts always to do the right thing? By definition, experts have accumulated a lot of specific knowledge. While this knowledge informs an expert, it can also distort his decisions. When a person has accumulated a vast amount of highly specific human capital, he has a vested interest in the success of the area in which that human capital is located. Oil drillers tend to support oil exploration; financial economists, financial derivatives; nuclear engineers, nuclear power. Without wars, who needs generals?

This conflict of interest is more common than we might want to admit. Sometimes it is obvious. My parents in Italy had a friend who was a geologist. One day, he was asked by his employer to evaluate the profitability of the mine he was working for. He determined that the mine was unprofitable and duly reported it. The result: the mine was closed and he was fired. His family considered him a fool, not a hero, and the marketplace did not compensate him for his honesty either: he became a schoolteacher at a considerably lower salary.

Sometimes the conflict is less clear. Consider an expert in software royalty transfer pricing. Inevitably, one of his large clients would be a multinational company such as Microsoft, with a web of subsidiaries throughout the world. Microsoft Ireland, for example, might pay Microsoft USA for the right to sell software. The less Microsoft Ireland pays its American counterpart, the more the overall profits will occur in low-corporate-tax Ireland, rather than in comparatively high-tax America. The determination of these prices thus has a huge impact on Microsoft's overall tax bill. Large multinational corporations and their main auditors are the main employers of the economists who specialize in this field; the Internal Revenue Service, which challenges the assumptions that the corporations make to minimize their tax liability, hires far fewer.

So let's say you're a tax accounting professor trying to decide what multinationals should be able to charge in terms of transfer prices. If you take a very rigid view, you might perhaps be hired by the IRS as an expert witness. If, by contrast, your position makes it easier for multinationals to reduce their tax liability, you can (and will) be hired by the richest corporations in America. Will these considerations play any role in your writing?

ESPRIT DE CORPS, INBREEDING, AND GROUPTHINK

So far, I have reasoned like an economist and focused only on economic incentives. Yet the failure of experts to see the obvious, as in the example of the housing bubble, could be the result of other incentives as well. As social psychologist Irving Janis pointed out, deeply cohesive groups often reach a consensus without critically testing their ideas, a phenomenon that he labeled *groupthink*. Groupthink happens when group members desire to minimize conflict within the group, and it is exacerbated when the group feels superior to the outside world, since any member who challenges the consensus runs the risk of being excluded from the group and thus losing the status that it confers.

It is hard to imagine an institution that better embodied the principles of competence and efficiency than the German army in the early twentieth century. But despite their superior training and considerable experience, German generals developed an abominable strategy in World War I. Plan A was to win the war with a massive and decisive attack against France. Plan B, however, was to "bleed France white." The Germans knew that in the previous fifty years, more German children had been born than French children, so they concluded that in a war of attrition in which they killed as many soldiers as they lost, they would eventually prevail. In other words, the official strategy of the German army was to wipe out an entire generation, not only of their enemies but also of their own citizens. The plan was implemented in the Battle of Verdun in 1916, which lasted ten months and caused huge losses on both sides. Casualties are estimated at between 600,000 and

800,000 men, almost equally distributed between the French and the German armies.[12] How could a group of highly intelligent and competent people arrive at a plan that any ordinary human being would have rejected as crazy?

German generals were not unique in their folly. During World War I, French, English, Austrian, and Italian officers sent hundreds of thousands of men to die with a purpose no grander than conquering a few yards and making themselves look good in the eyes of their superiors. No surprise that France's prime minister at the time, Georges Clemenceau, concluded that "war is much too serious a matter to entrust to military men." In the end, the German strategy failed because it was not only criminal but stupid as well: it ignored the risk, which later materialized, that the German people would revolt against the prolonged, senseless carnage.

It is perhaps not surprising that the German plan was formulated by generals who all came from the Junker elite and, thanks to their past successes, felt invincible. But Janis actually coined the term *groupthink* to explain a number of American foreign-policy disasters, such as the failed Bay of Pigs invasion and the military strategy in Vietnam. Indeed, the phenomenon is pervasive in modern societies, where decisions are delegated to highly specialized groups who feel superior to the rest of society because of their technical training.

Ironically, the more meritocratic an organization is, the more it can suffer from this problem, especially when it tries to replace compensation with prestige. One issue that every organization faces is how to attract, retain, and motivate all the people whose specialized talents it needs. One strategy is to dangle the prospect of significant compensation in the future. This method works, but it is expensive, since that compensation must be paid eventually or the system will collapse. Alternatively, an organization can offer prestige. The head of a primitive tribe is not significantly richer than the other members, but he has more prestige.

The value of prestige, however, is culturally determined. A person values it only to the extent that the group of people she values and respects considers it worthwhile. Hence, every organization that wants to use prestige as an incentive has to create a strong sense of belonging and superiority in its members. A stock market speculator does not need social recognition: his proceeds are what motivates him, and in fact, those proceeds have to be large enough to outweigh the disdain with which many view him. By contrast, soldiers, scientists, and professors receive a lot of their "compensation" in the form of social recognition.

It is easy to see why the higher ranks of a hierarchy support such a system of prestige: they receive enough benefits (at least prospectively) that they are better off keeping the system in place than rejecting it. But what about the rank and file? For a young officer, the chance of becoming a decorated general is low; he has to recognize others much more than others will ever recognize him. For this reason, all these organizations foster an *esprit de corps* that creates a sense of superiority in their members. The young officer may feel inferior to many other officers, but at least he can feel superior to civilians—just as a young professor feels superior to her students and the young scientist feels superior to people who make money. There is an old joke that academic feuds are so intense because the stakes are so low. Like all good jokes, it contains an element of truth. Academics have to feel that their questions are important; otherwise, how could they justify to themselves that they make so little money?

If the problem of *esprit de corps*–fostered groupthink is severe in a formal, homogeneous group like the military, it is even worse in informal groups, whose membership can quickly be revoked by consensus. A dissenting officer can be prevented from advancing in his career, but he cannot be ejected from the military, unless he violates its formal rules. By contrast, self-appointed groups of experts quickly ostracize dissenters. John F. Kennedy adviser Arthur Schlesinger recalls remaining silent during the cabinet's discussion of the Bay of Pigs invasion for fear of being cut out of the inner circle.[13]

The problem also becomes more severe the more a group is threatened from the outside. Entertaining critics' hypotheses is seen as betrayal of one's group, and thus dealt with severely. Something like this happened to the military in the case of Vietnam: as antiwar protest increased, the Department of Defense became more insular.

Traditionally, this problem has been much more severe in Europe than in the United States, partly because of the sheer size of this country.

In a small country like Belgium or the Netherlands, the political elite is likely to come from a single cultural milieu, if not from a single school. The size and diversity of the United States have prevented Americans from creating a homogeneous elite. The centralization of education in Continental Europe has also contributed to this cultural inbreeding. Until Nicolas Sarkozy, all the French presidents of the Fifth Republic had come from the École Nationale de l'Administration, as did many ministers and top bureaucrats. In Europe, this problem is exacerbated by a sense of superiority felt by the intellectual elite toward ordinary people, an attitude dating back to the Middle Ages. Even a communist as committed as Vladimir Lenin theorized that the intellectual elite ought to lead the ignorant masses toward his vision of their own good.

Unfortunately, the idea that a small, enlightened elite should guide the ignorant people to what is good for them, even at the cost of misleading them, has become more prevalent in America too. This paternalistic view among political and economic leaders emerged in all its clarity during the discussion of the 2008 financial bailout. As with a patient, when the economy is sick, we naturally seek the help of experts. These experts can use their knowledge to explain the available options to politicians and voters, or they can use it to disguise the real costs of political decisions. During the 2008 financial crisis, as the average American balked at the magnitude of resources transferred to the financial industry, political leaders and their preferred experts did everything in their power to make their achievement less visible to voters.

CONCLUSIONS

As the division of labor increases specialization, the interests of the specialized, technically competent elite diverge from those of the rest of the people. As I have explained in this chapter, the causes for this divergence are various, but the outcome is always the same: the experts' interests increasingly align with those of the powerful incumbents, or at least begin to diverge from those of the rest of the population. This is true for all experts, including academic economists, who have an incentive to be influenced by the very business agents they study. Not only does this divergence lead to bad decision making, with the interests of entrenched business trumping support for the free market; it also engenders public mistrust of experts and of merit-based systems. And a sense of fairness and trust is essential for American capitalism to thrive.

A divide between the intellectual elite and the people can easily fuel the most dangerous forms of populism, especially as the perception of corruption and the consequent resentment against Washington are soaring. If the intellectual elite cannot be trusted, anti-intellectualism prevails, and the quality of the political debate deteriorates. This deterioration, in turn, gives the intellectual elite another reason to feel superior, a feeling that exacerbates groupthink and fuels even more populist reactions.

The solution is not to get rid of experts; that cure would be worse than the disease. The solution is to understand the potential biases and create a system of checks and balances. Only with a high degree of popular control does a meritocratic system avoid degeneration into an oligarchy. The solution is also that experts—especially those, like myself, with extensive connections with the business world—recognize these risks and fight against them. The danger of capture makes it all the more important, too, that data be readily available to all and that intellectual debate and competition be vigorous, as it is in most American universities. We will return to these issues later in the book.

7

THE TIME FOR POPULISM

The people are now contending for freedom, and would to God they might not only obtain but likewise keep it in their own hands.

—Anonymous, "The People Are the Best Governors," 1776

"THE TELECOMMUNICATION REVOLUTION MADE AMERICA, and the world, a much smaller place, facilitating large-scale organization and centralization. Corporations grew exponentially amid traumatic spasms of global capitalist development. . . . The rich amassed great fortunes, a prosperous section of the middle class grew more comfortable, and hard times pressed on most everyone else."[1] This passage describes not the beginning of the twenty-first century but the end of the nineteenth and the conditions that, according to historian Charles Postel, laid the groundwork for a populist movement in the United States: globalization, a telecom revolution, and a widening income gap.

Those conditions closely resemble the conditions prevailing today. And once again, some form of populism seems inevitable. For promarket forces, this situation represents both a threat and an opportunity—a threat because populist movements tend to emphasize redistribution and egalitarianism, which can impede meritocracy and thus destroy incentives and diminish economic growth; and an opportunity because a populist revolt can provide the political resources to fight crony capitalism. When diffuse interests confront concentrated ones, the former generally lose, as we've seen. The fight against crony capitalism can be won only if the public joins the fight, shaming those who abuse their power and speaking out against the damage that crony capitalism inflicts on us all. The current moment could hardly be more favorable. Public resentment against the bank bailouts and the Bush and Obama administrations' favorable treatment of finance is running high. A concerted campaign against the corruption in Washington should find a sympathetic reception.

In any country other than the United States, *promarket populism* would be an oxymoron. Promarket ideas tend not to be very popular, and in the short term, populist movements can get easy consensus by pushing for massive redistributions of wealth. The United States has a more positive populist tradition than other countries do, however. By understanding this tradition, we may be able to channel the new populism into saving rather than destroying free markets.

THE GOLDEN AGE

The term *populism* is often used pejoratively; indeed, it can be an effective label with which to delegitimize a movement. Movements and parties often label themselves "popular," not "populist," to avoid this stigma. Yet it is fair to say that all forms of populism share an exaltation of "the people" and some form of resentment against the "dominant elite."[2]

Historically, populism surfaces when a sizable percentage of a country's population becomes economically disenfranchised. This is what happened to small farmers at the end of the nineteenth century in America; to the small bourgeoisie wiped out by inflation in pre-Nazi Germany; and to the middle class in Latin America after the commodities booms of the 1920s and World War II left it much poorer. Populist resentment and protest tend to be triggered less by the actual state of living conditions than by the decline (or relative decline) of those conditions. And such decline, unfortunately, is visible in today's America.

Let's take a short trip in time back to the end of World War II, when America enjoyed a huge victory dividend—one that especially favored the middle class. From the mid-1940s to the beginning of the 1970s, US GDP grew at an average of 3.7 percent per year, and income inequality fell. In 1939, a typical high school graduate earned 29 percent less than a college graduate; in 1975, he earned just 22.5 percent less.[3] In 1975, too, the average American was earning 74 percent more than his father had.[4] The American Dream seemed within everyone's reach.

As Adam Smith taught, the wealth of nations is ultimately determined by their productivity. And the United States boasted a gigantic productivity advantage relative to the rest of the world, which allowed it to distribute the newly created wealth throughout its population. One reason for the advantage was America's protection of property rights—a rarity in the world of that era. In 1946, only 6 percent of the people in the world lived under even somewhat democratic regimes.[5] With Mao's victory in China, 34 percent of the world's population was under the boot of communist regimes.[6] Moreover, several Western democracies (such as France and Italy) found themselves threatened from within by strong communist parties. What company would choose to move to a country where the communists might take over any day?

Also contributing to America's productivity was its workforce. Thanks to its democratic (indeed populist) tradition, the postwar United States was also one of the most educated countries in the world. In 1950, when 44 percent of the world's population was illiterate and only 8.2 percent held high school degrees, the corresponding figures in the United States were 2.2 percent and 37 percent.[7] Again, what company would want to relocate to a country where most of the population was illiterate?

The United States had still more factors increasing its productivity. For one, the physical destruction of war had left it nearly unscathed. Whereas 16 percent of the industrial plants in Germany, 26 percent of those in Japan, and 8 percent of those in France had been destroyed, the American industrial base was fully intact.[8] Furthermore, the military effort had compelled American companies to modernize and improve their productivity, making the United States by far the top industrial force in the world. Also, a postwar commodities' glut lowered the real prices of oil, iron ore, and other inputs. In fact, the real prices of industrial commodities halved between 1950 and 1970, enabling the US to improve its standard of living quickly.[9]

In short, America had a stable environment, advanced technology, and an educated workforce. Those three conditions were then rare, if not unique, in the world, and they explain why US companies had little desire to outsource their operations. America had a monopoly (or quasi-monopoly) on safe and efficient places in which to produce, and the wealth flowing from this monopoly benefited the entire nation.

The post–World War II generation flourished in these favorable market conditions—but it also took the liberty of appropriating some of the benefits belonging to future generations. Critics of America's Social Security system have called it a Ponzi scheme, which is not as ridiculous as it may sound. In a Ponzi scheme, earlier investors get paid with the money deposited by later investors, with the very first investors enjoying an entirely free lunch and handing the bill to the people who follow them. If enrollment is mandatory, a Ponzi scheme can continue for a long time—in the case of Social Security, as long as the economy and the population continue to expand. Provided that future generations are much richer or much more populous than the current one, the scheme works.

However, if economic growth or population growth—or, worse, both—slow down, the magic disappears. The generation in the workforce contributes more than it ever expects to reap in the future, simply to compensate for the slowdown. We see this reality unfolding today not only with Social Security but with other entitlement programs, such as Medicare.

THE WORLD IS CATCHING UP

The good news is that, over the last sixty-five years, American values have spread across the globe. Most communist countries and autocracies have become democracies. Today, 55 percent of the people in the world live in democracies. Now that China has embraced capitalism, only 2 percent of the people in the world live under truly communist regimes.[10] And much of the world has embraced basic market principles. Generalized education has become the rule, not the exception: a full 71 percent of the people living in OECD countries have high school degrees.[11] In short, America has succeeded in nation-building after all—not by force but by example.

The bad—or, better, the challenging—news is that this global progress has shrunk America's comparative advantage. In part, we have ourselves to blame. The percentage of college graduates in the United States has not increased much over the last thirty years, and the quality of education that non-college-graduates receive has decreased.[12] Rather than recognize that this historical anomaly is over, too many Americans feel entitled to prosperity without an education. But much of the blame (or, rather, credit) for this American decline belongs to other nations. It's a lot easier to catch up than to keep the lead. When you're catching up, you can look around and figure out what works and what does not. If you're in the lead, it's harder to know where to go and much easier to make mistakes.

An example of the United States' relative decline is the recent history of the New York Stock Exchange. Until the end of the millennium, the NYSE was the gold standard in the stock-exchange world. During the 1990s, the number of foreign companies listed on the NYSE quadrupled;[13] meanwhile, the European exchanges, including London, saw declines in their share of world companies listed. In the first decade of the new millennium, the tide turned. At the beginning of the 2000s, 82 percent of the equity raised by the initial public offerings of foreign companies outside their domestic markets was raised in the US; at the end of the decade, the figure was only 10 percent.[14] In 2000, new foreign listings in the NYSE outpaced foreign "delistings," or removals from the NYSE, by a 3.5-to-1 ratio. In 2007, the balance was reversed and foreign delistings exceeded foreign listings by a 14-to-1 ratio.[15] What happened?

According to many commentators, the relative decline in the attractiveness of the US market can be blamed on excessive financial regulation.[16] But the relative improvement in the rest of the world's exchanges is an important reason as well. One way to measure this improvement is to examine stocks listed in more than one exchange, since most of the trades in these stocks will naturally migrate to where they can be executed more cheaply. In the early 1980s, more than half of the trades in these stocks took place in the United States. But by the end of the 1990s, the fraction of trades taking place in local exchanges had grown larger than the fraction taking place in the US.[17] This suggests that at the beginning of that decade, it was cheaper to trade in New York, and by the end, in the local exchanges. Exploiting the second-comer advantage, foreign exchanges had installed more efficient trading platforms than those in the United States. Many of the managers of these foreign exchanges had received their training in US business schools and had learned how to organize and market exchanges. The local regulators learned better rules from the United States, too. Competition intensified.

THE MODERN FARMERS

As the world catches up, the telecommunications revolution has been obliterating geographical distance. This process of globalization is not all that different from the one that occurred in the nineteenth century, when railways, steel hulled steamships, and the introduction of the telegraph integrated the world economy to a greater degree. All of a sudden, farmers had to stop producing for local markets alone and instead respond to world prices. The first to exploit the opportunities offered by this integration made millions; most of the rest got squeezed.

The populist party that emerged against this backdrop viewed its primary targets as railroads and banks. The movement was a visceral reaction to the messengers of globalization: the railroad companies buying wheat for the global market and the banks enforcing the loans that farmers could no longer pay.

The modern "farmers" reeling from globalization include high school graduates not all that different from the middle-class people who in a previous generation enjoyed very comfortable lives. When Robert Mc-Namara joined the Ford Motor Company in 1945, under 1 percent of the firm's managers had college degrees;[18] nowadays, a person can't even get an interview without one. But the newly economically displaced also include college-educated engineers and accountants—and soon lawyers, teachers, and even doctors. If railways and steamboats integrated markets by shattering transportation costs, the technology revolution is making distance itself less and less relevant. It used to be that most services, from fixing computers and tutoring to accounting and legal services, required the provider's physical presence. A manager in Palo Alto couldn't hire a secretary in Bangalore, even though such a secretary would be far cheaper than one in Palo Alto. But as communication technologies improve, a secretary sitting 10,000 miles away will soon be almost as convenient as one sitting outside your office. Secretaries in Palo Alto will find themselves competing with secretaries in Bangalore. This will depress the salaries of the American secretaries and increase the salaries of the Indian ones. It is a great opportunity for the Indian middle class and a great threat to the American middle class.

This foreign challenge is quickly expanding to almost all services, including more knowledge-intensive ones. As videoconferencing becomes more sophisticated and cheaper, teaching, tutoring, and legal services will be done at a distance. In 2001, the first transatlantic *surgical* procedure took place: using fiber optics and a robotic surgical instrument, a doctor in New York performed a gall bladder operation on a patient in Strasbourg. While these operations are still experimental, we are not far from the time in which a local technician will insert an endoscopic camera and a top surgeon thousands of miles away will perform the operation.[19] While this process, in America, will open extraordinary opportunities for the most talented workers in their fields—they will see demand for their services in every corner of the globe—it will have a negative impact on the salaries of their more ordinary counterparts.

THE POPULIST REACTION

Not surprisingly, worries about the economic effects of globalization are reflected in declining public support for free trade. In 2001, according to a regular survey conducted by the Pew Research Center, 49 percent of Americans were in favor of the North American Free Trade Agreement

(NAFTA), which liberalized trade among Canada, the US, and Mexico, while only 29 percent were against it. In 2010, only 35 percent supported NAFTA and 44 percent were against it—and 55 percent (wrongly) believed that NAFTA had produced a net loss in jobs, with only 8 percent thinking it had generated new jobs. The loss of support for free trade is even stronger among Republicans than among Democrats. In 2010, only 28 percent of Republicans thought NAFTA a good idea, and support was even weaker, 24 percent, among Tea Party supporters.

As I've shown, a major factor supporting the American free-market system is a public consensus that wealth is the just compensation for hard work and, as such, is attainable by anybody who puts in the effort. A December 2011 Pew survey shows that a large percentage of Americans still believe this to be the case, but the proportion is dropping fast. In 1998, 74 percent of Americans agreed with the statement "Most people who want to get ahead can make it if they are willing to work hard." As of 2011, that figure had fallen to 58 percent.

Doubtless contributing to this decline is the widespread perception that banks and other large firms have been playing according to a different set of rules. Several years after the subprime crisis, no mortgage brokers have been convicted for fraudulent misrepresentation of data on loan applications. This is odd, given research showing that 30 to 70 percent of early payment default can be attributed to a fraudulent misrepresentation on the original application.[20] Small wonder, then, that the level of trust toward these institutions has plummeted. In a BBB/Gallup poll administered in April 2008, 42 percent of the respondents said they trusted financial institutions and 53 percent said they trusted large companies. In a similar poll taken eight months later, those percentages dropped to 34 and 12 percent, respectively.[21] Three years after that (in October 2011), the percentage of people who said they trusted banks had fallen a bit more, to 33 percent, while the percentage who said they trusted large companies had risen, but only to 16 percent.[22]

The question, then, given these trends, is no longer *whether* populist pressure will have a strong influence on policy decisions but *how*. Will it work to destroy or to improve the market system that has brought so much well-being?

WHICH POPULISM?

Outside the United States, populism is generally associated with two equally bad extremes. On the one hand, there is *reactionary populism*, which can develop when Machiavellian leaders stoke primitive feelings—racism, fear, religious intolerance—to build support for an otherwise unpopular regime. An example is Peronism, the movement started in 1940s Argentina by Juan Perón, at the time the secretary of labor. Peronism exploited Argentinean nationalism to promote a form of corporate nationalism, blurring distinctions between corporations and government. The Fascist and Nazi movements were more frightening forms of reactionary populism.

On the other hand, there is *left-wing populism*, which plays on envy and class warfare, pitting have-nots against haves in an effort to destroy meritocracy and introduce a new, political allocation of resources. The most extreme form of left-wing populism was Mao Zedong's mad Cultural Revolution, which, in the years between 1966 and 1976, wiped out China's intellectual elite and cost the country millions of lives.

America, too, has had its share of ugly populism, including that of the Ku Klux Klan and segregationist politician George Wallace. But there is another, more positive strain in American history, extending back to the American Revolution itself, in which the elite and nonelite formed an alliance against the colonial power.

Far from populists themselves, the Founding Fathers designed a system of checks and balances to prevent a mob-led degeneration of the new republic.[23] Nevertheless, there were populist elements in the colonists' fight against the British Crown, which they perceived as a conflict between liberty and power.[24] With the election of Thomas Jefferson as president in 1800 and the subsequent demise of the Federalist Party, the populist strains of the American Revolution became mainstream. These populist elements resurfaced with the election of Andrew Jackson in 1828, and later with the creation of the People's Party (1891), with which the Democratic Party fused in 1896, nominating William Jennings Bryan as its presidential candidate.

In fact, rather than the exception, populism has been the rule of American politics. The two exceptions have been periods of unprecedented growth, prosperity, and social mobility: the frontier era, which lasted until 1890, and the industrial golden age between 1945 and 1970.

Thanks to this tradition, American populist political movements have tended to be quite different from those elsewhere.

For example, the political goal of the People's Party, which played a significant role in US history between 1891 and 1908, was not to overthrow the existing political system but to improve it through economic and political reforms. The People's Party protested against banking and railroads, the big economic powers of the day, for the same reason that American colonists protested against the powerful East India Company a century earlier: they believed that these interests unduly influenced the political process and rendered state and federal governments "corrupt, oppressive and unrepresentative of the people."[25]

Furthermore, the People's Party was not anti-intellectual. In fact, it came to be known as "a reading party" and a "writing and talking party."[26] Its members *were* anti-elite and believed that the elites had been captured by the dominant economic interests. The party's fundamental message was "This is *our* polity, in which we, the democratic sovereign, have a right to practice government by the people; but we have been shut out for power by corrupt politicians and an unrepresentative elite who betray our interests, ignore our opinions, and treat us with contempt"[27]—a message that resonates to this day.

Yet despite this legitimate tradition, the term *populism* still has a negative connotation for many Americans. Partly this is because some of the nation's populist movements have been represented by flawed or destructive personalities—from Louisiana governor Huey Long, who was accused of bribery and dictatorial tendencies, to the anti-Semitic priest Father Charles Edward Coughlin. Another reason is that populist movements, above all in Latin America, have a terrible economic record. Populist programs that focus on economic redistribution, as many outside America have, can have a positive short-term effect on the private consumption of the poor, who naturally tend to consume a greater percentage of their income than the wealthy. Together with massive government spending, though, redistributive programs have created huge fiscal deficits—deficits that eventually force the government to cut expenses and raise taxes. Then, as the economy struggles, the very workers who are the populists' constituency find themselves worse off. Income redistribution also reduces the incentive of companies to invest, which in turn reduces workers' productivity and their real wages.[28]

If it is well understood that populist economic policies unleash such problems, why don't populist leaders change the policies? A recent paper hypothesizes that the policies are necessary for populist leaders to be elected in the first place.[29] In divided societies where the power of the entrenched elite is large, politicians need to signal to voters that they aren't in cahoots with that elite. Unless they advocate policies that benefit the lower class immediately, even at greater cost later on, populist leaders won't be able to differentiate themselves from the ruling elite. In short, the most damaging forms of populism manifest themselves in societies where a closed elite rules, detached from the rest of the population.

Only in a country with a credible populist tradition can populist movements avoid radical and counterproductive programs. It is thanks to America's moderate populist tradition that we have a Bill of Rights. It is thanks to this tradition that we invented antitrust law before economists fully worked out the reasons that it was a good idea. And it is thanks to this tradition that senators are no longer nominated but elected, a process that limits corruption.

PROMARKET POPULISM

Even in the United States, populism has typically not been promarket. At a time when markets weren't that competitive, the populist revolt against the excessive power of large corporations brought us the first government agency (the Interstate Commerce Commission) and the first regulation to keep railway prices low. Squeezed by the globalized markets, farmers looked to the government for protection. The public perception was that the interests of ordinary people were better protected through the political process than through the marketplace. For this reason, American populism tended to support an activist government.

Today, the situation is quite different, opening the possibility of a fully promarket populism. The perception that Americans have of markets remains positive. According to a survey conducted as part of the Chicago Booth/Kellogg School Trust Index, 46 percent of Americans agree with the statement "The free market system is the best way to protect the interest of ordinary Americans," while 22 percent disagree. The public's trust in government, by contrast, is low. Over 50 percent of Americans declare that they trust the government very little or not at all. This lack of trust is due at least partly to the perception that the government acts in the interest of a few large corporations or special interests, rather than in the interest of the country as a whole. In December 2008, for example, when Americans were asked in whose interest they thought Treasury Secretary Henry Paulson had acted during the financial crisis, 50 percent responded, "in the interest of Goldman Sachs."[30] To a similar question asked about President Obama in December 2009, 32 percent responded, "in the interest of the financial industry," and 22 percent, "in the interest of the unions." Support for big business is virtually nonexistent. Only 16 percent of Americans trust large corporations (a figure lower than the percentage who trust the government), and 53 percent agree with the statement "Big business distorts the functioning of markets to its own advantage."

Is it possible to build a populist political agenda that reflects this support for free markets and distrust of government and big business? Is it possible to design policies that reset the economic balance in favor of the ordinary American without massive government intervention, which would interfere with economic freedom and suppress growth? In short, is it possible to recapture the lost genius of American prosperity?

PART TWO

SOLUTIONS

FOR THOSE READERS WHO ARE ALREADY ANGRY, I HOPE THAT MY no-holds-barred exposé resonates with your frustrations. For those who were not angry when you picked up this book, I hope my exposé has made you so.

The degeneration of the US free-market system into crony capitalism should anger any person who loves freedom and democracy.

The purpose of poets is to provide humans with words for their feelings. The more prosaic purpose of social scientists is to provide a framework for interpreting—and, more important, addressing—economic and social problems. In a democracy, comprehension of problems and their causes is a necessary, albeit not sufficient, condition for change.

Yet understanding is not enough; a cure must be found as well. Accordingly, the rest of this book outlines my proposed remedies. Some of these are original; others I borrowed. But they have one important element in common: they all reflect an effort to use free markets and competition to fix the economic and social problems we are facing—rather than sidestepping them.

These problems have given rise to two frequent reactions. One is to blame the free-market system and try to fix the problems through heavy reliance on government intervention. This course fails to realize that the government is part of the problem rather than part of the solution. The other reaction is to deny that the problem exists or that it can be solved. In some cases this denial results from obliviousness, or even desperation. In others, however, it is a callous strategy to undermine the call for change.

I want to provide an alternative to blame and denial. My aim in the first part of the book was to convince you that America has a big problem that needs to be addressed—now. In the second part I hope to convince you that the problem can be addressed without renouncing a principle that most of us hold dear: the principle of free markets. The changes I advocate are meant to enhance freedom, not repress it.

Another element my solutions have in common is that they all rely on people's desire for freedom.

8

EQUALITY OF OPPORTUNITY

*You cannot lift the wage earner up by pulling the wage
payer down.*

—Abraham Lincoln

S I EXPLAINED IN CHAPTER 2, DEMOCRACIES CONSTANTLY
wrestle with the tension between providing the right
incentives—to build human capital, to invest, to work
hard—and assuring that the benefits of the free market are
widely shared, so that people maintain their faith in both the efficiency
and the fairness of the system. Without some inequality, there are no incentives: people go to college and study hard not just because they love
learning but also because they expect to earn more money afterward.
Without the promise of a higher reward for good performance (or threat
of a lower reward for laxity), most people will not exert extra effort.

Yet high income inequality implies that a few people receive a disproportionate payoff but many get little or no reward, depressing the
incentives of risk-averse individuals. Pronounced income inequality
yields bad political consequences, too. Political support for a meritocratic system dwindles if most people feel that they are receiving little

from it and that an elite group is gaining disproportionate political power and can rig the system to its advantage.

If we do not care about maintaining a system of incentives, there is a simple solution to excessive income inequality: income redistribution through taxation. However, this solution, tried in various forms in socialist and social-democratic countries, has weakened incentives to create wealth and consequently impaired nations' possibilities of prospering and growing. If winning golf players had to add strokes to their totals so that everyone got the same score, the best golfers would soon lose their incentive to play hard. Instead, golf equalizes the starting points of the players by imposing handicaps. An analogous mechanism for the economy, encouraging more equal opportunity, would offer, I think, the best approach to making markets more inclusive, while preserving the incentives that make us grow.

THE DISTURBING PICTURE

In Chapter 2, I presented a chart illustrating the divergence between salaries and productivity between 1946 and 2009. Productivity (the dashed line) kept growing, while real wages (the solid black line) declined a bit over time. Now take a look at Figure 3.

The first rule of empirical economic analysis is that when you find a stunning result, check the data. Nine times out of ten, the "stunning" result turns out to be a data problem. The data might not be false but also may not show what you think. In this case, part—though not all—of the surprising result is an illusion.[1] In this graph, in addition to wages, I plot compensation (the dotted line), where compensation is the sum of what firms pay for workers, rather than what workers take home. For the past thirty-five years the dotted line has been in the middle: not as steep as productivity but not as flat as real wages. What is the difference?

Part of it is a by-product of how the government reports the issue of pay. Year-end bonuses have become more important, but for historical reasons they are not included in the definition of wages. Still, much of the observed divergence is due to a real phenomenon: firms' contribution to workers' health care has been increasing over time to become a bigger percentage of compensation. If workers feel poorer, it is because

Figure 3. Productivity and Average Real Earnings

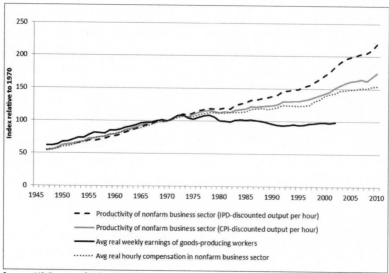

Source: US Bureau of Labor Statistics.

rising health insurance premiums have been swallowing up most (if not all) of their real wage increases in recent years. Between 2003 and 2010, premiums for family coverage rose 50 percent.[2] Workers don't feel the benefit of health insurance in their biweekly check—they feel themselves struggling harder to keep up.

A second reason for the difference between rising productivity and falling pay is technical. As economists explain, productivity is adjusted by nonfarm business output price—the price of goods and services produced by businesses in the United States—while the wage data are adjusted by the better-known consumer price index.[3] The grey line on the graph reflects productivity adjusted by the consumer price index, and that closely matches compensation, at least until the new millennium.

Behind this dry technicality lies a real problem. As it turns out, one of the major differences between the two series is that the nonfarm business output does not include nonprofit institutions, such as universities and nonprofit hospitals. Between 1977 and 2009, the real average cost of university tuition more than doubled,[4] and at top colleges, the increase was even greater. If we look from 1920 to 2000, the real cost of Harvard tuition increased ten times.[5] For many Americans the cost of this increase has been ameliorated in part by expanding public and private scholarships; for many others, it has not.[6] While this cost increase is reflected in the consumer price index used to transform the nominal wage into real wages, it is not reflected in the adjustment of productivity, whose growth would look less steep if adjusted by the same formula used to calculate real wage growth.

Thus this difference reflects something that ordinary Americans feel: college has become relatively more expensive for typical workers, making it more difficult to provide for their children's future. Furthermore, even after we correct the data, the gap between compensation and productivity is still there. Until 2000, data correction can account for most of the gap; after that, a significant part of the gap is real.

If the first golden rule of economic data analysis is to check the data when you find a stunning result, the second is to check whether the same fact is present if you look from a completely different perspective. Because money does not just disappear, the difference between productivity and compensation should appear somewhere else: in profits. Since the early 1900s, economists have liked to study how total production is allocated between labor and capital. If the divergence between wages and productivity is real, the share of gross domestic product (GDP) going to capital should be increasing over time, and the share going to labor should be shrinking. While this distinction is muddled by stock options and bonuses (which count as return to capital, even though they are given to workers, at least a particular category of workers), the share going to labor is indeed decreasing. In 1970 the labor share of manufacturing sector output was 40 percent, while in 2008 it was only 25 percent.[7] This phenomenon is particularly pronounced in the first decade of the new millennium.

To understand why this is happening, we need to turn to basic microeconomics.

OF FARMS AND EBOOKS

When Alfred Marshall wrote *Principles of Economics*, the foundation of modern economic analysis, in 1890, the United Kingdom, the world's leading economic power, owed 11 percent of its GDP to agriculture and 36 percent to manufacturing.[8] Thus it was only natural that much of Marshall's analysis and modeling focused on the economics of manufacturing and farming.

Consider the simplest farming technology. A farmer plants wheat. The more fertilizer he uses, the more wheat he gets, but at a decreasing rate. The first $100 worth of fertilizer per a given acreage, let's say, yields $150 of extra wheat. The next $100, only $120. If he keeps increasing the fertilizer, the amount of extra wheat produced starts to be worth less than the cost of the fertilizer. Even without knowing calculus (which Marshall introduced to economics), a smart farmer knows to stop adding fertilizer when the cost of an extra unit of it equals the net revenue—the price he gets for the wheat less the cost of the labor he hires to harvest it—generated by the extra bushel of wheat that this fertilizer will yield. (This is the famous "marginal revenue equals marginal cost" rule.)

The economic system that results from aggregating many small farmers is extremely well behaved. Since it is costly for a farmer to flood the market with cheap wheat—he faces an increasing marginal cost of production—it is hard for any single farmer to gain market power. Furthermore, a small increase in the price of wheat will induce farmers to increase the amount of fertilizer they use, increasing the supply of wheat, with equilibrating effects.

In farming (and traditional manufacturing), when innovation (like the mechanical reaper) increased productivity, the demand for unskilled labor dropped while the demand for skilled labor rose. The new machines required skillful hands for operation. The farmer's fixed capital investment in them was so large that it was profitable for the employer to compensate the workers more in order to keep the machines running properly. This is the great intuition behind Henry Ford's $5 a day compensation policy:[9] if you pay more than the base minimum wage necessary to attract workers to you—the so-called market-clearing wage—you will elicit more effort from them.[10]

For this reason, during much of the twentieth century, moderately educated, law-abiding Americans and some Western Europeans were overcompensated for their skills. This brings us back to the concept of rent. American-like workers living in American-like capitalist systems were scarce in the world in the second part of the twentieth century. As already noted, the rest of the world's good fortune in catching up has meant a relative decline in the level of wages the American middle class can command.

But innovation has intensified this squeezing of the American middle class. In the traditional snail-mail world, where books were sold in bookstores, readers relied on their local booksellers for recommendations. There was a job for a reasonably educated, well-read person to provide those recommendations. For the authors and the publisher, it was just a tax—but a necessary tax to reach the customers.

In a world of eBooks—where books are acquired online, and recommendations are gathered and read online, or automatically compiled based on the number of downloads—the role of local bookstores and the people who work in them has shrunk severely. Readers get their books more cheaply online, and temporarily (until the bulk of the market has gone online and competition in the online market has become more intense), the publishers might be able to make more money. The clear losers, though, are the middlemen—the traditional booksellers of yesteryear.

THE ECONOMICS OF WINNER-TAKE-ALL

Progress has always had its victims. Mechanized looms destroyed most textile artisans, trains replaced most coachmen, computers replaced most order clerks. Yet today we are experiencing more than normal progress; we are experiencing a change in the nature of the economics of production.

Consider the typical twenty-first-century product: software. A lot of software, from word processing to social media websites, has a characteristic that traditional goods do not: the more people who use it, the more it is worth (the technical term for this is *network externality*). This means that sustaining multiple producers in the same market isn't easy. Whoever produces the best application in a certain category will conquer the entire market—and not just the US market but the global one.

In the farming example, the slightly less efficient farmer was making slightly less money than the more efficient one. In the extreme version of software technology, by contrast, the slightly less brilliant programmer makes nothing, while the more brilliant one makes a fortune. This is what my late colleague Sherwin Rosen defined as an economy of "superstars" and what Cornell economist Robert Frank calls the "winner-take-all society."[11]

This phenomenon is not limited to goods with technical network externalities (such as software) but extends also to goods with social externalities—goods that are worth more in the eyes of consumers when they become popular. In a clever experiment, some psychologists showed how strong this effect is.[12] They asked students to rate unknown songs, allowing them to download the ones they liked the most at the end of the experiment. To show the effect of social buzz, they let one group of raters see how many times a song had been downloaded before they could rate it; the other group was not allowed to do so. Both the ratings and the market share of downloads were more volatile when raters could see the record of previous downloads. Early winners greatly benefited from the initial buzz and gained a disproportionate market share. This social-snowball effect creates an outcome that is not exactly winner-take-all (there is still a bit of room for the losers), but it is awfully close: the winners enjoy a disproportionate share of the market and the profits, and the rest get the crumbs. What the authors showed that is particularly interesting is that the really good songs make it anyway and the really bad ones lose anyway. It is the ones in the middle that get lucky or unlucky. But this is exactly where most of us are.

Finally, a winner-take-all economy can arise even in sectors where there are no network or social externalities, but where the fixed cost of production is very large and the marginal cost very low, often zero. Consider, for example, a software application with little or no network externalities—let's say an iPhone application to keep track of a person's caloric intake.

This application costs a lot to design and test, but once it's completed, it costs nothing to copy; its marginal cost of production is essentially zero. Consequently, whoever produces the best application in a certain category is able to conquer the entire market by giving it away. And this, again, is not just a US market but a global one. Once she has conquered the world with her application, the software inventor can charge producers of diet foods to advertise on her application. With hundreds of millions of targeted customers throughout the world, she will make a fortune. An application that was nearly as good as hers would not cut it. For most goods this would not be the case, as we willingly trade price for some quality: I will buy a slightly lower quality good if it is properly discounted. But if an app is free, why shouldn't I get the best one?

In principle, the producer of the second-ranked software could try to attract customers by offering them cash rebates on the revenues of future advertising. For example, Amazon.com sells a lower-priced version of its Kindle eReader that shows ads to the customer. The problem is that the model is credible only if the software, as may be the case with Amazon's, has a chance to succeed. But slightly inferior software is unlikely to conquer a significant market share, so its advertising will not be that valuable. The promised rebates will be worth little because there will be few profits to rebate.[13]

This situation is not unique to software but is spreading to movies, songs, and entertainment, as well as to drugs, high-tech products like iPods, telecommunications, cars, and (with the advent of eBooks) even to books.

This change in the nature of markets explains a good deal of the gap between productivity and wages. In the winner-take-all economy, the technology or design embedded in the product partly explains the higher productivity. The iPhone that sells for $399 has an estimated production cost of $188. The $211 difference results from the pricing power Apple has, thanks to its superior technology and design. The Chinese worker who produces the iPhone, however, has little bargaining power vis-à-vis Apple. Thus the company can appropriate a return on design and innovation, creating a gap between the increase in the value of the productivity and the wage, as we see in Figure 3 on page 125.

THE VALUE OF BOSSES

Part of the gap between labor productivity and wages goes not to investors (traditionally called capital) but to high-level executives, who are technically part of labor but are not considered in the traditional version of wages. This phenomenon is probably one of the most controversial aspects of increasing income inequality: the rising compensation of top executives.

Behind this controversy lies a deep ideological divide about the function of managers. Traditional economists see them as training, allocating, and coordinating the workforce.[14] Marxist economists have tended to deny that they add any value at all. They regard managers as opportunistic rent seekers, whose power allows them to subtract some of the value their subordinates create.[15] While less extreme, the non-Marxist Left tends to echo the Marxist interpretation: it perceives managers not as adding value (at least not as much as they get paid) but as grabbing the value that the overall organization produces.[16]

Such radically different interpretations cannot be reconciled on purely theoretical grounds. To settle the question requires data on labor productivity and job assignments and good econometrics to analyze them—both of which we lacked until recently. Companies balked at sharing data with researchers, who, in any case, lacked the necessary methodology. Recently, both these problems have been solved, at least when it comes to lower-level bosses—the supervisors. There must be sufficient turnover to allow us to tease out, in a statistically reliable way, the contribution of workers under different bosses, and the different contribution of various bosses assigned to the same workers.[17]

One study looked at a technology firm and found that bosses (supervisors, in this particular case) have a large effect on the productivity of their subordinates. Replacing a boss who is in the bottom 10 percent of the ability distribution with one who is in the top 10 percent increases the team's total output as much as adding an extra worker to a team (from nine to ten). The marginal product of a boss—the amount of output that a boss adds to team production—is about twice that of a worker. In the company in question, this ratio matched the ratio of the average compensation received.

The most interesting result, though, was that while a better boss makes all workers more productive, the best workers feel the effect most profoundly. In other words, there is an extra return from matching the best bosses with the best workers. If we were to apply the same result to football, this would imply that the total benefit of having Tom

Brady, one of the best NFL quarterbacks, coached by Bill Belichick, one of the best at his profession, is more than the sum of the benefits of having Tom Brady and Bill Belichick separately.

This extra payoff that the right match generates creates a compensation issue. Who captures the added value of putting these two together? Not Brady, who would be less productive with any other coach. Not Belichick, who would be less successful without his star. In this case, the payoff will probably accrue to the owner of the New England Patriots, who had the vision, resources, or luck to put them together. You can see how this would be a problem in companies with diffuse ownership. The knowledge of how to combine the best supervisors with the best workers belongs not to the CEO but to the company itself, and hence to its owner. Yet if the owners are dispersed (as are the shareholders in most US corporations), it is easy for the CEO to capture it.

This appropriation is all the easier because it is very difficult to measure performance for top managers (unlike supervisors), since general market conditions matter so much and there are not a lot of people in similar situations who can help separate signal from noise. Think of all the variables that go into Tom Brady's success, such as the quality of the players around him, the competitiveness in his division, and so on.

The combination of extra profits and the lack of objective data about who or what ultimately produced them creates an enormous opportunity for discretion. This is where power and social norms play a big role. When an ordinary worker bargains for her salary, there is very little room for discretion. The employer generally knows her productivity, and that sets a cap on what the firm is willing to pay.

When it comes to top-level executives, though, that number is much harder to assess. In a competitive market, where there are no extra profits, the value of the executive contribution cannot be vastly overestimated because if the executives are overpaid, other workers will receive too little and eventually will complain or leave. If the firm has market power, however, a CEO can easily appropriate some of the extra return without harm to the firm.

The same is true for the extra payoff generated by the right match. If the firm, as an organization, can find the formula that makes everybody more productive, who will appropriate this extra return? This is where CEOs' power and influence play the biggest role. No board worth anything will knowingly reward the CEO too much. But in the presence of ambiguity, they find it easy to overattribute successes to the CEO, while underattributing the failures. These impulses explain the extreme rarity of relative performance evaluation in CEO compensation, one of the great puzzles in the literature on this subject.[18] Economic theory holds that executive compensation should try to filter out all the external shocks that are beyond the control of any executive and that affect performance of all firms in the industry but are not determined by any of them—an increase in the price of crude for oil companies, for example.[19] Similarly, a standard fairness argument points out that an oil company CEO should not be compensated for the increase in crude prices (which is not due to his merit), nor should he be penalized for their decline (which is not his fault). Most CEOs do get rewarded for luck, though, especially in the absence of a board with the proper incentive to monitor.[20]

In sum, bosses are valuable, and some are very valuable. The late Apple CEO Steve Jobs obviously comes to mind. Those who are valuable should be appropriately rewarded: this is one of the fundamental principles of a meritocracy and of a capitalist economy. Yet compensation for top executives is not necessarily aligned with their productivity. Unless properly monitored, top executives can easily appropriate a disproportionate share of the value created by the organization as a whole, increasing the income inequality and the perception of unfairness, which undermines support for free markets.

LOSERS' RESPONSE

Whether this is strictly a winner-take-all market or, more broadly, an economy with a disproportionate return to superstars, the consequences are similar: there are big winners and big losers. This is true of any period of economic change. The current changes, though, are creating many losers and a few conspicuous winners. This is not a recipe to maintain social consensus. To add insult to injury, luck seems to play a bigger role in this disproportionate success—again, not a good recipe for maintaining social consensus. How will the losers respond?

Thus far, the political response has been fairly muted, because most of the burden has been borne by low-skilled non-college-educated workers, who have a relatively weak political voice. These are the people who have been most negatively affected by foreign competition and outsourcing and are least likely to benefit from the big payoffs provided by an economy of superstars.

Over time, however, the identity of the losers will change. As the competitors become more highly educated, the cost will be borne by those higher up the ladder, who hitherto have been the big beneficiaries of the process, as their relative wages increased while those of the rest of the population stagnated or fell. Computer scientists have already experienced the wage pressure arising from foreign competition. Accountants, lawyers, doctors, and teachers are next. These groups have greater political clout and will not go down without a fight. They will likely start to lobby aggressively to introduce barriers to trade.

This pressure will find support among many American businesses. As competition intensifies and globalizes, the importance of political connections increases, and foreign competitors are at a natural disadvantage in lobbying efforts. Already, businesses that are closer to the government have suffered less than others from foreign competition. In fact, with intense competition keeping the prices in other sectors low, they have benefited doubly.

Italy presents the most extreme example of this involution. As it opened up to foreign competition, the biggest industrialists moved their investment from internationally competitive sectors such as textiles and computers, where they felt at risk, toward regulated utilities, where they could count on a helping hand from the government. The result has been more, rather than less, corruption.

THE EFFECTS OF AN ECONOMY OF SUPERSTARS

The economy of superstars prevailing in many markets not only creates winners and losers but also changes incentives throughout society. Competition for the prize pushes investments up. When car companies were developing products for the US market alone, they could not afford to spend a lot of money in developing one single model. Today, the cost of developing a car is easily over half a billion dollars.[21] At the same time, returns have become more uncertain. This problem is not so worrisome when it comes to physical capital investments, such as investment in developing a car model or in advertising a new song, especially if capital markets work properly. Imagine that several companies try to develop a new search algorithm at the same time. As long as they finance themselves with equity, investment risk can be diversified in the stock market. All of us who invest our retirement savings in stock market indexes diversify this risk. It does not really matter to us who succeeds, as long as one of the companies in our portfolio does and compensates for losses among the others. With all its excesses, the Internet boom of the late 1990s showed that the equity market was willing to provide great sums of money to companies playing this winner-take-all game, whether in telecommunications, software, or online shopping.

Problems arise when the investments are in human capital. Unlike investments in physical capital, investments in human capital are difficult to finance with an equity stake. If a promising young student tried to finance her education by selling a fraction of her future income, she would find it close to impossible. If you pledged 30 percent of your future income to a financier, your incentive to be paid under the table would go up, and it would be too costly for the financier to prevent this behavior by monitoring you. Such a scheme would lead to inefficiency and lower returns to the financier. Anticipating these problems, the financier would demand a high stake in the human capital, making the deal very unattractive.

Because of these difficulties in equity financing, most investments in human capital are financed through loans. This mode of financing works when the return on investment is equally distributed. But when the return is skewed, as in economies of superstars, it becomes problematic. To the people who cannot repay their loans, it is no consolation to know that there are superstars who could pay their own loans a thousand times over.

Not only does this risk increase the burden of college debt for most Americans; it also increases their anxiety (what economists call *risk aversion*). We could motivate people equally well by offering them a bonus of $10,000 or a one in a hundred chance of a bonus of $1 million.[22] Yet the second option generates more anxiety. This anxiety is magnified by another feature of the winner-take-all game: the advantage of a head start.

If the differences between the prizes offered at a golf tournament are small, the monetary advantage of receiving a higher handicap is limited. But in a winner-take-all tournament, even small advantages that only slightly change the probability of winning can be valuable, because the expected benefit is the change in probability multiplied by the prize. If the prize is very large, the benefit of a head start will be too.

As a result, parents are spending vast resources to give their children a small head start. Data show a remarkable increase in the amount of time that parents, especially highly educated ones, dedicate to child-related activities.[23] College-educated mothers now spend twenty-five hours a week taking care of their children (the equivalent of a part-time job), more than twice what their mothers spent thirty years ago. While less dramatic, a similar increase occurred for fathers, especially college-educated fathers. Interestingly, this increase is almost entirely due to time spent with older children, including coordinating and transporting them to their activities.

This increase has not occurred among Canadian families, even highly educated ones, and the remarkable divergence between the two countries induced an economist couple to explore possible reasons. The most plausible one is that in the United States, parents spend more time with children trying to improve their chances of getting into a good college. In Canada, college admissions are less competitive than in America. It's reasonable to conclude that the greater parental involvement in America is the rational response to a surge in competition for college admissions.[24] While the number of college applicants has doubled since the early 1970s, school size has changed very little, making acceptance harder to win. Keeping applicant quality constant, the acceptance rate at selective private schools fell by 22.5 percent between 1972 and 2004.[25]

The rational response of parents and children has been to invest more time in activities that can enhance their record. The amount of time parents spend with older kids is only one manifestation. As the *New York Times* describes it, "Once, summer for teenagers meant a season of menial jobs and lazy days at the local pool. But for a small but growing number of college-bound students . . . summer has become a time of résumé-building academic work and all-consuming, often exotic projects to change the world."[26]

Parents' desire to provide their children with a head start begins at birth. In London, some women about to give birth take nursery school applications with them to the maternity room.[27] They wait for the baby's delivery only because the application requires a birth certificate. Everywhere, parents scramble for the best preschool, the best middle school, the best high school—all to ensure that their children get into a good college. They know that Ivy League colleges will give their offspring a better post-college job-search network, and that the lifetime earnings of grads from the most expensive colleges tend to be higher than those with diplomas from less exalted schools.[28]

The distortions produced by an economy of superstars tend to compound over time. The more unequal the rewards are, the more universities will try to admit future winners, hoping to receive some of their future donations. Over time, this selection creates a substantial gap in resources between first- and second-tier universities. In 1990 Harvard (the richest university) had a $4.6 billion endowment, while Mary Baldwin College (the 300th richest) had only $18 million. In 2007 Harvard's endowment had grown to $34.6 billion (7.5 times), while Mary Baldwin's had grown only to $30 million (1.7 times).[29] These differences, besides creating a strong winner-take-all competition in academia, generate a substantial gap in the quality of the faculty. Hence, the importance of admission to Harvard over Mary Baldwin grows. Winners in the admissions sweepstakes pass their good fortune from generation to generation. Besides the great advantage they already have in economic and social status, children of Harvard alumni have a legacy admissions advantage to a much better school, gaining a significant head start over the children of Mary Baldwin's alumni.

The biggest cost of a winner-take-all economy, in the presence of differential head start, is that it diminishes hope. Children born to uneducated low-income parents have the odds so stacked against them that many of them give up on school and then on work as well. In part they are discouraged by America's movement toward a knowledge economy, which makes it more difficult for uneducated people to find work, but also by the decreasing return on effort for the uneducated. Between 1973 and 2010, the male labor-force-participation rate went from 79 percent to 70 percent, largely because the number of less-educated men grew. In the 1970s, only 6 percent of them were out of the labor force during prime working years (twenty to forty-five years old); in 2010 the percentage went up to 14 percent.[30] The risk is that this phenomenon will spread to the middle class. High school dropouts will not be the only ones left behind; high school graduates and those with only a few years of college will join them.

THE POLITICS OF AN ECONOMY OF SUPERSTARS

The other major cost of an economy of superstars is political. In a traditional economy, the biggest and most successful businesses (which tend to be the most politically powerful) do not need government protection. Companies grew larger and more politically influential by being more efficient—by having the lowest cost of producing an extra unit (i.e., their marginal cost). Because their marginal cost was lower, these companies were not afraid to compete in a free market. They knew that if the playing field was level, they would gain. Thanks to the nature of technology, the free-market ideology fit with the interests of the winners in the marketplace, who tend to be the most politically influential businesses. Thus there was a natural coincidence between the interests of the most powerful capitalists and the flourishing of free markets. This brought the diffusion and the triumph of free-market ideas.

In a winner-take-all market, the winner is not necessarily the best, as the aforementioned song-download experiments showed. So, too, did the victory of the VHS videocassette technology over the superior Betamax system, and of the Microsoft operating systems, first DOS and then Windows.

The resulting equilibrium is very dangerous. The incumbent large firms are politically powerful but not necessarily the most efficient. Thus they have a strong incentive to manipulate the power of the state to preserve their market power through political means. The winner-take-all economy, in other words, breeds crony capitalism.

Even when the winners *are* the most efficient firms, winner-take-all markets need political support. Think about drug companies that invest billions of dollars in research and development to produce a new drug. When the drug gains approval, the marginal cost of production (for them as for everybody else) is nearly zero. To recoup the cost of the investment, the drug company needs strong patent protection. Since legislation as well as litigation affects patent rights, each drug company must have lobbyists in addition to a strong team of lawyers. The distinction between a drug company lobbying to protect legitimate rights and excessive ones is often in the eye of the beholder. The same is true for software patent law. Some claim that the excessive enforcement of patent law in software is a strong disincentive for innovation.[31]

This tension is particularly strong in innovative sectors. Companies such as Microsoft and Google have succeeded because they have been astonishingly innovative. But once they reach a critical mass, they find it difficult to sustain the innovative spirit. Thus political lobbying becomes a seductive option as they seek to sustain their market position against the threat of new entrants. In the 2007–2008 political cycle, it's worth noting, both Microsoft and Google appeared in the list of top political donors, with $5 million and $2.6 million, respectively.[32] Their competitors, weak in Washington to begin with, have become even weaker.

Ironically, similar mismatches between political (or military) power and economic efficiency have occurred internationally. When countries with powerful militaries were the most efficient producers, free trade spread. When Japan resisted opening its markets in the mid-nineteenth century, the United States sent Commodore Perry to force them open. When China resisted the drugs the East India Company exported, the British sent troops to open up that market. When in the 1980s Japan resisted opening up its financial markets to US firms, the United States flexed its political muscle to gain entry.

Now, the situation is different. While military and political power is still concentrated in US hands, economic efficiency is not. Brazil is the most efficient producer of sugar, but it does not have the muscle to force the United States to lower its tariffs.[33] The differences between the most efficient producers and the most politically (and militarily) powerful ones is as problematic as the divergence between the most efficient producers and the ones that have the greatest power in Washington. In both cases, free markets suffer.

THE WRONG FIXES

One natural political response to this state of affairs is protectionism. Given the economic fundamentals, there has been surprisingly little pressure for that so far. One possible explanation is that support for protectionism is strongest among low-skilled manufacturing workers, who have little political influence and whose cry for government aid has made little impression on an intellectual elite that, by and large, has benefited from free trade and the exportation of American values and culture all over the world.

The balance of power may change as those who wield political influence begin to feel the effect of free trade. When accountants, lawyers, and professors start to lose their jobs or see their compensation cut because of foreign competition, they will lobby to protect the domestic market. Already, Internet firms provide legal services, and in time Chinese or Indians trained in US law might do the work from thousands of miles away.[34] Can online college courses featuring foreign professors be far behind? Interestingly, by that time the workers might turn in favor of free trade: they have nothing more to lose, while they can benefit from the falling price of professional services.

Protectionism is not the solution, because the problem arises not from free trade (though free trade amplifies it) but from the nature of the technology. Let's go back to the golf tournament example. Imagine that, tired of foreigners dominating the Masters Tournament, Americans decided to prevent them from participating. Initially the effect might seem positive, since American stars would see their odds of winning roughly double. Over time, however, the tournament would lose prestige. Foreign golf fans would stop watching it, and foreign sponsors would stop endorsing it. Even the best American golfers would desert it. Why waste time in a regional competition, when other tournaments (like the British Open) gather the best of the best? The only beneficiaries of the protectionism would be the current also-rans.

The same is true in the industrial sector. Protectionism will not permanently solve the problem of low-skilled workers or benefit the US economy overall. But it might temporarily benefit a few incumbents: from the low-skilled workers nearing retirement who receive a year or two more of employment to the accountants, lawyers, and consultants who make a good living today thanks to their established relationships that marketplace competition will disrupt tomorrow.

The second obvious fix is to slow down or stop technological change—the cause of increasing income inequality. Why not deal with it directly? This is a time-honored strategy. When the steam engine was invented, stagecoach owners lobbied to require that all trains be preceded by a horseman waving a flag for "security reasons." While the measure did not change the future of trains, it did slow down their adoption, with little benefit for anyone except the coachmen.

There is a natural tendency to idealize dying professions—a century ago farmers, today booksellers. But this sympathy is a way of expressing nostalgia for old ways of living, nostalgia that disappears as the people who lived that way die. American readers, for instance, have sympathy for the disappearance of booksellers but could hardly care about specialized newsagents, who disappeared a generation ago. By contrast, in Italy, until recently, newspapers could be sold only in specialized stores. Italians who read a newspaper thus had a personal relationship with their newsagent, who is often the first person to greet them in the morning—and they regret the disappearance of newsagents as online newspapers have spread. In another generation, booksellers in the United States will be as out of fashion as newsagents and coachmen.

The Italian example also suggests how costly these restraints to competition are. In all other countries where newspapers were once sold in specialized stores, specialized newsagents have mostly disappeared, minimizing the social cost of the introduction of online newspapers. In Italy, by contrast, the aggressive defense of the newsagents' monopoly increased the number of young people who dedicated themselves to that occupation, increasing the social cost inflicted by online newspapers.

Unfortunately, the American way of dealing with the dislocation that technology creates is not much better. In the first six years of the new millennium, a very loose monetary policy (over)stimulated the demand for housing, causing the construction sector to expand. This boom halted the slide in wages among less educated men[35] but merely borrowed demand from the future, making the problem worse in the long term. Furthermore, the temporary increase in low-skill wages has induced more young people to drop out of school to enter the low-skilled labor pool, exacerbating the problem. Worse, once young people are out of school for a few years, they find it much more difficult to go back, and their disadvantage becomes permanent.

The same is true for the Obama administration's stimulus policies. If a problem is temporary, stimulus policies can alleviate it. But this problem is structural, and a temporary stimulus actually makes it worse in the long run, to the extent that it affects wages.

THE WORST CRONYISM

The solution is not to restrain competition and markets but to enhance them, and not only in the private sector, where too-big-to-fail bankers or uneconomic sugar or ethanol producers or inefficient "green" energy manufacturers lobby heavily to enjoy gains at the expense of the rest of the population. But since, as all middle-class American parents know, education is the key to competitiveness, perhaps the most destructive cronyism that uses lobbying to extract money from the American people in exchange for a product that doesn't meet their real needs is in the public school system. In the 2007–2008 electoral cycle, the National Education Association, the union representing public school teachers, was the largest lobbyist in America, spending $56 million.[36] More important, as the teachers union defends the status quo in education, it is killing the American Dream for much of the population.

Look at the abysmal state of American primary and secondary schooling. In the last decade, the Organisation for Economic Co-operation and Development (OECD) has made a Herculean effort to establish unbiased measures of student achievement across the more developed countries. It gave a battery of tests, purged of any cultural bias, to a representative sample of fifteen-year-old students from forty-one countries, ranging from Serbia (with only a $3,000 average per-capita income) to Luxembourg (with $49,000 average per-capita income). The results of the OECD Programme for International Student Assessment (PISA) are depressing.

American students score below average in every subject but reading, where they are barely above average. In problem solving, American students rank thirtieth out of forty-one, below Russia and barely above Portugal; in math, they are twenty-ninth, below Latvia and just above Portugal; in science, they are twenty-third. Since there is a strong correlation between quality of education and income per capita (richer countries have more resources to spend on education), the relative position of the United States looks even worse when we adjust for per-capita income. In problem solving, the United States is thirty-seventh, scoring worse than Mexico. Similarly, in math it is fifth from the bottom, barely above Mexico but below Indonesia.

Most people blame a lack of funding for these dismal results. Yet the United States spends more per student than almost every other country, with little to show for it. Between 1980 and 2005, public spending per US student increased 75 percent in real terms, with little or no impact on performance.[37] The problem is not a lack of money but inefficient teaching methods. As America measures and improves productivity in other sectors, education stagnates.

While test scores are a decent way to assess student knowledge, they are a very noisy measure of teacher performance. Even the worst teacher in the world with a class of wealthy children on the Upper East Side will score better than the teacher of a class of single-parent kids in the Bronx. The real measure of a teacher's productivity is her ability to improve a given student's scores. Using data from two large Tennessee metropolitan school systems, a now-famous study shows that if two average eight-year-old students are given two different teachers, at the end of the year the one with the better teacher will end up in the ninetieth percentile of the performance distribution, while the one with the worse teacher will land in the thirty-seventh percentile.[38] These effects are cumulative over the years, and there is little evidence that effective teachers subsequently can offset the damage produced by ineffective ones.

For disadvantaged children, the effect of teacher quality is even stronger. A study shows that during an academic year, some teachers are able to produce one and a half years of achievement gain, while others with equivalent students produce only a half-year of gain.[39] If a single year can create such a difference, imagine what happens if differences compound year after year. Soon the unlucky children are so far behind that they cannot recover.

Interestingly, whether a teacher has a master's degree does not seem to correlate with his performance.[40] Whereas the first few years of experience do improve a teacher's skills, after year five there seem to be no further gains.[41]

So, what makes Finland perform so well and the United States so poorly? A study by the international consulting firm McKinsey & Company suggests a simple answer: teacher selection.[42] In Finland the selection process is very intense. Aspiring teachers take numeracy, literacy, and problem-solving tests. Interviewers then assess their motivation to learn, communications skills, and emotional intelligence. Only one out of ten candidates makes the cut. Some see this as a form of regulation, and if it amounts to a formal list of requirements, it is. Quality-based selection is meritocracy in action.

Clearly the pool of candidates must be large and deep. Higher salaries attract better candidates, but higher salaries without better selection are a waste of money. As it happens, Finnish teachers are not paid particularly well by international standards.

Education economist Eric Hanushek has proposed a simple method to improve performance: eliminating the worst teachers. He estimates that eliminating the least effective 6–10 percent of teachers would increase American PISA scores by fifty points (i.e., one-half standard deviation).[43] He also shows that such an increase is associated with a 0.87 percent higher annual GDP growth. If this seems a small achievement, consider that the OECD average annual growth in GDP per worker in the past two decades has been 1.5 percent. Thus this increase in PISA score would translate into a 58 percent higher per capita GDP growth per year; or, put in other terms, it would reduce the number of years it takes to double the GDP per capita from forty-seven to thirty.[44] This is an achievable goal, since Poland improved its performance in reading by twenty-nine points in only six years. While Hanushek does not estimate the impact on income distribution of such a change, all the evidence suggests that it would substantially reduce wage inequality.

Unfortunately the policy currently prevailing in America is quite the opposite. The most common probationary period for tenure is just three years of experience, when a teacher is still learning the job. Performance evaluations are cursory and read like news from Lake Wobegon, where all teachers are above average.[45]

In addition to jeopardizing American competitiveness, this poor performance kills the American Dream. The 90 percent of children who do not have high proficiency levels in math at age fifteen do not stand a chance of attending top colleges and, in a competitive labor market, have little chance of landing a high-paying job.

VOUCHER-BASED OPPORTUNITY

The abysmal state of education is the result of the massive state involvement, allowing lobbying and cronyism to capture unearned rewards for the incumbents—the teachers' unions. Education should, in my opinion, be state-funded, even more so today than in the past, to equalize starting points. Yet there is no reason it should be state-provided. We see in the education sector the same corruption that we observe when the government intervenes in any other industry. The fact that the incumbents come in the shape of union members rather than capitalist plutocrats should not alter our conclusion: the problem is the same.

A version of Milton Friedman's idea of school vouchers can help solve this problem. The school voucher idea is politically charged, as is both the research trying to assess its impact and press reports of its findings. Moreover, comparing the performance of students in a voucher program with students in public school, as some researchers do, is misleading, since the population in the two samples may be very different.[46]

The proper way to control for student characteristics is to assign students to the voucher program or the public school program randomly. Studies that use this method find students who participate in the voucher program do better[47] or are at par with those who attend public school.[48]

Even more important than the effect of vouchers on individual students is their effect on the entire school system, in which competition should trigger improvements. While the results are mixed on this test,[49] one must realize that most voucher experiments have a design flaw, in that the public schools' survival and the salaries of their teachers are guaranteed, no matter how poorly they compare. For vouchers to reform the system in a real way, not only must students have freedom of entry into well-functioning schools but poorly performing public school teachers must be at risk for losing their jobs.

To create a market for education, however, we need more than just the vouchers. We need a system to help families select the better teachers. Fortunately, a recent study finds that "providing parents with direct information on school test scores resulted in significantly more parents choosing higher scoring schools for their children."[50] Horatio Alger's Ragged Dick rose to respectability by learning the three Rs with the help of a roommate; today, the education required to enter the middle class isn't so easily obtained. Even more troubling than its below-average PISA scores, the United States is among the top twelve nations having high variability of scores, alongside countries like Brazil, Indonesia, Mexico, and Tunisia. High variability means that a share of the population performs significantly subpar. This group is denied its chance at the American Dream before its members even start working. Clearly, we need a better school system, particularly for the poor, and the best way to create one is to give low-income children access to better schools through a voucher program or other choice initiatives.

A voucher system can also address the profound inequality in starting points. Given the intensity of the game and its winner-take-all nature, inequality at the start can drain motivation and induce many people to drop out. The wealthier and more educated the parents are, the more the children in primary and secondary school benefit from test-preparation courses, application-enhancing extracurricular activities, and individualized tutoring. Attempts by colleges to undo this unequal preparation are insufficient. Private elite universities give a 310-point SAT boost (on a 400–1600 scale) for African American students but only a 130-point boost for low-income students. Unfortunately, an economically disadvantaged childhood can lower a student's expected SAT score by 399 points, while being African American predicts a score just fifty-six points lower. Higher-value vouchers for people who start from less privileged conditions, regardless of their race, is the best way to address this inequality.

The voucher system favors children of concerned parents who can choose appropriately, but it can leave behind those who have parents incapable or unwilling to supervise their children's school choice. To address this problem, I envision match-specific vouchers—i.e., higher dollar vouchers for better schools that admit more disadvantaged students. The better schools, therefore, would be financially incentivized to rescue poorer-performing students at risk.

THE NEED FOR A SAFETY NET

In Chapter 4 we saw that harsh punishment in case of failure can be a strong deterrent to take any risk. This disincentive is especially strong when the odds of success are lowest. So a winner-take-all economy discourages people from investing in human capital when the consequences of failure are very harsh. A safety net is thus not only a mechanism to ensure political consensus for free markets;[51] it is also a way to encourage people to invest in their future. The sure way to fail is not even to try, and without a safety net to protect them from the costs of failure, many people won't try.

One crucial element of this safety net is reducing the burden of personal debt when the borrower is unable to repay. Good bankruptcy laws do not leave room for abuse but are not too harsh, either. A second element of this safety net is unemployment insurance coupled with retraining opportunities. Like school vouchers, retooling vouchers should pay schools commensurately with the success they achieve in training the unemployed to find new jobs. These interventions should be aimed at protecting individuals, not firms. In a free market, inefficient firms have to fail, but people do not have to suffer. In fact, getting rid of inefficient firms is easier when their individual workers don't face destitution.

But the transfers that exist today provide subsidies to powerful firms rather than protection for individuals. For example, if we add up the average amount spent per person in Medicare and Medicaid, the income of the lowest 20 percent of the population increases by 50 percent.[52] This is no small contribution, but it is not necessarily the contribution people want, and it is often hard for them even to see. The Congressional Budget Office estimates that recipients value these contributions at less than half their real cost. Thus, according to the CBO, half the value of the transfer implicitly is wasted (at least as far as the recipient is concerned). Why? Because many of these subsidies are designed to allow drug companies and doctors to make more money, rather than to provide the most desired benefits to recipients.

CONCLUSIONS

A divergence between productivity and wages exists, and it is particularly pronounced at the beginning of the new millennium. Shifting the blame to technology does not solve our problems. Increasing income inequality is undermining the popular consensus in favor of a free-market system.

In this chapter we have just scratched the surface of what needs to be done. It is not enough to try to equalize the starting points by reforming the educational system in a way that increases the quality of teaching. To reduce the pernicious effect of an economy of superstars, we need to promote competition in those markets where it is deficient—the subject of the next chapter.

9

FIGHTING INEQUALITY
WITH COMPETITION

*The market, already a wonderful mechanism, ... can
produce even more wonderful outcomes if we will manage to improve and reform the institutions, the norms,
the laws in which it is enclosed so as to reach higher
ideals of life.*

—Luigi Einaudi, economist and former president
of Italy (1948–1955)

N THE LAST CHAPTER, I SUGGESTED SEVERAL REASONS WHY
the American middle class feels squeezed: the rising cost of college education, the rising cost of health care, and an economy that
increasingly rewards only superstars. Fixing these problems, I
suggest, requires introducing greater competition into each area.

CRONY CAPITALISTS ARE US: ACADEMICS ...

Earlier, we saw that the most dangerous crony capitalists are those who
can wrap their requests for protection and subsidies in a noble cause.

Since few goals are nobler than education, academics make some of the worst crony capitalists of all.

The market for higher education is far from competitive. A combination of government subsidies and industry-controlled accreditation makes entry for new educational institutions extremely difficult. Consider accreditation first. Vocational schools and for-profit universities rely heavily on federal student loans that enable their students to pay tuition. But the federal government will only provide loans to attend schools that have been accredited—and accreditation boards are typically staffed by the deans of existing schools, who have an interest in protecting their franchise from further competition. The fox is in charge of the chicken coop.

This shielded market position applies to nonprofit colleges and universities, too. Comparing a reputational study of American universities in 1906 with the influential *U.S. News & World Report* school rankings for 2011, two education professors found that only one private university, Cornell, had dropped from the top thirteen.[1] (By comparison, only one of the twelve top companies on the Dow Jones Industrial Average at the beginning of the same period was still there at the end: General Electric.) Among the top ten liberal-arts colleges in *U.S. News,* only one change has taken place in the last twenty years.

This stasis at the top is due less to the accreditation barrier than to the superstar nature of the academic business. The schools with the best reputations attract the best students. The presence of these bright students attracts the best faculty. But the stasis is reinforced by huge government subsidies, even to the less exalted colleges. Lacking any threat to their survival, colleges have no reason to compete aggressively, including on prices, which grow and grow. The government subsidies come in many forms. Recall that universities were among the pioneering beneficiaries of earmarks. In 2010, they received $2 billion in such transfers, including $14 million for a Research Center for Southeast Weather and Hydrology at the University of Alabama and $4 million for the National Center for Natural Products Research in Oxford, Mississippi.[2]

Nor are federal earmarks the only higher-ed subsidies. Student loans are subsidized as well. According to the Congressional Budget Office, the federal direct loan program costs taxpayers 12 percent of the amount lent.[3] With student loans reaching $107 billion in 2010–2011, the total cost for taxpayers that year was $13 billion. To these subsidies we need to add student grants. In 2010, 8 million students received Pell Grants, for a total of $28 billion.[4] Thus including earmarks, the total amount of subsidies to university education was $43 billion a year, even before we start counting tax subsidies (for college funds); tax breaks (for example, the fact that returns from university endowments are not taxed); and subsidies dedicated to research.

Too often, the significant unintended consequences of these subsidies are ignored. The first is the effect that they have on the equilibrium price of the subsidized goods. Standard microeconomic analysis tells us that when you subsidize demand for a good whose supply does not respond much to its price, there is a small effect on the quantity of the good and a big effect on its price. The problem for colleges is worse than it is for, say, housing, since in most US cities, the housing supply does respond to prices. The same cannot be said for the supply of college educations, given space constraints to the expansion of existing colleges and the difficulty of starting new ones. So the effect of the education subsidies has been a limited increase in college enrollment—but a significant increase in price. As noted in the previous chapter, the real average cost of university tuition has more than doubled. These subsidies thus translate into high profits at for-profit colleges or into high faculty salaries at nonprofit colleges. Though I teach in a business school, I benefit indirectly from this inflation, since it has caused the salaries of all academics to rise.

The second unintended consequence of the education subsidies is a distortion in the credit market. Since the government guarantees all student loans, lenders have no incentive to restrict lending. All of the burden of making the right decision falls on the borrowers. Student loans are not easily dismissible—not even in bankruptcy (a provision strengthened by the 2005 Bankruptcy Reform Act). Unfortunately, eighteen-year-old kids with zero business experience aren't particularly good at judging the profitability of an investment without expert advice, and when they do get expert advice, it generally counsels taking the largest possible school loan. Thus students go heavily into debt, and many have a hard time repaying.

The stock of student loans has reached $1 trillion.[5] The fraction of borrowers in default rose from 6.7 percent in 2007 to 8.8 percent in 2009. The situation appears ripe for another debt crisis, one in which Sallie Mae—which originates, services, and collects student loans—plays a role similar to the one played by its cousin Fannie Mae in the last crisis; colleges play the role of the banks profiting from the subsidies; and students play the overleveraged homeowners.

If we have learned anything from the housing crisis, it's that we should stop subsidized loans. But what about students suddenly unable to afford tuition? A potential solution to this problem would be an equity-financing contract. Students would receive school funding by promising to the lender a fraction of their future income or, even better, a fraction of their increased income as a result of having attended college. Such contracts would have two advantages. They would share the risk of failure across students, with superstars who make large salaries helping pay the cost of financing for less lucky ones. More important is that they would provide lenders with an incentive to counsel students. Since they would profit from good educational investments and lose from bad ones, financiers would become informed about the relative benefits of various colleges. These informed advisers would create more informed demand for the schools, which would exert pressure on them to contain costs and improve quality. With these incentives in place, we could easily dispose of accreditation, eliminating another barrier to entry and source of corruption.

Why would we need government involvement in higher education at all in this scheme? Because the equity contracts would require a verification of the income of alumni. This would be too expensive a procedure for financiers to undertake, but they could easily piggyback on the IRS's monitoring of taxable income—especially after the definition of taxable income is greatly simplified, as I will explain in Chapter 12.

Cost- and quality-conscious buyers could promote much-needed innovation in the industry. While most industries have undergone dramatic change in recent years, higher education is stuck in the past. Harvard Business School professor Clayton Christensen has called for "disruptive change" in college classrooms, taking advantage of online technology.[6] I don't know whether online technology is the solution. I do know, however, that positive change is desperately needed and that an end to subsidies and fostering competition will help make it happen.

... AND THE HEALTH-CARE INDUSTRY

Between 1999 and 2009, the median real income of a typical family of four increased by a mere 1 percent. If we subtract the cost of health insurance, it actually fell by 5 percent.[7] But does it make sense to subtract the cost of health insurance? The increase in the cost of health care is already factored into the inflation adjustment; why should we subtract it again? After all, we don't subtract the cost of, say, college when we measure income.

The answer is that in the United States, health care, unlike most other goods and services, is not purchased in a free market. Most employees have little choice: they *must* buy employer-provided coverage. This employer-sponsored system has two major defects. It distorts the choice of employment opportunities and it hides the real cost of health insurance from the true payers. Further, even before Obama's Affordable Care Act became law, the US health-care system was significantly distorted by government intervention, which boosted demand for services, prices, and industry profits, but didn't necessarily improve the quality of health care. Only 15 percent of the funds used to purchase health insurance is controlled by beneficiaries, while 33 percent is controlled by employers and 52 percent by the government.[8] While employees end up paying the cost of this insurance through reduced wages, they fight employers' efforts at cost containment, which they perceive as cutting their compensation. Anticipating that they must rebate part or all of any health-cost savings to workers, the employers have no incentive to contain costs.

Not only has this avalanche of money failed to improve the quality of health care; it may have worsened it. A recent study, for example, shows that states with higher Medicare spending have lower-quality care.[9] Decades spent on empirical work have made me reluctant to interpret any correlation as a causal link. Still, the study convincingly documents the mechanism through which this counterintuitive effect takes place. There are certain simple, well-established procedures, such as beta-blockers after heart attacks and eye exams for diabetics, that are cheap, have desirable medical benefits, and rarely have any contraindication. States where more physicians are general practitioners, as opposed to specialists, tend to use these high-quality, simple procedures more frequently. But states that spend more on Medicare seem to have a higher ratio of specialists to general practitioners than states that spend less. One could conjecture—though the authors do not—that specialists routinely push for more advanced and expensive treatments, with questionable benefits to patients.

How did we end up in this mess? The health-care industry has succeeded in hiding the cost of its services to the average American. Most employed people who are lucky enough to have health insurance are unaware of its real cost, since the employer pays for the largest share of the burden with pretax dollars. The system is reminiscent of sales taxes in Europe, which are embedded in the final price of goods. In the United States, by contrast, sales taxes are added to the price when the consumer buys a product, which helps keep the tax burden visible and, since people can more easily object to increases, sales taxes low. Why shouldn't the same rule apply to health care? Greater visibility of costs would lead to more pressure to contain those costs.

Between 1974 and 1982, the RAND Corporation randomly assigned people to different kinds of health plans and followed their behavior over time.[10] The study unequivocally showed that cost sharing reduces the overuse of medical services. Most recently, Indiana adopted a consumer-driven health plan, with high deductibles linked to a health savings account 55 percent of which is funded by the state. A Mercer Consulting study found that the Indiana progam reduced claims by 10.7 percent and costs by 15 percent.[11] There is no evidence of reduced quality of health. The savings seem to result from patients' switching from brand drugs to generics and from specialists to generalists.

One solution to the problem of ballooning medical costs is to empower consumers. While most would remain unable to tell which procedures work best, their freedom of choice would generate a market for trusted experts. Similarly, most consumers cannot rate the quality of dishwashers or cars, which is why we have businesses like *Consumer*

Reports, which provide ratings for their subscribers. You wouldn't trust the government to rate cars (especially now that it's in the business of producing them with General Motors). Why would you trust it to rate your health care?

ACTIVELY PROMOTING COMPETITION

In the previous two sections, I presented examples of how government subsidies and regulations reduce incentives for comparative analysis and thus, ultimately, competition. In these cases the solution is obvious: remove those subsidies and/or regulations and the benefits of competition will flow. A more difficult question is whether the government can have a role in actively promoting competition. Let's postpone for a moment the question of whether a captured legislator would do it and instead focus on whether she could do it, were she inclined.

In an ideal market with no friction the role of the legislator would be strictly limited to defining property rights, a role I will deal with momentarily. In the real world, however, there are important frictions we cannot ignore. These frictions are particularly pronounced in the consumer sector. The growing field of behavioral economics has revealed that consumers do not always behave rationally.[12] Most human beings (myself included) are overly optimistic about their ability to pay their bills on time, they forget to cancel their undesired subscriptions that are automatically renewed, they tend to be overly optimistic about their future finances, and so on. These human weaknesses would not amount to major personal financial losses if businesses did not prey on them systematically.

Credit card contracts are designed to profit from optimists who do not pay their bills on time, mortgage teaser rates are introduced to take advantage of naïve people who discount the future excessively, and free introductory offers that automatically charge your credit card after a short grace period are conceived to exploit our forgetfulness. Unfortunately, competition does not address this problem.[13] As long as there are enough consumers who are overly optimistic, there are no incentives for credit card companies to offer lower rates on outstanding balances or mortgage companies to avoid teaser rates.

The reason competition doesn't take care of these predatory practices is simply that most people do not jump on these attractive offers because they are not paying close attention to their finances. The people who do grab these offers are the hyper rational, penny-pinching consumers, whom companies do not want to attract because they are not very profitable. So if anything, competition encourages companies to win the business of the inattentive by offering even lower teaser rates for mortgages and jacking up late fees even higher for credit cards.

One could take a benign view of these practices and conclude that customers will learn over time. For example, having learned for myself, I now refuse to enroll in any subscription that renews automatically, no matter how attractive the offer is. After all, one of the fundamental principles of commerce is *caveat emptor* (buyer beware). If we want to protect the customers from their own missteps, we would eliminate their incentive to shop wisely, which is one of the pillars of a market-based economy. But isn't there a middle ground between nannying consumers and leaving them unarmed against increasingly more sophisticated companies?

Harrah's Entertainment (now Caesars Entertainment) increased revenues 104 percent by applying modern marketing techniques to gambling. Harrah's searched its database for customers "who displayed avid-gambler traits such as hitting slot buttons quickly" and extended them an offer that induced them to gamble more often.[14] If a gene for gambling or alcohol addiction is identified in the future, would it be socially desirable for companies to target genetically predisposed addicts with their ad-hoc marketing material?

This question is not just a legitimate consumer protection concern; it is an economic efficiency concern as well. The effort spent designing more sophisticated offers to dupe customers is a social waste. In addition, the free entry into the credit card market translates into excessive entry, evidenced by the tons of credit card offers mailed to us. And early innovators will undoubtedly use part of their profits lobbying legislatures to protect them from new entrants into the market.

In most cases, the regulation required to limit these distortions would be minimal. Prohibiting teaser rates, for instance, does not really limit competition; it focuses competition on the actual rate paid over the life of the mortgage rather than just the rate paid over the first year. Requiring companies to remind customers just before a subscription automatically renews is not a major burden. In other cases, the solution is more complicated: for example, how to avoid exploiting addiction.

In any event, it is unlikely that a captured legislator would take action against these practices. In fact, there is good reason to fear that any legislative interference would only further distort the market. A much more effective tactic would be to heap shame on these behaviors, which will be addressed in Chapter 10.

REINVENTING THE ANTITRUST

In Chapter 3 I discussed how antitrust laws benefit a competitive economic system. Traditionally, however, the Department of Justice and the Federal Trade Commission have pursued antitrust cases based on a purely economic analysis of the costs and benefits of, let's say, a merger. Yet much of this book illustrates how potent—even in economic terms—is the political influence a business can acquire. The magnitude of this influence depends crucially upon a business's resources and its sheer size (hence potential voters).

The current antitrust mind-set ignores these aspects. In particular, it ignores the enhanced political power that a merger can confer. If two banks merge and become the biggest regulated entity of a state regulator, empirical research tells us that the state regulator will become more lenient,[15] conferring on the merged entity an advantage vis-à-vis the competition. Thus, even if the merged bank does not have any market power in the traditional sense of the word, it can still gain an unfair advantage.

If antitrust analysis took this into account, many mergers considered welfare-enhancing today would appear to be welfare-reducing instead. They would be stopped or subjected to restrictions. For example, mergers that lead to excessively powerful political entities could be subject to limitations on the amount of lobbying they engage in. This would be a radical departure from the status quo.

COMPETITION IN THE INFORMATION ECONOMY

In the traditional manufacturing economy, basic property rights were all that was needed. And, government's ability to affect the distribution of income by meddling with the definition of property rights was very limited.

But in an information economy, goods are immaterial. Thus, minor changes in the definition of what constitutes property and how it is enforced can have tremendous consequences on a firm's profitability.

Consider, for example, privacy law. Regulations on what Google can and cannot do with the billions of data it handles can dramatically alter Google's profitability. Another example is antipiracy law. In January 2012, Congress considered two different proposals to strengthen copyrights on the Internet. While combating online piracy and copyright infringement is a worthwhile goal, these proposals went too far in that the Department of Justice would have been empowered to shut down any website posting a link to pirated movies. While large companies, such as Facebook and Google, will be able to afford the teams of lawyers necessary to defend their sites, small startups will not. This will most likely have a chilling effect on competition and a big effect on the distribution of income.

Consider, also, patent and copyright laws. In both cases a delicate balance is required between protecting innovators and overprotecting them. Protection is necessary to stimulate innovation. But the temporary monopoly this protection creates for the innovator generates inefficiencies, as monopolies always do. In addition, overprotection of innovators exacerbates the superstar effect on the economy and taxes ordinary citizens because lower prices are not available to them.

Although traditionally the United States has struck a good balance with patent and copyright laws, that has not been the recent case. The best example of this new imbalance is the Copyright Term Extension Act (CTEA) of 1998, which extended copyright terms in the United States by twenty years. For example, under the old copyright protection an author's work was protected for fifty years after his death, but now it is protected for seventy years. There are costs (disincentives to produce) and benefits (the good that comes from diffusion of one's work) to the extension. Yet there were no incentives in the new law for work produced prior to it; only inefficiencies resulting from its restriction. Hence, there was no valid economic reason to extend this benefit to work already produced. But the CTEA did cover existing work, and that reflects the power of corporate lobbying.

In fact, the CTEA is also known as the Mickey Mouse Protection Act, because it granted a twenty-year extension to the Walt Disney Corporation's monopoly on its famous cartoons. This is essentially a tax imposed on Mickey Mouse lovers for the benefit of Disney shareholders and CEO Michael Eisner, who, after twenty-one years at the helm of Disney, walked away with $612 million.

FIXING CORPORATE GOVERNANCE

Reducing the cost of health care and college would make America's increasing economic inequality less painful but not attenuate it. To take a step in that direction requires fixing corporate governance in America, since bad corporate governance leads to many of the problems we have examined, including outsize executive pay, heavy lobbying, corporate malfeasance, opaque management, and cronyism.

But what's wrong with the way companies are currently run? At first, it might strike you as the very definition of a market operation. Firms are run by boards; board members are supposed to act in the interest of shareholders; if a board member fails to do so, his reputation will suffer, and he will receive fewer offers to join other boards, decreasing his future income.[16] With such a strong motivation to run a company well, why do board members fail so often?

The reason involves the word *reputation,* and the assumption above that board members have an incentive to maintain a reputation for competence. In the real estate market, home inspectors are supposed to work for the buyers. Yet most of the inspectors' referrals come from real estate agents, who work on commission—and if an inspector finds a problem that dissuades a prospective buyer from making the purchase, the agent pockets no commission. Real estate agents are obviously more likely to recommend inspectors who seem thorough but don't raise too many questions. Of course, not all inspectors succumb to this problem, as I discovered when I selected an inspector with a sterling reputation for honesty. The seller's real estate agent cried after seeing whom I had chosen. If there were enough fastidious buyers like me, a market for thorough inspectors would form. This may not be such a big problem in the real estate market; home inspection fees aren't so impressive that they can bend many people's integrity. It is a huge problem, however, in the market for corporate board members. Like home inspectors, most board members care about their reputation in the eyes of the people who nominate and elect them.

Elections for corporate boards resemble parliamentary elections in the former Soviet Union. The number of candidates equals the number of seats. Thus voters cannot really choose; they can at most complain by withholding their votes. The vote, however, is public, so investors who vote against management run the risk of retaliation if the incumbent management is renewed. To add insult to injury, the list of candidates is chosen by the current board members. While most companies nowadays have a nominating committee that excludes the incumbent CEO, candidates are usually vetted by him anyway. Dissenters are generally ostracized and not renewed.

Robert Monks is a Harvard Law School graduate who worked at the Department of Labor under Ronald Reagan. He has been a relentless critic of corporate governance practices, not only in books and publications but also in practice. In 1998, Nell Minow, another shareholder activist, told me about Monks's experience of being ousted from a corporate board for being too critical. After Monks raised some concerns about the board's practices, the chairman asked a consulting firm to do a board review. The result of the review was exactly what the chairman wanted it to be; indeed, the consulting firm reported that the board was functioning perfectly well—except for a certain disruptive presence. While not named, everybody knew who that was. Monks was not renewed at the next election.

When Minow related this story to me, she refused to reveal the name of the company. Many years later, however, she did: it was Tyco, home of one of the major corporate scandals of the new millennium. And the chairman who maneuvered Monks off the board was Dennis Kozlowski, currently serving a twenty-five-year sentence at the Mid-State Correctional Facility in Marcy, New York. His crimes range from receiving $81 million in unauthorized bonuses to squandering company money. To the public, Kozlowski is known as the guy who paid $1 million for an ice replica of Michelangelo's David urinating Stolichnaya vodka at his second wife's fortieth birthday party.[17] The total cost for the party ($2 million) was billed to shareholders as expenses for a shareholder meeting.

Corporate corruption and fraud occur when controls are weak, and controls are weak when the people in charge have no incentive to challenge the CEO. Yes, there are many serious board members who do their jobs well—but they do so *despite* the incentives. Just as home inspectors care less about their reputation with buyers than about their reputation with real estate agents, corporate board members care less about their reputation with shareholders than about their reputation with CEOs.

The way to fix this problem is to appoint board members who are accountable not to CEOs and the other board members but to the shareholders. Currently this is not possible because of regulation introduced by the Securities and Exchange Commission. This rule was generated by concern that politics could disrupt the corporate world. During the Vietnam War, many political activists turned shareholder meetings into forums for protest, and even today, politically engaged groups try to push their agendas at the expense of shareholders. If any shareholder could ask for a referendum on any cause, the cost of administering such a direct democracy would be enormous.

As is often the case, a good reason provides cover for a bad one: protecting the incumbent managers from competition. Currently, incumbent boards have everything tilted in their favor. For example, they can present a slate of board members to be mailed to all shareholders at the company's expense. To do so shareholders have to mount a very expensive proxy fight, bearing a cost that can discourage action. How can we change this situation without opening up the board to politics? The solution is very simple. It is sufficient to make it easy for shareholders to present some candidates to the board and reserve some seats for them, as long as they gather a sizeable consensus.

The need for an initial quota—a restriction I generally oppose— arises from the need to jump-start the market for board members who care about their shareholders' opinion of them. If an isolated company were to introduce institutional investors' representatives on the board, it would be of little use. Since it would be the only company with that kind of arrangement, the board members would still have no incentive to criticize management. Their future career opportunities would still depend on the CEO's goodwill. The rule would work only if applied to many companies at once; hence, the quota. In ten years, the quota might become unnecessary, as an active market for truly independent board members develops.

The high voting threshold for these seats—it should be at least a third of shareholder votes taken—would keep them from falling under the control of activists with little ownership and a misguided agenda. While organizing is costly for institutional investors, voting isn't. Hence, while the barriers to entry in the form of the percentage of shares required to present a list should be low, the voting requirement should be high. This is exactly the opposite of what we observe today: the barriers to entry are enormous while the votes necessary to be elected are few.

Institutional-investor-appointed board members would become natural advocates for shareholders' interests. Some legal scholars would then find it in their interest to cater to that constituency. The legal doctrine would follow. At least as far as corporate governance was concerned, the free market would finally have its lobby.

CONCLUSIONS

As children grow into adults, the process is not always pretty. Sometimes their feet and hands grow more quickly than the rest of them, resulting in the temporary awkwardness natural to the phase of life known as adolescence. The US and world economy are now in this adolescent phase, growing from mostly local economies into a fully global one. While this process has brought tremendous improvement to the world, it has also created difficulties.

For a doctor to try to stem the disproportionate growth of a teenager's feet would be malpractice. Yet if the teenager's spinal column starts to bend into scoliosis, the doctor needs to intervene. Trying to stop globalization or to "correct" market choices would be economic malpractice. Yet, intervening to minimize the side effects and to ensure a healthy degree of competition in every sector is not only good policy: it is a necessary one. In what follows I will highlight the areas of necessary intervention.

10

THE NEED FOR A MARKET-BASED ETHICS

It can plausibly be argued that much of economic backwardness in the world can be explained by the lack of mutual confidence.

—Kenneth Arrow, winner of the Nobel Prize in Economics

AT THE UNIVERSITY OF CHICAGO'S BOOTH SCHOOL OF Business, where I teach, students don't just register for classes—they bid for them. True to market principles, Chicago Booth organized this system to maximize student satisfaction. By creating a market in which students compete for the opportunity to take classes with the professors they like best, Chicago Booth ensures the class assignments that maximize students' desires.

To function properly, this market, like all markets, requires not only official rules but social norms as well. For evidence of the importance of social norms, consider a problem we encountered with the bidding system. The system gives each student a fixed number of bidding points at the beginning of his two-year program. Students can then use these points to bid for the courses they like. The "cost" of a given course is set by the number of students bidding for it and how many points they bid: less popular courses go for zero points, while more popular ones require students to dip into their precious points. When the demand for a course exceeds the supply, only the students who made the highest bids get to take the class. Each quarter features three rounds of bidding; after each round, students who win spots in a class can, if they like, give those spots to other students in exchange for points.

Years ago, students discovered a loophole in the system. The first round of bidding for the fall quarter took place before the first-year students showed up on campus—we wanted to give second-year students time to plan. As long as first-year students were bidding for first-year courses and second-year students for second-year courses, no problem arose. But second-year students soon realized that they could bid for popular first-year courses before the first-year students arrived and then "sell" them back at higher prices. This increased their number of points, which they could use to bid for other courses.

When this tactic—*arbitrage,* an economist would call it—became known, the faculty was divided on how to treat the students who had taken advantage of it. Some were furious and wanted to punish the students who gamed the system. Others thought that the students should be not punished but congratulated for their cleverness. I was not so sanguine. I thought it was unfair to punish the students, since they hadn't broken any rule. But their opportunistic behavior had undermined the system, creating no benefits for the rest of the business school community and in fact producing a net loss.

This apparently simple question—Should we, as teachers, condemn, condone, or praise their behavior?—raises a broader one. Should economists be ivory-tower scientists who teach facts and not morals? Or should we take a moral stand—and if so, which one?

AMORAL FAMILISM

One of the most influential books I read in graduate school was *The Moral Basis of a Backward Society,* written more than fifty years ago by Edward Banfield, a political scientist at Harvard University.[1] Banfield's wife was Italian, and they decided to spend a year in her small home-town in southern Italy. Banfield used this time to study the local habits. He grew curious about a particular question: why was this agricultural village so economically backward?

His answer was something that he labeled *amoral familism*. The villagers, he saw, pursued their own self-interest and that of their imme-diate family in a way that prevented cooperation. Southern Italian farm-ers, each owning minuscule plots of land, could never cultivate them efficiently because they were unwilling or unable to cooperate with neighboring farms. There was little civic engagement. And this amoral familism was self-fulfilling: since everybody looked after his own narrow self-interest, the widespread mistrust was justified, as was the general lack of hope that things would improve. The village was economically backward and seemingly doomed to remain so.

Banfield's description resonated with me. Though I had grown up in northern Italy, my paternal grandfather is from Sicily, where I had sev-eral relatives. These southern relatives of mine, I recalled, distrusted not just northerners but everybody. They feared being cheated—*fatti fessi* (being made fools). It was more than the fear of an economic loss. It was an injury to their personal pride. Their desire to avoid being cheated was so strong that they never made a deal with anybody.

Trained as I am in economics, I believe that individuals' pursuing their own interests leads to the common good. That's what Adam Smith taught us, right? So why, then, did things prove otherwise in Banfield's southern Italian town?

THE IMPORTANCE OF TRUST

Let's try to understand the institutional context in which economic transactions take place. Just as fish are unaware of the water in which they swim, so we are frequently unaware of the institutional structures surrounding us, not just in terms of law but also in terms of norms and beliefs. One of the most important of these norms is *trust*. "Virtually every commercial transaction," wrote economics Nobel Prize winner Kenneth Arrow, "has within itself an element of trust."[2] When we de-posit money in a bank, buy a share of stock through a broker, purchase a good over the Internet, or refinance a mortgage, most of us do not read the intricate details of the contracts we are signing. In bridging the gap between the knowledge that we have and the knowledge that would be required to make a decision in a fully informed way, we rely on trust. We trust our counterparties or, more broadly, we trust the system as a whole. We trust banks to let us withdraw our money, we trust the stockbroker not to abscond with our money, we trust the Internet vendor to deliver our goods, and we trust the Internet encryption system not to leak our credit-card information. Trust facilitates transactions because it saves the costs of monitoring and screening; it is an essential lubricant that greases the wheels of the economic system.

Of course, when millions of dollars are on the line, trust on its own becomes insufficient. Lawyers are paid handsomely to review contingencies, and sophisticated contracts are put into place to protect the contracting parties. But in millions of everyday transactions, there is neither time nor resources for people to practice any serious due diligence. If trust is there, the transaction takes place. If it isn't, there's no deal. Millions of small transactions that never take place because of the absence of trust translate into billions of dollars lost to the economy and diminished human welfare.

Trust comes in two forms in economic life. First is the *personal trust* forged through a history of interactions, typically between partners, friends, or close business associates. This kind of trust is both positive and negative. It helps those who have built it up but can hurt those who find themselves excluded from the group and even discriminated against. While it benefits early economic development, personal trust may hinder development as an economy becomes more complex and requires communication and exchange among remote individuals and groups.

For modern economies, therefore, the second type of trust— *generalized trust*—is essential. This is the trust that people have in a random member of a group or society, somebody they don't know and don't necessarily expect to run into again. It allows markets to develop, trade to prosper, civilization to advance. And it is what is so desperately lacking in southern Italy and in much of the less developed world.

To measure generalized trust, many researchers (including myself) regularly include an odd-looking question in a popular survey, the

World Value Survey, conducted in many countries around the world. The question is, "Generally speaking, would you say that most people can be trusted or that you need to be very careful in dealing with them?" In Sweden, 68 percent of people answer that most people can be trusted; in Brazil, only 9 percent do.[3] Perhaps Swedes are more trusting than Brazilians because law enforcement in Sweden is more effective than in Brazil. The average Brazilian would then be foolish to trust others as much as a Swede does because the opportunities to cheat profitably in Brazil are greater than in Sweden.

Interestingly, though, a Swede who visits Brazil does not immediately adjust his level of trust, nor does a Brazilian who visits Sweden. In fact, people from countries with high levels of trust tend to extrapolate their high trust to countries with low trust levels, and vice versa.[4] Immigrants to the United States take several generations to reach the average level of trust prevailing in America.[5] Thus trust is not simply an outcome of a society in which nonlegal mechanisms get people to behave cooperatively: it is a long-lasting characteristic.

Generalized trust is mostly the product not of observations that people have collected but of preconceptions that they hold. Some of these preconceptions are rooted deeply in the past. When French managers are surveyed about whom they trust, for example, they rate their British counterparts second to last (above only Italians); every other European group rates the British much higher. The British managers reciprocate, trusting French managers less than their counterparts from other countries do. In my research, I have shown that countries with a long history of wars, like England and France, trust each other less, which stands to reason.[6] Countries with the same religion trust each other more. And it's even the case that countries whose populations look more alike trust each other more. This latter tendency may be left over from prehistoric times, when early human beings, needing to decide whether a stranger approaching in the savannah was a friend or foe, relied on somatic characteristics.

All of these attitudes influence economic decisions, even those made by sophisticated players. The lower relative levels of trust between France and Great Britain lead them to trade less and invest less in each other. When trust is low, a potential investor will compare the due diligence costs of an investment with the expected benefit. If the costs are large enough, the investor will pass up even highly profitable projects. Sometimes an absence of trust makes good sense, as in the case of too-good-to-be-true Internet offers, whose profitability few people spend time investigating. But lack of trust where it might be warranted may lead to considerable losses.[7] In 1980, IBM, desperately looking for an operating system for its PCs, invited Gary Kildall, the founder of Digital Research, to a meeting. Fearing that IBM would extract all the surplus from any possible negotiation, Kildall declined to attend the meeting and consequently missed the opportunity that eventually went to Microsoft.

CIVIC CAPITAL

Trust is just one example of what I call *civic capital*,[8] the values and beliefs that foster cooperation. One clever study unveiled a different variety of civic capital by examining the behavior of UN diplomats in New York.[9] Until 2002, when the law was changed, UN diplomats from other countries were exempt from paying parking tickets. The New York City police, though, regularly issued them tickets, which piled up unpaid. The only obstacle to free parking was each diplomat's civic sense. During a five-year period, the study showed, Italians accumulated fifteen tickets per diplomat, German diplomats one, Swedes zero, and Canadians zero. Fortunately for my national pride, Italy wasn't the worst offender, though it performed poorly when compared with other developed countries. Brazilian diplomats, meanwhile, accumulated thirty tickets per person. Kuwait, at the bottom of the list, racked up 246!

Why do people with identical incentives behave so differently? This is a flagrant violation of an economic idea—admittedly, an extreme version of it—that all rational individuals respond to incentives in a similar way. Is the Swedish diplomat less rational than the Kuwaiti one? No; she merely incorporates civic values into her decision. Swedish diplomats are willing to sacrifice their own self-interest, at least when the stake is small. I am not claiming that the rules of economics do not hold in Sweden. Quite the contrary: it is precisely because Swedes can be relied upon not to be too opportunistic that markets work better in that country than in Italy, to say nothing of Brazil and Kuwait. Such civic capital is as important a factor of production as physical and human capital. In countries or regions where it is higher, one finds less corruption and greater public safety. Public administration works better, and private companies can grow more efficiently.[10]

To increase physical capital, we know, you invest in machinery. To increase human capital, you invest in training. But how do you increase civic capital?

WHERE DOES CIVIC CAPITAL COME FROM?

Research on how civic capital is accumulated is still in its infancy. We know that one kind of civic capital, a general willingness to cooperate with others, is enhanced by particular episodes of successful cooperation. In one study, Colombian welfare mothers were required to participate in meetings where they discussed topics of mutual interest. Two years later, these women as well as a control sample were asked to participate in an experimental game that measured their willingness to cooperate. The mothers who had earlier participated in the meetings exhibited 30 percent more willingness to cooperate.[11]

Again, history clearly plays a fundamental role. Political scientist Robert Putnam conjectured that the differing attitudes exhibited by northern and southern modern-day Italians had to do with the free city-states that formed in northern Italy after the fall of the Holy Roman Empire. Those city-states did exhibit a high level of cooperation.[12] But can an experience more than five hundred years old really leave traces today? With two Italian colleagues, I tried to find out.[13] Not all important cities in northern central Italy became free city-states. Both Faenza, a town of 54,000 thirty miles southeast of Bologna, and Senigallia, a town of 44,000 sixty miles south of Faenza, were important medieval towns. But Faenza became a free city, while Senigallia never did. And in all our measures of present-day civic capital, Faenza beat Senigallia. The number of nonprofit organizations per capita was 42 percent higher in Faenza, and participation in public referenda there was 89 percent (versus 86 percent in Senigallia). Faenza had an organ donor organization, while Senigallia did not. And so on.

Other researchers have found a similar persistence in civic capital. The level of trust among different African ethnicities today reflects their ancestors' chances of being captured and sold as slaves between the fifteenth and early nineteenth centuries. Because selling people to slave traders had a high payoff, indigenous people would sell members of their own ethnic group, close friends, and even relatives. The climate of suspicion that resulted seems to have carried over into mistrust of local leaders and others today.[14]

Civic capital is hard to build up but relatively easy to depreciate. As mentioned above, it takes several generations born in the United States for an immigrant Italian family to reach the average level of trust in America (I'm counting on my grandchildren). But a single prominent politician can undermine trust for an entire group. In March 2011, a coauthor and I commissioned a survey of US citizens to analyze the effect that the extravagant personal life of Italian prime minister Silvio Berlusconi had on Americans' trust of Italians and their willingness to buy Italian products.[15] Half of the subjects, chosen at random, were *primed,* as psychologists call it, by being reminded that Berlusconi had been indicted for sex with a minor. The other half were not so primed. The survey was then performed, and it turned out that the primed group reported a lower level of trust—a statistically significant one—toward Italians than did the control group. This difference in trust also translated into a lower willingness to buy Italian products. Given a choice between a German car and an identical Italian car that costs $1,000 less, only slightly more than a third of nonprimed Americans chose the Italian option. Among the primed group only 20 percent did so.

AMERICA'S ORIGINAL ADVANTAGE

The level of civic capital in a country can affect views of government—and how government is perceived can in turn influence civic capital. The first time I experienced a hurricane watch in the United States—I was in Boston—I was shocked by how faithfully people took the advice of local authorities to stay at home, tape the windows, and so on. My instinctive reaction when I received any official instruction was to doubt it and possibly do the opposite. If an Italian mayor had told me to tape my windows, I would assume that his brother sold tape. My skepticism was reinforced by my knowledge of what happened to Italians who did follow official instructions. During a fire in one of the major tunnels under the Alps, for instance, the drivers who followed official instructions and went to the public shelter died from lack of oxygen; those who decided to walk out on their own survived.

This fundamental difference in attitudes stems in part from the American and Italian experience of government. Most Americans (especially those who have not felt the sting of racial discrimination) perceive the government as serving the people, however imperfectly. For Italians, government is the expression of the will of the latest dictator or boss. When I was born, Italy had been a democracy for less than twenty years. My mother remembered the Nazi occupation, and her grandmother, who had helped raise her, remembered when Austrians ruled her city, Venice. The effect of all these rulers on civic capital is described beautifully by Martin Scorsese, an Italian American, in his film *My Voyage to Italy*. He says, "The lesson of survival that has been passed on for centuries and that was carried over to the new world by Italian immigrants is a pretty brutal one: you think twice before you trust anybody outside your own family. Think about it. Your country, your homeland, changes hands again and again over thousands of years. So who can you trust: the government? The police? The Church? No, only your family, your own blood."

Education also contributes to American civic capital. Italian schools try to inculcate their students with blind obedience and respect for authority. For example, students must stand up when the teacher walks in as a sign of respect, and they are punished for asking provocative questions. While I was fortunate enough to attend a gentle Montessori elementary school, some of my friends actually had to endure corporal punishment in their classes. In the United States, by contrast, I have watched my children be treated by their schools as citizens in the making, not dumb subjects. Asking tough questions is rewarded, not punished. Children learn that it is their duty to stand up and speak out against unjust acts—even those committed by the teachers, who, like all human beings, are not perfect. A recent paper documents the way teaching practices differ across countries: students work in groups more often in Nordic countries and the United States, while in eastern Europe and the Mediterranean, teachers spend more time lecturing and students copying from the board.[16] The paper also finds that various measures of civic capital are higher in countries where there is more group work and lower where teachers lecture more.

Like trust, a tendency to be engaged and critical is a component of civic capital. An engaged citizenry will complain a lot. Though such complaints have costs—from the time and effort spent to file the written complaint to the risk of retaliation that the complainant faces from his superior—they also make authority accountable and provide essential critical feedback. This can increase the support for, and the functioning of, markets. Even the most visionary business leaders can make mistakes and find it difficult to identify them if they receive only positive feedback. Criticism is extremely useful to society in general, which is why Americans try to teach it as a value in school. We condemn those who are afraid to speak out, and we celebrate people like Rosa Parks who have shown the courage to stand up against injustice.

MORALS AND MORTGAGES

A good example of the way civic capital affects the economy is strategic mortgage default: the decision to walk away from a mortgage because it exceeds the value of the house, even when the mortgagee has the ability to pay. If too many underwater homeowners—the nation is filled with them in the wake of the financial crisis—decide to abandon their mortgage commitments, the results could be catastrophic. The more people walk away, the more houses get auctioned off, further depressing real-estate prices. This additional decline would push more homeowners into negative territory, leading to still more defaults. Thus, society has a strong incentive to prevent strategic default from getting out of hand.

The law, however, doesn't provide much incentive for people to stay put. It's true that thirty-nine states permit a lender to come after a borrower's other assets and income if he defaults. And it's also true that even in the eleven states that don't allow that, the restriction applies only to original home loans used to purchase property, not to home-equity lines of credit, while there is some legal uncertainty regarding mortgages issued to refinance existing mortgages. Nevertheless, lenders rarely slap borrowers with a deficiency judgment—a court injunction to pay the difference between the face value of a mortgage and the proceeds that the lender earns by repossessing and selling the house. The procedure is costly and generally not worth the expense because of the limited assets that most Americans own aside from their homes.

The tax code likewise doesn't impede people from defaulting strategically. Until recently, it's true, people had to pay taxes on any forgone debt. If you walked away from a house worth, say, $100,000 less than you owed the bank for it, that $100,000 was essentially income, and you had to pay income tax on it. However, in December 2007, Congress made mortgage debt cancellation nontaxable for personal residences. Congress's aim was to facilitate the renegotiation of underwater mortgages, but the move had an unintended consequence: reducing the cost of walking away.

What does prevent people from strategic default, it seems, is their sense of what's right. More than 80 percent of Americans think that it's immoral to default on a mortgage if you can afford to pay it, according to a recent paper by Luigi Guiso, Paola Sapienza, and myself, and these people are 77 percent less likely to declare their intention to default strategically than people who don't find the act immoral.[17] Perceived social norms also seem to affect the propensity to walk away: knowing somebody who defaulted strategically, or living in an area where many people have done so, makes a person much more likely to declare his willingness to follow suit.

Seeking to undermine the social norm to repay mortgages, as some economists and journalists have done by saying that it is the rational course of action for underwater homeowners to default strategically, is thus a very bad idea. You might just as well say that when a theater is going up in flames, it's rational to trample other people in rushing to the exits.

ETHICS AND ECONOMICS

Most economists recoil at the word *ethics*. Like all the social sciences, economics became a "legitimate" discipline when it distinguished itself from moral philosophy. Adam Smith, a moral philosopher, started the field when he decided to analyze the production, distribution, and consumption of goods and services apart from moral considerations. Economic analysis of the behavior of economic agents should start not from moral considerations (how people *should* behave) but from objective ones (how they *do* behave), just as the analysis of atoms starts not from the way they should behave but from the way they do behave. Consequently, economists are hypersensitive about letting moral considerations back into their discipline.

However, this position is hypocritical. First, physicists don't teach atoms how to behave. If they did (and if atoms had free will), the physicists would be concerned about how the atoms being instructed could change their behavior and affect the universe. Economists should have that concern for the people they teach. Experimental evidence suggests that people who choose to study economics not only are more selfish to begin with, but *become* more selfish and less concerned about the common good by studying economics.[18] So economics does seem to teach people how to behave, even inadvertently.

Second, economists routinely engage in normative analysis—how things ought to work. Indeed, an entire branch of economics, *law and economics*, rationalizes laws on the basis of economic principles. Why are economists happy to say what the optimal laws are from an economic standpoint but afraid to say what the optimal social norms are for a successful economy?

Last but not least, economists who reject morals are hypocritical because the distinction between positive ("scientific") and normative analysis is sometimes so tenuous that it gets lost on most students. My colleague Gary Becker pioneered the economic study of crime, one of the contributions that earned him the Nobel Prize in economics.[19] In determining the resources that society should allocate to fighting different types of crimes, Becker employed a basic utilitarian approach in which people compare the benefits of a crime with the expected cost of punishment (that is, the cost of punishment times the probability of receiving that punishment). Becker's model had no intention of telling people how they *should* behave. But a former student of Becker's once admitted to me that many of his classmates were remarkably amoral. He attributed this to the fact that they took Becker's descriptive model of crime as prescriptive. They perceived any failure to commit a high-benefit crime with a low expected cost as a failure to act rationally—almost a proof of stupidity. The student's experience bears out the experimental findings that I mentioned above.

The idea that people act in their own self-interest is a useful methodological assumption, of course, and it has brought tremendous insights. But it must be placed in context. It may be useful to know that most market mechanisms operate when everyone acts in narrow self-interest, but that doesn't mean that markets always *prosper* when people act in narrow self-interest. Above all, the fact that Smith taught that economic systems can work effectively when people pursue their own interests is not the same thing as saying that they *should* pursue their own interests. Greed isn't good. Smith would have been the first to oppose anybody who said that it was.

It is also not empirically true that all individuals always operate in narrow self-interest. The real question is whether there are sustainable social norms that can nudge people to act in a way that benefits society when narrow self-interest fails to deliver a desirable outcome. If so, what are those norms? And who has an interest in codifying and teaching them?

HOW TO DETERMINE SOCIAL NORMS

I am not a moral philosopher, and consequently I have no particular competence to determine what is ethical and what is not ethical. As an economist, though, I *am* able to identify behaviors that are welfare-enhancing and those that are not. For instance, I can contrast the Chicago Booth students' arbitrage, which generated no gain for the school or the student community, with financial arbitrage, which provides useful social functions. Most traders do not have to worry whether prices are aligned because arbitrageurs do the job for them. This alignment ensures that corporations can finance themselves at the lowest possible cost, with greater benefit to society. Speculators may earn a greater return than the benefit they generate to society warrants (hence their lousy reputation), but at least their work isn't completely at odds with the greater good. While self-interest motivates both types of arbitrage, only the latter demonstrates Adam Smith's "invisible hand," the self-interest of the agent leading to a benefit to society.

One way of putting the difference between these two situations is that in financial arbitrage, individual incentives are aligned to societal incentives; in the students' arbitrage, they were not. When a theater catches fire, the individual incentive is to rush to the exit as fast as possible. Yet if everyone in the audience rushed at once, the crowd near the door would allow fewer people to escape—indeed, many could die. Not surprisingly, there are social norms against this behavior. People who violate those norms are judged rude, egotistical, ill-behaved, or in certain cases even negligent. The individual and social incentives aren't aligned.

Economists have a way of determining whether a policy intervention is economically efficient: it must increase the utility of at least one person while not decreasing the utility of anyone else (economists call this *Pareto optimality*, after the Italian economist Vilfredo Pareto). If we applied this criterion to social norms, we would consider a norm economically justified if, followed by all, it made no one worse off and at least some better off. A social norm against financial speculation, for example, fails to satisfy this criterion, since it would leave speculators worse off. By contrast, a norm against rushing to the exits in a burning theater would be justified, since if everybody followed it, everybody would be able to exit safely.

Economically based social norms allow small communities to solve the free-rider problem mentioned earlier. Think, for example, about donations to build a gym in your kids' school. The typical economic argument is that the probability is minimal that your small donation will make any difference about whether the gym gets built or not. Knowing this, you are better off not contributing, since if the gym does get built, your kids will get to enjoy it regardless. If everybody reasons this way, of course, the gym will never be built.

But this argument ignores the fact that your donation may create social pressure for others to donate. This increases your individual payoff from donating. If the effect is strong enough and the community is small enough (so that inducing a few other people to donate increases the proportion of people who contribute), then donating is in your personal interest. Particularly if the cost per person of building the gym is less than the benefit each one would receive from it, this social pressure—that people should donate an amount similar to what their acquaintances donate, if they can afford to—fits the economic criterion for a good social norm, since nobody is made worse off and many are made better off.

Some economically useful norms are shared by most religions. My research has found that on average religious people exhibit attitudes that are conducive to better market functioning.[20] Yet this is not true of all moral and social norms. In many African countries, for instance, people who become rich are expected to support all their relatives. By acting as a high marginal tax rate on entrepreneurship, this practice is harmful, from an economic point of view.

Thus there is no perfect coincidence between social norms and economically useful norms. Nevertheless, sensible social norms can be useful in getting individuals to internalize the likely consequences of their actions. While most economists advocate taxation and regulation to deal with these consequences, I prefer (when feasible) to rely on norms, which draw their power from social consensus rather than from the political process. The problem lies in identifying who has an interest in creating this social consensus.

THE ROLE OF BUSINESS SCHOOLS

Most successful firms tend to develop a corporate culture that centers on key values that are shared by the employees and enforced throughout the organization. Integrity, for example, is a value identified by 70 percent of the companies belonging to the Standard and Poor's 500 Index.[21]

In part, these values are meant to make companies look good, but there is more to them than that. Employees often face trade-offs between the company's interests and their own. Should I push for higher sales at the end of the quarter to make my yearly bonus, even if this reduces the quality of the product? Should I overlook the declining value of the company's assets, so that the reported profits are not affected, leading to a higher bonus? Should I discount my product so that I can temporarily boost sales and sustain the perception of high growth that supports my stock price (and thus my stock options)? While incentives can be designed to minimize these problems, they can hardly eliminate them; the problems are inevitable, short of a complete identification between the individual goals and the corporate goals. So companies create values that draw the line beyond which trade-offs aren't acceptable. When a company touts excellence as a value, for instance, it communicates to its employees that no compromises will be allowed in the pursuit of excellence. The same could apply for integrity and other values.

The role of these values is twofold. First, they establish a rule of behavior for employees who might not know how to operate in certain situations. Second, they make it easier to screen out employees whose own values are most at odds with the company's. It is much easier for a firm to enforce a zero-tolerance policy than a more nuanced one. Thus the corporate world does recognize the benefits of internal norms.

When it comes to market-wide norms, however, no company is big enough to reap the benefits of creating a better market system. Why should any company care about making norms that enhance the functioning of the whole market? Companies, as we saw earlier, prefer to consolidate their market power. So who does have an interest in creating market-wide norms?

Business schools. They have the greatest interest in the long-term survival of capitalism, especially the superior American version of capitalism. They are—or should be—the churches of the meritocratic creed. So they should lead the effort to impose some minimal norms for business—norms that discourage behavior that is purely opportunistic even if highly profitable. For this reason, we should have frowned on the Booth students who exploited the loophole in the bidding system. We should likewise frown on behavior that we recognize as detrimental to the long-term survival of the free-market system.

Asking business schools to stigmatize all behavior that does not maximize welfare would be absurd. They shouldn't be expected to shame or criticize a company for using the market power that it has legitimately acquired through innovative patents. They also shouldn't be expected to denounce a company for taking advantage of the tax loopholes present in the system. I regularly teach my students how to exploit the tax benefits associated with corporate borrowing, and I don't consider it unethical. The preferential tax treatment of debt is—at least in principle—designed to stimulate companies to borrow more, just as the deductibility of mortgage interest is designed to subsidize people who borrow to buy a house. While I do not consider it a good law, I do not feel bad about advocating its use as long as it is on the books.

There is a difference, however, between taking advantage of existing tax loopholes and lobbying aggressively to have those tax loopholes created or expanded. What about marketing policies targeted to prey on addiction or to induce young customers to smoke? Is making money the only metric we should reward and admire in business leaders?

Business schools have a powerful enforcement mechanism: the way they treat their alumni. The schools celebrate their most prestigious alumni, for instance, and they reward the others by providing access to a valuable network of connections. In awarding prizes to outstanding alumni who adhere to economically useful norms, and by expelling from the network those who do not, they could send a powerful message. But they generally choose not to do so. In fact, they often seem to tolerate, if not foster, business behavior that is immoral and sometimes even illegal.

Consider the insider trading case involving the Galleon hedge fund. Raj Rajaratnam was convicted and sentenced to eleven years in prison; McKinsey director Anil Kumar pleaded guilty, and Rajiv Goel, a managing director of Intel, pleaded guilty too. They had all been classmates in the same business school earlier in their lives. Was this just a coincidence? Unfortunately, academic research seems to suggest that university friends, such as Kumar, Goel, and Rajaratnam, may well share confidential information.[22] The research shows that portfolio managers place larger bets on firms with directors who are their college friends and acquaintances, earning an 8 percent higher annual return on these investments. A benign interpretation of these results is that college friends know each other well; thus a portfolio manager would have an advantage in judging the quality of a CEO he went to school with. But this benign interpretation is difficult to reconcile with the finding that the positive returns are concentrated around corporate news announcements. Why would your intimate knowledge of the CEO's personal qualities help you earn a better return . . . right around the time of a corporate news announcement? Isn't it more likely that some information has leaked your way? Business schools should do more to eradicate such behavior.

While insider trading is illegal and should be punished by the law, behaviors that are legal but not socially desirable could be effectively stamped out with a shaming from the business community, including the business school alumni network. Money should not be the only criterion of success by which alumni are recognized. A business school would never honor a businessman who made his fortune selling pornographic movies. Why should it honor somebody who has become wealthy preying on people's addictions or marketing a financial instrument designed to dupe unsophisticated investors? In fact, business schools should actively shame this kind of behavior by criticizing it publicly.

Most business schools do offer ethics classes. Yet these classes are generally divided into two categories. Some classes simply illustrate ethical dilemmas without taking a position on what people are expected or not expected to do. It is as if students were presented with the pros and cons of racial segregation, leaving them to decide which side they wanted to take. Other classes hide behind *corporate social responsibility,* saying that social obligations rest on firms, not individuals. I say "hide" because a firm is nothing but an organized group of individuals. As the 2010 Supreme Court decision *Citizens United v. Federal Election Commission* affirms, we should not impose burdens on corporations that we do not want to impose on individuals. So before we talk about corporate social responsibility, we need to talk about individual social responsibility. If we do not recognize the latter, we cannot talk about the former. Business schools should stand up for what they think is the individual responsibility of a good capitalist.

CONCLUSIONS

The question posed at the beginning of this chapter—Should we, as teachers, condemn, condone, or praise their behavior?—led us to a consideration of social norms. Not cutting in line is a useful social norm that elementary school teachers happily teach our children. Similarly, there are several types of norms relevant to the flourishing of a market economy that we can and should teach. One of them, a limit on lobbying, is the topic of the next chapter.

11

LIMITS TO LOBBYING

*If any of the great corporations of the country were to
hire adventurers who make market of themselves in this
way, to procure the passage of a general law with a view
to the promotion of their private interests, the moral
sense of every right-minded man would instinctively
denounce the employer and employed as steeped in
corruption, and the employment as infamous.*

—Supreme Court justice Noah Swayne
in *Trist v. Child* (1875)

NOWHERE IS THE NEED FOR SOCIAL NORMS MORE important than in the area of lobbying. On the one hand, members of the world's second-oldest profession do play an important role in our political process. The expansion of state functions has made it all but impossible for any elected representative to keep up with all the issues she is required to vote on, and lobbyists can help fill in the information gap. "Lobbyists are, in many cases, expert technicians," admitted then-senator John F. Kennedy while advocating limits to their power, "and capable of explaining complex and difficult subjects in a clear, understandable fashion."[1]

On the other hand, in economics, there is no presumption that the level of lobbying produced by the private sector is efficient. And evidence is mounting for the deleterious effects of at least some lobbying, especially when it is unbalanced. Most of the benefits from lobbying come from competition among different interests. If this competition is missing, lobbying can become akin to legalized corruption.

NOT ALL LOBBYING IS CREATED EQUAL

What is lobbying? In a narrow sense, lobbying seeks "to petition the Government for a redress of grievances," as the First Amendment puts it in protecting that right. Yet in the broadest sense, lobbying is any general advocacy. Since I am advocating a particular type of change in this book, one could consider it a form of lobbying. My advocacy can affect my future career opportunities. My ability to promote the book will be affected by how much its content pleases or displeases various interest groups. Yet as a tenured academic, I am in a privileged position. I do not need this book for my career. The potential compensation I forgo by writing it instead of, say, consulting, exceeds not only my advance but probably any royalties I will earn. I am writing this book because I believe in what I have to say.

Some kinds of advocacy are paid for more directly and thus are less free. Twice in my career, I have been approached by companies to write newspaper op-eds for pay. In each case, I was chosen because my position was congenial to the firm that was offering to pay me. Thus I would not have had to bend my principles. In both cases, though, I declined. It's not that I object to being paid for my expertise; indeed, a few times I have provided expert testimony, a paid advocacy position. But in legal cases, it is common knowledge that witnesses get paid; the opposing lawyer knows the exact amount and can challenge it if he likes. Further, in court, each side can hire expert witnesses. But newspaper op-eds have neither cross-examination nor disclosure, so I didn't feel it right to accept the offers.

Being a "hired gun" in such a fashion can raise troubling questions. For example, after a civil war began in Libya in 2011, it was revealed that several US and UK academics and public intellectuals had met with Libyan dictator Muammar al-Qaddafi in 2006 during a mission organized by the Monitor Group, a Boston consulting firm. The British press reported that the objective of the Monitor Group, which was paid more than £2 million by the Libyan government, was to "identify and encourage journalists, academics and contemporary thinkers who will have interest in publishing papers and articles on Libya."[2] After these trips to Libya, several of them wrote articles in European and US newspapers praising Qaddafi's "conversion"—without mentioning that they were working under contract with the Monitor Group to interact with Qaddafi, as reported by *Foreign Policy*.[3]

Special-interest advocacy is something different: direct lobbying for a particular initiative, such as the adoption or removal of emissions standards. This lobbying doesn't try to hide that it is paid work, but it claims to follow ethical rules. A lobbyist "should seek to provide factually correct, current and accurate information," states the ethical code of the American League of Lobbyists.[4] Yet lobbyists aren't known for providing a complete or accurate picture. Is withholding information a violation of the ethics code? A still more important question: Who enforces these norms?

Fund-raising for political candidates, in principle, is distinct from standard lobbying. But while one may not link a campaign contribution to a particular vote or position, the quid pro quo is clearly implied. Lobbyists don't merely act as conduits between donors and candidates; they themselves make political donations. In fact, on average, lobbyists' contributions to campaign funds exceed by 50 percent the contributions made by their own clients.[5]

Gifts from lobbyists—invitations to luxurious parties, gifts of exotic trips (often disguised with some business pretense), lifts on corporate jets, and invitations to corporate skyboxes during major sports events—occupy an even lower rung on the moral ladder. It is hard not to call these gifts bribes. The only difference is the absence of an explicit condition—a quid pro quo. Fortunately, the similarity between lobbyists' gifts and bribes has not gone unnoticed. Members of Congress must disclose any gift with a monetary value above $50.[6]

WHAT'S THE EVIDENCE?

What evidence do we have that the current level of lobbying is excessive? Until the 1995 Lobbying Disclosure Act, data on lobbying were hard to come by. As the data have become available, independent researchers have begun to make sense of them, but it's still not easy to prove the corrupting influence of lobbying beyond a reasonable doubt. It's taken some inspired research to bring us answers.

Three researchers from the London School of Economics decided to look at what happens to a lobbyist's income when the politician he formerly worked for retires or loses his seat.[7] If lobbyists are mostly about informing legislators, the researchers posited, their business should not suffer, since their ability to inform should not be affected by the death or departure of a former employer. If undue influence is present, however, then the loss of connections would be important. The researchers' highly suggestive data show an average 24 percent drop in revenue for a lobbyist when his former boss loses or relinquishes a US Senate seat.

A similar study looked at the issues lobbyists cover when a previous employer in the political world changes jobs—for example, moving from a committee related to health care to one that covers defense.[8] It found that lobbyists switch issues following the reassignment of their former employers. Thus the most valuable component of a lobbyist's human capital is *whom* he knows, not *what* he knows. This result is hardly consistent with the claim that lobbying is mostly about information.

Yet these studies do not completely rule out the information hypothesis. Lawmakers depend on having reliable information, and trusted connections can be a mechanism to convey information reliably. This idea is expressed in a statement by House Speaker John Boehner: "Many lobbyists are of the highest integrity and feel as much of a duty to the House as a democratic institution as they do to their clients. But there's every incentive for those with more questionable ethics to shortchange us and the House. And absent our personal, longstanding relationships, there is no way for us to tell the difference between the two."[9] Relationships are important to make the information transmitted credible. So if a lobbyist loses revenue after his former employer leaves Congress, perhaps that simply means that the lobbyist's valuable credibility suffers from lack of that legislative relationship. Maybe lobbyists shift fields of expertise as their contacts do because relationships are harder to build than knowledge about a particular field. Even sophisticated researchers have a tough time disentangling the informational role of lobbying from the market-distorting one.

The best way to tell whether lobbying carries undue influence is to test whether it sways actual votes. TARP provides a good recent example; one study that controlled for ideology found that congressmen who received the greatest political contributions from the financial industry were the most likely to vote for TARP.[10] And it wasn't simply that representatives already predisposed favorably toward the financial industry received more money. If that were the case, the correlation would have held with congressmen retiring in 2008—but it didn't.

UNFAIR COMPETITION

Twice a year since 1656, the city of Siena, Italy, has hosted Il Palio, a very special horse race. The picturesque setting—Siena's medieval central square—is beautiful, the customs associated with the race are fascinating, and a colorful show precedes the main event. In addition, there are almost no rules. It is not illegal to bribe jockeys or drug horses. Jockeys can hit each other's horses or try to unsaddle each other. A horse can win the race without the jockey, as long as it crosses the finish line first. The city is divided into seventeen equal areas, called *contrada*. Each supports the race through voluntary donations. The horses are randomly assigned to the *contradas* just before the race.[11] Ostensibly, the goal is to prevent richer *contradas* from having an unfair advantage because of their ability to acquire the best horses. Maintaining this balance has helped make the event one of the oldest competitions in existence.

Thus even ruthless competitions can be balanced if the resources invested in them are relatively balanced. That truth applies to lobbying, too. If various interests compete, using roughly similar resources, to transmit information to legislators, the legislative outcomes will be efficient.[12] But *do* the competing groups have roughly similar resources with which to compete? As I explained in Chapter 5, the free-rider problem makes it difficult for dispersed groups to raise a large amount of money, while it is quite easy for a focused interest to do so. So the lobbying game is heavily tilted against dispersed taxpayers. As a colleague of mine concluded after spending some time in Washington, "Truth is just another special interest—and a very poorly funded one."

Further, is it really the case that all the money spent in lobbying is spent on transmitting information? From the point of view of efficiency, we want both sides of an argument to be conveyed so that a legislator can make an informed decision. Because the competitors want to win, however, they need to outspend their rivals. As economist Gordon Tullock, whom we met earlier, realized long ago, this problem isn't unique to lobbying but applies to all games in which the winner is rewarded disproportionately with regard to the other competitors. These are also known as winner-take-all games; sports competitions are a good example.

Winner-take-all games create a wedge between social incentives and individual incentives. In sports, most of the fun for fans—the social incentive—comes from the approximate evenness of opposing teams or competitors. It would be much more exciting to watch two decent college teams face off than to watch Kobe Bryant play one-on-one with me. Yet each individual team has the incentive to stack everything in its own favor. "The main waste" in such circumstances, writes economist Robert Barro, "is that owners and players (and prospective players) use too many resources in the process of improving skills."[13] Lobbying is to the political game what building an unbeatable team is to professional sports: if money can buy success, lots of money will be spent.

To prevent lack of balance, even a conservative economist like Barro, who is critical of regulations and wage restrictions, is willing to endorse restrictions, such as salary caps. Without salary caps, teams will overtax their fans in an attempt to outspend one another, but games will be no more exciting. And teams from richer cities will outspend everybody else so much that the entire sport will suffer.

Can a similar approach work for lobbying? One simple way to minimize the distorting effect of large political contributions and level the playing field would be to impose a progressive tax on these contributions. If the tax applied to individuals as well as to corporations, it would not violate the spirit of the *Citizens United v. Federal Election Commission* Supreme Court decision. As I will explain in Chapter 13, this would be the ultimate "good" tax, improving incentives instead of distorting them as the income tax does.

THE REGULATION CONUNDRUM

Nowadays, most economists who oppose regulation aren't endorsing the idea that unregulated markets always deliver the best outcomes. Rather, they mistrust the political process that shapes regulation. If the regulatory process is captured by vested interests, the regulatory fixes may in fact be worse than the market failures. This position owes much to Nobel Prize winner Ronald Coase, who warned economists against comparing real-world market distortions with ideal government fixes—a mistake he labeled the *Nirvana fallacy*. To avoid committing this fallacy, we need to compare real-world market distortions with real-world fixes. This reduces the attractiveness of regulation without necessarily eliminating it, as Coase recognized.[14]

Adopting this perspective would discourage attempts to reduce the inefficiency introduced by lobbying. If we want to regulate lobbying because we think that it distorts the political process, why do we think that the distorted political process can ameliorate the problem by regulating lobbying? If the decision-making process is the problem, it can hardly be the solution.

While the idea of regulating lobbying appeals to many, it is extremely difficult, if not dangerous. First, candidates will regularly renege on it once elected, as President Obama did.[15] Second, any but the simplest proposal would be massaged so heavily in Congress that the outcome would be ineffective or worse than the status quo. In writing legislation, the devil is invariably in the details. The details here are just too subtle to become a public political issue. Lobbyists gain a tremendous advantage by understanding and maneuvering the details in legislation to the advantage of their clients. If lobbyists have an information advantage in general, they certainly have it on the intricacies of lobbying itself! No one can beat them at their own game.

Here social norms can help. The biggest advantage of social norms is that they are generated from the bottom up—from the institutions of civil society—rather than from the top down. Unlike laws, norms aren't designed by experts behind closed doors but emerge from a population's social awareness. In this respect, they are democratic, not only in their design but even more so in their enforcement. While legal norms need some consensus to be enforced (if everybody revolted against paying taxes, no police force could compel them), it is paramount for social norms. Compliance depends on the voluntary participation of the vast majority of the population. Thus without broad consensus, norms are vacuous. This makes it a tall order for small, interested groups to create and enforce norms that are at odds with the beliefs and values of the majority. It is impossible, for instance, to sustain a social norm to help bankers every time they get themselves into trouble. By contrast, it is much easier to sustain a norm to help poor people who find themselves in need through no fault of their own. The reason is that the first norm is not only unfair but also inefficient, in the sense that if consistently applied, it will make society worse off. The second, to the contrary, will make society better off.

The second advantage of social norms over top-down laws or regulations is that their mechanism of enforcement is decentralized. Intentions aren't easy to prove in court but are usually apparent to close observers. While the court of public opinion can and does make mistakes, so do legal courts. But because the court of public opinion can only punish through ostracism, its mistakes are less costly than those made by courts.

Social norms can thus afford to be broader than laws, making it harder for people to skirt them. There is an old Italian saying: The moment a law is passed, the way around it is found. This attitude reflects not only Italians' pessimistic view of the quality of their laws but a shortcoming of all legal codes. In the United States, most judicial decisions are determined on the basis of precedents and ultimately on the judge's sense of fairness (common law). But in Italy, like the rest of Continental Europe, judges are required to apply the law rigidly (civil law)—and laws thus tend to be minutely detailed. Consequently, amoral people can satisfy the letter of the law while violating its spirit. The best lawyers in Italy (or the worst, depending on your point of view) are those who can play this game most skillfully.

American common law occupies a place somewhere between legal statutes and social norms. That, in my view, is the reason why institutions and law enforcement seem to work better in common-law countries, a well-established empirical fact.[16] The decentralized nature of common law makes it less subject to capture. To get your way in litigation in a civil-law country like Italy or Brazil, it is sufficient to influence legislators, since judges apply the law, no matter how unjust or corrupt it is. By contrast, in common-law countries, you would have to influence the judges, too, a process that is more difficult, time-consuming, and expensive.

In fact, social norms can be understood as the most extreme form of common law. In many US states, elected judges rule on the basis of their sense of fairness. In the court of public opinion, we ourselves are the judges. Can an effective social norm arise against companies or individuals who spend too many resources lobbying? How might it work?

THANK YOU FOR SMOKING

I have never smoked cigarettes and rarely a cigar, but I like to hold one in my mouth. One day I was driving my son, then eight, to a friend's party. A student who had just had a baby had given me a cigar to celebrate the happy event, and I was holding it in my mouth unlit while driving. As we approached the party, my son asked me to put the cigar away: "I don't want my friends to think you're smoking." What had transformed smoking from the cool activity in James Dean and Humphrey Bogart movies into a social taboo?

A first step in that direction was achieved with the 1964 surgeon general's report, which stated that cigarette smoking was responsible for a 70 percent increase in the mortality rate of smokers over nonsmokers. The report changed Americans' view of the health consequences of smoking. In 1958, only 44 percent of Americans believed smoking caused cancer; in 1968, 78 percent did.[17] The report reduced the number of smokers, but it did not create a social norm against smoking. Because the harm— it was thought—was limited to the smoker, it was considered his own business. The turning point came in 1986 with another surgeon general's report, this one focusing on the damage of *secondhand* smoke and saying that smokers were causing health damage to nonsmokers, what in economics we call a negative externality. This is the situation in which social norms are most effective. Fifteen years later, the anti-smoking norm had become so widespread that even my eight-year-old son had fully absorbed it.

The tobacco industry spared no resources fighting back, as humorously portrayed in the 2005 movie *Thank You for Smoking*. Despite one of the most massive disinformation campaigns ever organized, the truth prevailed. While lobbying by health groups contributed to the release of key government reports, these reports would have been unthinkable without the scientific work underlying them. Earlier I described the problem of academic capture. That capture, however, is far from complete. Why?

COMPETITION IN THE ACADEMIC MARKET

What forces prevent full academic capture? And how can we strengthen them? As we saw in Chapter 6, the major difference between regulators and academics is that an academic's career depends on publications in peer-reviewed journals. To win promotion, faculty members must publish a certain number of articles. Even after tenure, a professor's salary depends on the existence (or at least potential) of outside offers, which in turn depend on her reputation in the profession. An academic's reputation is highly correlated with the number and the quality of her publications (often measured in terms of citations).

While the peer review process is affected by many biases, it does favor new ideas. The easiest way for a referee to reject a paper is to say that it has no new results. Thus in academia there is a strong incentive to search for new ideas and to reject old ones.

As more articles are written defending a particular position, debunking it acquires a higher payoff. When I advise students, I tell them that there is little payoff in proving a paper wrong, unless the paper is famous. That fact may generate perverse cycles and fads in the academic market for ideas, but it also acts as a counterbalance to capture. The moment a theory starts to win influence in the academic market, a counterbalancing incentive to debunk it arises. The theory of efficient markets was celebrated with statements like "there is no other proposition in economics which has more solid empirical evidence supporting it."[18] But a couple of years later, the first "anomalies," pieces of evidence of market inefficiency, started to emerge. This is why academic research was able to demonstrate the dangers of smoking, despite the large resources that the tobacco industry channeled into grants.

The most dangerous biases do not come from factual errors: competition in the academic market can quickly expose them and fix them. They come from implicit shared assumptions that are hard to challenge. Most of the findings in economics are derived under the assumption of perfect competition, in part because it makes those results sharper and more elegant; allow for monopoly power, and the results become quite different. As a result, the conventional wisdom is shaped by the competitive paradigm and often leads to the wrong policy conclusions, since we live in a world in which many firms have so much market power that competition is far from perfect. Think about an employment subsidy. Under perfect competition, it makes no difference whether you hand such a subsidy to firms or to workers. In a less competitive market, however, whoever receives the subsidy captures most of it. Yet firms lobbying to receive subsidies can say with a straight face that economic theory shows that the subsidy they receive will fully benefit their workers.

It is more than just a desire for new ideas that drives academic research to defend the public interest. Most academics enter their profession attracted more by glory than by money. After all, there are better ways for educated people to become rich than to enter academia. While there is more money in fighting for vested interests, there is more glory in fighting for the public.

This is no accident. Once again, social norms are trying to fix a market failure. Because there is often more money in defending vested interests, people tend to look down on lobbyists. Children dream of finding a cure for cancer, not of helping tobacco companies avoid taking responsibility for causing cancer or of reducing a company's liability for polluting the environment. In this respect, social norms increase the prestige of certain activities and consequently the supply of high-quality people who want to undertake them. Business schools have a responsibility to contribute to shaping these norms. Since they have a long-term interest in the survival of a vibrant capitalism, they should consider what social norms help secure that end. For example, should someone who edits a major business journal also be a business consultant? In today's world, finding a profitable investment strategy is considered true scholarship, while designing a new finance instrument that works, like the microcredit institutions designed by Muhammad Yunus, is not. Is that just?

Unfortunately, some disciplines or subdisciplines become so narrow that they end up being self-referential. The academic stops trying to find the cure for cancer in favor of becoming the most cited scholar. To protect themselves from irrelevance, scholars develop standards of scholarship that allow them to exclude outside challenges. When I watched the dialogue between two Latinists in Tom Stoppard's play *The Invention of Love,* I laughed: their idiosyncrasies and obsessions in trying to define scholarship seemed silly to me. Yet I realize that the idiosyncrasies and obsessions of my own field may be even more laughable. Preventing academia from drifting into irrelevance is one of the top priorities to reduce capture.

COMPETITION FOR NEWS

A desire for fame drives the media as well.[19] Newspapers, magazines, and television are often accused of being fully captured by advertisers and being the instruments of special-interest propaganda. Yet there are forces, as in academia, that push in the opposite direction too. After all, CBS finally aired the controversial *60 Minutes* interview with Jeffrey Wigand, the tobacco industry whistleblower. Part of Wigand's leaked deposition was published in the *Wall Street Journal.*[20] If all newspapers were captured by advertisers, which newspaper would be more captured than the *Wall Street Journal*? What pushed the *Wall Street Journal* to publish that story and CBS to air it?

Why journalists pursue these stories is obvious. The prospect of a scoop and a Pulitzer Prize makes investigative journalism attractive. The Watergate articles they wrote made *Washington Post* reporters Bob Woodward and Carl Bernstein famous. They got everything a journalist ever dreamed of: money and fame. By definition, a scoop means publishing an important news story. Spinning a story in favor of a lobbyist, however, is hardly a scoop. Uncovering how special interests manipulate regulation and legislation is. While journalists seek scoops for their own advancement, they provide a service to society at the same time: they inform people by collecting, verifying, and summarizing relevant facts.

But what's in it for the newspaper or the broadcast station that publishes the news? Making a profit is capitalism's basic goal. Profit-maximizing media are in the business of attracting the largest possible audience.[21] The cost of producing a program remains the same if the number of viewers increases, but the revenues, whether from sales or from advertising, go up. So any media owner interested in making money will obviously work to expand his audience. The easiest way to do so is to tell stories that the public wants to hear. Lobbyists spend massively to try to spin the news. According to *Vanity Fair,* Brown & Williamson (B&W), Jeffrey Wigand's former employer, hired special investigators at consider-able expense to spread rumors about him, trying to undermine his credi-bility.[22] But the campaign failed because the story of Wigand as an honest whistleblower was much more interesting to the public than was that of Wigand as a pathological liar. Thus it was in the newspaper's interest to verify the allegations, as the *Wall Street Journal* did with the Wigand story. Once the rumors spread by B&W were found to be unsubstanti-ated, all the effort B&W put into denigrating Wigand only confirmed that he was telling something important that B&W did not want the public to know. Thus media that want to maximize sales and viewership must pro-vide information that is of interest to the public at large.

Advertising pressure can offset some of this effect. For instance, as I mentioned in the introduction, newspapers with a diversified advertis-ing base, such as the *Wall Street Journal* and the *New York Times,* seem uninfluenced by how much mutual-fund advertising they contain.[23] By contrast, there is evidence that specialist magazines are influenced by this spending. The reason, once again, is market power. Specialized magazines, to survive, depend on a handful of advertising companies and therefore cannot afford to displease them. Generalist newspapers operate in a more competitive market, and competition once again pro-vides freedom. The most unbiased information again comes from the least specialized sources.

In addition to reporting news, the print media can attract readers. By making information entertaining, they can help overcome the so-called free-rider problem in information gathering. Everyone benefits from informed voters, but one's individual benefit is generally smaller than the cost of collecting the information. Even if the cost of gathering the information is paid for, the individual cost of processing it—say, the time involved in reading or viewing the news—might still exceed the individual payoff from becoming informed.

I might never have known much about the Wigand case if not for *The Insider*, a popular movie starring Russell Crowe. Similarly, comedy programs like *The Daily Show with Jon Stewart*, by making news fun to watch, can help keep people informed. Sometimes this is serendipitous. Other times it's the work of a political entrepreneur who tries to inform people by entertaining them. For example, newspaperman William Randolph Hearst commissioned novelist David Graham Phillips to write the famous muckraking series *The Treason of the Senate*, which I will describe in a moment. Hearst was a Democrat with a clear political agenda.

Media can do so much because voters' "rational ignorance," their lack of economic incentives to become informed, lies at the heart of the power of vested interests. If voters are ignorant about what is best for them, lobbyists find it easier to persuade elected representatives to vote their way. But elected representatives do respond to voters when those voters are informed. This is hard to prove in the age of national TV and the Internet. Does media content affect voters or does voters' demand for information drive media content? To sort it out, we briefly have to go back to the early twentieth century. Institutional change can make a difference, though it may be difficult to bring about.

THE MUCKRAKING EXPERIENCE

For evidence that the importance of money in Washington is nothing new, consider the following accusation launched by David Graham Phillips:

> Treason is a strong word, but not too strong, rather too weak, to characterize the situation in which the Senate is the eager, resourceful,

indefatigable agent of interests as hostile to the American people as any invading army could be, and vastly more dangerous: interests that manipulate the prosperity produced by all, so that it heaps up riches for the few; interests whose growth and power can only mean the degradation of the people, of the educated into sycophants, of the masses toward serfdom.[24]

Phillips used these words to describe the US Senate in 1906. At that time, the majority of senators were appointed by state governors, not elected by the people, and hence not accountable to voters. Several attempts to amend the Constitution to allow for the direct election of US senators had failed. In 1902, when the Senate finally allowed a roll call vote, the proposed amendment failed by a significant margin. In 1911, the amendment returned to the Senate floor and passed, becoming the Seventeenth Amendment. What happened during those nine years that forced a third of the senators to switch their votes?

The answer lies in the 1906 publication of Phillips's series *The Treason of the Senate,* which exposed the corruption in the upper house. The series was an instant success, bringing the circulation of *Cosmopolitan,* the monthly magazine that published it, to 450,000 and its readership to 4.4 million people at a time when the national presidential vote was 15 million.

Colleagues and I tested whether other exposés in muckraking magazines affected voting on major regulatory legislation in the Progressive Era. We found that the higher the circulation of the muckraking magazine in a representative's district, the more likely he was to vote in favor of the progressive legislation—but only if the issue had been taken up by muckrakers. It is not that districts where the magazines were sold elected more progressive representatives. When an issue received no attention from muckrakers, representatives voted as before. It was the muckraking that made the difference.

SHAMING

Exposing facts can also cause companies to change their behavior, as a few examples suggest. On April 12, 1990, the H. J. Heinz Company announced that it would sell only dolphin-safe tuna.[25] Within hours, two other tuna producers made a similar commitment. Shareholders were not happy with this decision, which was costly. Consumers were not thrilled either: some marketing studies showed that "if there is a dolphin-safe can of tuna next to a regular can, people choose the cheaper product even if the difference is just one penny."[26] So why did Heinz do what it did? Or consider what happened the following year, when Allied Signal, a large conglomerate, tripled its expenditures on environmental control facilities and voluntary cleanups that vastly exceeded legal requirements.[27] Why did it undertake significant costs, apparently against its own self-interest?

The simple answer is public shaming. The Heinz decision followed the 1988 broadcast of a video that showed tuna fishermen killing hundreds of dolphins. Similarly, the Allied Signal decision followed the publication of *Who's Who of Toxic Polluters* and *The Toxic 500,* publications created by environmental groups like the Natural Resources Defense Council and the National Wildlife Federation. The entire industry responded, with the Chemical Manufacturers Association developing a code for responsible manufacturing and making it mandatory for members—an instance of "draconian self-policing" viewed as "necessary to reverse the public's overwhelmingly negative opinion of the chemicals industry."[28] The publication of those lists was prompted, in turn, by the 1990 Pollution Prevention Act, which mandated disclosure of annual releases of each chemical by facility. As the Environmental Protection Agency noted, "The information is a lever for action, as citizens exact pledges from local manufacturing facilities to reduce toxic discharges."[29]

Public shaming works because most CEOs care about their firms' public image. Being labeled a dolphin killer or an environmental polluter tarnishes their brand image, which they spend so much money to create and maintain. For this reason, they are willing to pay attention to citizens' concerns, even if these concerns have no immediate impact on the demand for their products.[30]

In the same way, I believe, companies will pay attention to citizens' concerns about lobbying. For this to be true, though, two conditions must be satisfied. First, as was the case in 1990, the amount companies spend on lobbying must be made public. Public data allow researchers to conduct their analyses independently of vested interests and thus more objectively. Second, the damage inflicted by lobbying must be exposed and explained to the public, as environmental groups did when they published lists of the worst polluters. Fortunately, a group of activists has already started a campaign to transform the first condition.[31] With the proper incentives on the academic and media side, Justice Swayne's hope that we will "instinctively denounce the employer and employed as steeped in corruption, and the employment as infamous" may become reality.

IT TAKES ONE TO BEAT ONE

Just mentioning the term *class action* triggers for some the image of unscrupulous trial lawyers, hundred-million-dollar awards, and the soaring cost of medical malpractice insurance, which burdens all our health insurance bills. And if we are worried about lobbies, the trial lawyer's association is certainly a very powerful lobby.

Yet, with all their downsides, class action suits have an important benefit: they help level the playing field. Thanks to class actions, even small claims, having little potential on their own, can be effectively pursued through aggregation. This aggregation makes 1 million one-dollar claims as attractive for lawyers to pursue as a single claim of 1 million. For that reason, class actions ensure that individual rights are protected no matter how powerful the plaintiff is.

What speculation is for finance, class actions are for the law: the profit motive benefitting everyone, in the best tradition of Adam Smith. When channeled within proper rules, speculation provides liquidity to the market and accurate prices to investors. Similarly, properly regulated class actions help provide equal opportunities to the people, along with the defense of their rights. They are a pillar of capitalism for the people.

Ironically, according to some scholars, Progressive Era legislation created regulatory agencies in response to the perceived unfairness of the court system.[32] So how can the court system patrol and punish regulatory capture?

The relationship, in fact, is not such a contradiction. In a period when the adversarial process was heavily tilted in favor of the wealthy, regulatory agencies appeared to be a wise solution. At inception, regulatory agencies are generally staffed by highly motivated public servants. The revolving door leading from the agency to the lucrative private sector has not yet begun to operate, and the newly regulated industry has yet to figure out how best to cajole and corrupt the agency. Thus, the immediate effect of a regulatory agency, especially in the beginning of the twentieth century, might have been positive.

Over time, however, business grew much more effective at capturing regulatory agencies. By contrast, the judicial process has become more accessible to the common person, thanks to class actions becoming better established and much more diffused.

Class actions, however, have still more benefit in that they helped balance the intellectual battlefield. Writing in 1905 before the introduction of securities class actions, future justice Louis Brandeis stated: "Instead of holding a position of independence, between the wealthy and the people, prepared to curb the excesses of either, able lawyers have, to a large extent, allowed themselves to become adjuncts of great corporations and have neglected the obligation to use their powers for the protection of the people. We hear much of the 'corporation lawyer,' and far too little of the 'people's lawyer.'"[33]

This was obviously not just a problem of the lawyers but of any type of experts, as I discussed in Chapter 6. The existence of class actions thus creates powerful financial incentives not just for people's lawyers, but also for people's experts who can provide intellectual firepower in their defense.

CONCLUSIONS

Both economic theory and empirical evidence suggest that lobbying is excessive and corrupting and should be curbed. The 2010 *Citizens United v. Federal Election Commission* Supreme Court decision, however, means that lobbying cannot easily be restricted through legislation. Even had the Supreme Court ruled differently, it would be hard to distinguish efficient lobbying, which provides information to legislators, from inefficient lobbying. Above all, we cannot expect the political process, which is heavily influenced by lobbying, to restrain itself. That would be like expecting turkeys to vote for Thanksgiving.

Yet in spite of these long odds, the battle against vested interests is not necessarily a losing one. In a free, competitive society, countervailing forces always exist. They may not be strong enough to fix the problem, but they are there—and we can make them stronger. In this fight, the business schools that train many of the brightest businesspeople play a special role. Because they have a long-term interest in the survival of a vibrant capitalism, they should develop social norms for acceptable and unacceptable lobbying behavior and try to enforce them among their students. I dream of the day when my students will be as ashamed of spending large amounts on lobbying as my son is of my cigar.

12

SIMPLE IS BEAUTIFUL

*There are no easy answers but there are simple answers.
We must have the courage to do what we know is
morally right.*

—Ronald Reagan

RYING TO RESTRAIN THE ESCALATION OF LOBBYING through social norms can go only so far. We need to do more to solve the problem of legislators and regulators being captured by special interests. One intriguing solution, advanced by legal scholar Lawrence Lessig, is to reduce our elective representatives' need for corporate donations through campaign finance reform introduced by a constitutional convention.[1] But even if that proved feasible, it wouldn't solve the entire problem. Legislators and regulators need information to do their job. This is why even the most public-spirited regulators will succumb to the power of industry. One good approach to address this problem is to simplify the regulations whose growth and complexity feed the lobbying machine.

WHY SO COMPLICATED?

The more technical a law or a regulation is, the higher the need for industry expertise. Without this expertise, legislators risk making serious mistakes. Thus experts who advise the crafting of norms have a vested interest in making those norms complicated, because that increases the value of their expertise and human capital. It is possible that this is just an unwanted side effect of the experts' desire for precision. But when you read an op-ed written by the senior officers of one of the largest economic consulting firms asking for more cost-benefit analysis, it is difficult to conclude that it is serendipitous.[2]

In 2010, we saw the passage of the Dodd-Frank financial-reform bill, which was a staggering 2,319 pages long. Things were not always this way. The Glass-Steagall Act, which in 1933 separated investment banking from commercial banking, was just thirty-seven pages long. The act that created the Federal Reserve in 1913 ran to thirty-one pages. Even the recent Sarbanes-Oxley Act, which was written in response to the Enron and WorldCom scandals, was only sixty-six pages long. Tellingly, the Dodd-Frank bill was popularly called the "Lawyers' and Consultants' Full Employment Act of 2010." It may well have created more jobs than Obama's original 2009 stimulus package did.

Each page of regulation probably provides a year's worth of employment for several lobbyists and a couple of lawyers and economists. This gigantic waste is never properly factored into our economic analysis. But the biggest cost is the smokescreen that overregulation creates. For centuries, in Continental Europe, laws were written in Latin, a language that ordinary citizens could not understand. As institutions were democratized, laws started being written in the vernacular. Overabundant regulation, and the legalese that it is written in, achieves the same goal that Latin once did: to confuse the public. "When I was writing regulations," says one retired EPA regulator, "I was told on more than one occasion to make sure I put in enough loopholes. The purpose of the complexity is to hide the loopholes."[3]

Back in 2009, at the beginning of the financial-reform legislative process, I made a concerted effort to follow the debate. It was my area of expertise, so I wanted to know about it, but at a certain point I gave up. Except for a few selected passages, I read a summary of the final Dodd-Frank bill, rather than the full 2,319-page version, to say nothing of the sixty-seven studies that the bill mandated and the thousands of pages of further regulation that it authorized.[4]

During the debate, I was stunned by the popular support for the old Glass-Steagall Act. The more distant people were from the financial world, the stauncher their support for restoring the separation—which had been defunct since 1999—between commercial banking and investment banking. As an economist, I knew that the separation had costs as well as benefits, and in the absence of strong evidence that the benefits exceeded the costs, I went with my free-market assumption that the separation wasn't a good idea. The 2008 financial crisis did not change my views. While investment banks were among the biggest culprits in the crisis, the merging of commercial and investment banking activities, in my view, was not to blame. Bear Stearns was only an investment bank, not a commercial one, and it nevertheless got a bailout because the Federal Reserve deemed it too interconnected to fail. So what did it matter whether a commercial bank and an investment bank were jointly owned or simply joined at the hip by a web of financial contracts? Further, commercial bank JP-Morgan Chase subsequently bought Bear Stearns, reducing the public cost of intervention—another sign, I thought, that a forced separation between the two forms of banking was unwise.

So why was the 1999 repeal of Glass-Steagall so unpopular? Indeed, why is it still so unpopular that the Occupy movement demands that the separation be restored? For a long time, I thought they just didn't get it: I was an expert, and I knew best. But eventually I realized that *I* was the one who didn't get it. While Glass-Steagall may not be the most efficient form of regulation, it worked for more than sixty years. People sensed that the power of the financial industry had become excessive, and they wanted to contain it. They might not understand the sophisticated economic arguments, but they understood the bottom line: that the best is the enemy of the good, and that by trying to achieve the best possible regulations, we end up preventing the passage of feasible regulations.

The beauty of Glass-Steagall, after all, was its simplicity: banks should not gamble with government-insured money. Even a six-year-old can understand that, which is why former Fed chairman Paul Volcker endorsed the principle in 2009. But then the Obama administration transformed the so-called Volcker rule into 298 pages of mumbo jumbo.[5] Why? Well, as an economist, I have been trained to infer intentions from outcomes, especially when I'm considering smart and experienced people. So it seems a reasonably safe bet that the Obama administration endorsed the Volcker rule, rather than Glass-Steagall, because it knew that the Volcker rule was almost as popular but, unlike Glass-Steagall, required so many details to be implemented that it would never be enforced. In this way, the Obama administration could avoid displeasing the banking industry and get political consensus to boot.

The United States was born on the principle of no taxation without representation. It should add no regulation without representation. But if regulation is too complex, people have no way to understand it and thus cannot participate properly in democracy. Simplifying regulation, therefore, is essential to building a capitalism for the people.

SIMPLE IS BEAUTIFUL

Simple regulation is necessarily inefficient, at least in a narrow economic sense, as Glass-Steagall was. So why impose simplicity in spite of this inefficiency?

When I visited Stanford Business School many years ago, I was surprised to see that all of the offices in its new building were identical—a result that had cost money, thanks to the structure of the building. Why should socialism prevail with respect to offices? I was told that the dean, who had to assign the offices, wanted to avoid the headache of having to decide who would get the best ones. Faculty members' compensation is never disclosed, but office size is obvious. We professors are all extremely concerned about our prestige. If some offices were visibly more desirable than others, then each professor would lobby to get the best spots. The dean wanted to prevent that.

At the time, I thought these concerns were exaggerated, until Chicago Booth also constructed a new building for itself but decided to differentiate offices. To minimize lobbying, the dean announced that each faculty member would be randomly assigned a number within categories—presumably assistant, associate, full, and chair professor (though this was not explicit), and would choose an office sequentially. But when the selection order was announced, the most famous faculty members were first, suggesting that the process had not in fact been random. The school erupted. Emotions took over. One faculty member shouted "I hate you!" at another who had received a better office, ruining their relationship for quite some time. Some faculty members organized a simulation to try to figure out how this sequential procedure would have assigned offices. For days, the only topic of conversation was office assignments. Ironically, except for a few corner offices, the offices didn't differ that much. Most of the haggling was over nothing.

We might underestimate the cost of all this commotion because it was not easily measurable. But if you do factor in the time wasted in office-allocation simulations, along with the cost of tense relationships for years to come, you see that Stanford's choice was the more efficient one. This point has been recognized by a few economists.[6] When you factor in the enforcement costs and lobbying costs of regulation, many choices that looked inefficient at first become efficient in a broader sense. So when you simplify regulation, you might make it less effective in curbing the distortion you might want to curb, but you actually reduce its overall cost and make it more transparent. By ignoring enforcement and lobbying costs, policy makers fall all too often into the "Nirvana fallacy" of comparing real world markets with ideal regulation. Simple regulation stands a better chance to allow a comparison between real-world markets and real-world regulation.

In the context of regulation, however, there is one added benefit of simplicity. Not only does simplifying regulation reduce lobbying costs and distortions; it also makes it easier for the public to monitor things, reducing the amount of capture.

If you still fear the inefficiency of simple regulation, let me make one final argument. It is often *useful* to make an instrument inefficient when you fear that it will be used too much. Conservatives, for instance, oppose the introduction of a value-added tax because it raises revenue so efficiently, making it very easy for politicians to expand the size of government. The same logic applies here. Regulation that is a bit inefficient by design will reduce the overuse of regulation. Only the most compelling and useful regulation will survive.

SIMPLE ENFORCEMENT

One of the many benefits of simple rules is that they facilitate accountability. Complicated rules are difficult to enforce even under the best circumstances, and impossible when their enforcement is the domain of captured agencies.

Between the Federal Reserve, the Office of the Control of the Currency, and the State Regulators there are about 30,000 people in charge of supervising banks. Given this army, how is it possible that bank supervision is so ineffective? In March 2008 the market was predicting the probability that Washington Mutual would fail within a year, at 30 percent. Still the bank was left to operate until September 25 of that year. There is no political payoff for an early intervention, especially given the uncertainty that surrounds all such decisions. After the government took over Washington Mutual in 2008, there were still complaints that the action came too early. Preventive banking regulation is like pre-emptive war: There is no credit for the pain avoided, while there is plenty of blame for the pain inflicted. Experience shows that we simply can't rely on regulators to resist these pressures.

The alternative, however, is not to do away with regulation but to rely on simpler regulations that have other enforcement mechanisms. In Chapter 14 I will present a proposal on how to use the market to regulate banks without relying on ineffective banking supervisors. Similar ideas can also be applied to other forms of regulation. As I explained in Chapter 4, whistleblowers identify corporate fraud more effectively than the SEC does and at a fraction of the cost. And as noted above, a key advantage of a whistleblower-based system is that it is resistant to capture. Any employee can be a whistleblower, and it is too costly for the industry to buy them all off. Thus, antifraud regulation can more effectively be enforced by amply rewarded whistleblowers.[7]

THE SIMPLICITY OF ZERO

When it comes to enforcing rules, zero tolerance is often the only policy that makes sense: zero tolerance for crime in the street; zero tolerance for sexual harassment; zero tolerance for exceptions in a promotion system. Zero tolerance makes no allowance for trade-offs and therefore prevents an erosion of standards.

If a police officer observes a small criminal act on the street, should he intervene? Of course. But if he is allowed to use his own discretion, he will likely intervene to a lesser degree than the rule requires. Since he bears the personal and physical cost of intervening, consciously or subconsciously he will lean a bit too much against acting. Other officers observing his behavior might assume that his decision reflects the effective rule. When confronted by their own decisions, they will likely copy his leniency. Little by little the standards are eroded, unless a zero-tolerance policy dispenses with ambiguity.

We may recognize the damage that subsidies and loopholes do to a market economy, but there is resistance to adopting a zero-tolerance policy toward them. In isolation many of them seem worthy: a tax reduction to promote investments in the inner city; subsidized loans to help develop green energy and save the environment; a reduction in payroll taxes for young unemployed people. The problem is that when you open the floodgate there is no realistic restraint. Each industry, each large corporation, employs an army of lobbyists to pressure Congress on their merits. They flood newspapers with op-eds, some paid for directly, others indirectly. They advertise on television and start "grassroots" campaigns on the Internet. And who is lobbying for the other side? Nobody.

AN APPLICATION TO THE PERSONAL TAX CODE

How can we force regulation to be simple? With 60,000 pages and 3.4 million words, the tax code is the obvious place to begin. There are millions of justifications for exemptions and deductions. Individually, they may even make sense. But collectively, they do not. The deductions that make it into the code are likely to be those that benefit the most politically powerful groups. The existence of some deductions encourages everybody else to lobby for similar deductions, as in the case of the business-school office assignments. If there is a home-mortgage deduction, why not a deduction for motor homes? What about boats, cars, bicycles? The only defensible line is zero. The moment the door is opened to one deduction, we have a flood, and resources will be wasted on lobbying for deductions, as well as on the lawyers and tax accountants who exploit them.

Paradoxically, many of these deductions lead to results opposing their goals. Consider the mortgage-interest tax deduction, which defenders claim encourages homeownership and the attainment of the American Dream. The fact that the deduction is unlimited implies that it subsidizes the wealthy, who have large mortgages and consequently can take large deductions. In cities where real estate is limited—such as New York, San Francisco, and Boston—the subsidy will have the effect of raising home prices. Since the increase will be in proportion to the average subsidy, the less wealthy will wind up receiving less than the cost of home increases, *jeopardizing* the American Dream. Meanwhile, the subsidy induces excessive investment in housing and excessive leverage within the household sector, a problem that emerged after the 2008 financial crisis.

Further, the proliferation of tax deductions erodes the tax base and forces marginal tax rates to increase. As I will explain in the next chapter, higher marginal tax rates encourage people to evade and elude taxes. The most extreme form of tax elusion is substituting leisure for work. When I watch a movie, I do not get taxed; when I work, I do. Taxing income is equivalent to subsidizing leisure. The more I am taxed on work, the less work I do.

To get a sense of how deductions make marginal tax rates increase, I took 2008 tax returns and calculated what the marginal tax rates would have been if we had eliminated all deductions and raised the same amount of revenue. The result: people with household incomes below $30,000 would have been exempted from any tax. The fraction of income between $30,000 and $70,000 would have been taxed at 10 percent. The remaining marginal tax rates would have been 20 percent, up to $150,000; 25 percent, from $150,000 to $250,000; 30 percent, from

$250,000 and $500,000; and 35 percent above that.[8] In short, getting rid of all deductions would have reduced the marginal tax rate of all taxpayers by at least five percentage points, except for taxpayers making more than $500,000, who would see their marginal tax rate unchanged.

Far from being regressive, such a reform would decrease the tax burden of all households making less than $1 million a year. The additional tax burden for those in the income bracket between $1 million and $1.5 million would be $22,000 a year—probably close to what they currently spend on lawyers and tax accountants, who would be mostly unnecessary if we got rid of all deductions.

I do not claim that the rates used in my simulation are optimal. My point is simply that we can simplify the tax system without making it more regressive. The majority of proposals advocating simplification have suggested a flat tax rate, an idea that I will discuss in the next chapter. Here, suffice it to note that simplifying the tax code would be a good thing. The only argument against it is a Machiavellian one: tax loopholes make taxing less efficient and consequently reduce the risk that government will increase the tax rates. For this reason, it would be fair to introduce a constitutional amendment imposing a maximum marginal tax rate, something I will also discuss in the next chapter.

SIMPLIFYING CORPORATE TAXES

One change that would greatly simplify the tax code and avoid plenty of tax arbitrages is the equal treatment of personal income and capital gains. However, reducing the personal tax rate to the level of the capital-gains tax rate would create a large hole in the US budget, while increasing the capital-gains tax rate to the level of the personal income tax would discourage investments. Fortunately, this problem can be easily resolved by modifying the corporate tax rate. Currently, a dollar of profits is taxed 35 cents at the corporate level, and then another 9.75 cents (15 percent tax on the remaining 65 cents) when it is distributed in the form of a dividend or realized as a capital gain.

The problem with such a high corporate tax rate is that it is very distortive and all too frequently eluded. It's distortive because partnerships are heavily advantaged vis-à-vis corporations and so is debt, whose payments are deducted from the taxable corporate income. Also, large corporations with armies of lobbyists are very good at eluding this tax, while small firms have to pay it. A 2008 study by the General Accounting Office found that 55 percent of large US companies paid zero taxes at least one year between 1998 and 2005.[9] What's the impact of that? Well, in 1962 corporate tax revenues amounted to 39 percent of corporate profits and 16 percent of total tax revenues. In 2007, they represented only 29 percent of corporate profits and 10 percent of tax revenues.[10] This elusion is not the same in every sector. A *Bloomberg BusinessWeek* analysis, based on public filings, infers that on average semiconductor companies pay only 19.6 percent of their income in taxes, while telecommunication companies pay only 22.2 percent.[11]

One time-honored way companies reduce their tax liability is by hiring lobbyists to obtain special tax loopholes or to protect the ones they have. For example, in 2003 Tyco paid lobbyist Jack Abramoff's firm $150,000 a month to fight legislation aimed at the company, which reincorporated in Bermuda to avoid paying US corporate taxes.[12] The proposed legislation would have cost the company about $4 billion. Tyco's strategy succeeded. Another example of businesses buying preferential tax treatment is the dividend repatriation provision in the American Jobs Creation Act of 2004, which allowed US multinationals a one-time opportunity to bring home foreign earnings, paying taxes on only 15 percent of this repatriated income. A study finds that the ninety-three public firms engaging in lobbying for this provision spent $282.7 million on their persuasive effort, and won $62.5 billion in tax savings, with a 220:1 return on investment.[13]

The simplest solution to all these problems is to move most of the burden from the corporate level to the individual level. In fact, corporations have much stronger incentives to lobby for tax loopholes than individuals do. If corporate taxes were just 15 percent and dividends and capital gains were taxed at the personal tax rate (35 percent), a dollar of corporate profits would still yield the same tax contribution before reaching shareholders, but tax elusion and tax arbitrages would be more difficult.[14]

Elimination of the deductibility of interest from the definition of taxable corporate income could easily help lower the corporate tax rate to 10 percent without reducing tax revenues. Such provision would eliminate the distortions in favor of debt present in the current tax code, which disadvantages small firms (which are unable to borrow in the same proportion as large ones), and pushes all firms to borrow more.

THE SIMPLICITY OF CERTAINTY

At the end of 2010, there was enormous uncertainty about future taxes: were the Bush-era income tax cuts to expire, as planned, at the end of 2010, tax rates would increase for everybody—at the lower end of the income distribution from 10 to 15 percent, and at the higher end from 35 to 39.6 percent.

The greatest uncertainty, however, was over estate taxes. By 2010, they had been reduced to zero. Absent congressional action that year, they were to leap to 55 percent for estates valued above one million dollars in 2011. The change was so abrupt that a doctor expressed the fear that unscrupulous people might accelerate the death of sick rich relatives.[15] The estate tax reprieve was granted at the eleventh hour, but the income tax cuts were extended only for another two years, setting the stage for another last-minute fight in 2012.

Regardless of the merit of these tax cuts, one has to despise their temporary status: it generates great uncertainty, which is bad for the economy as well as for individuals (not to mention the old sick relatives). Unfortunately, the Bush tax cuts are not an exception. An increasing number of provisions in the tax code are designed to expire. A recent study shows that in 1991 there were about 40 expiring tax cuts, but in 2011 there were close to 400.[16] Why did the number of these measures increase ten times in twenty years?

One (not particularly noble) reason is that to federal bean counters, expiring tax cuts appear smaller than permanent ones. The Congressional Budget Office (CBO) computes its projections for federal spending and borrowing using 'current law' as a baseline. Thus, if a tax cut is set to expire in a given year, the CBO assumes that the expiration date will trump politics and the tax will be reinstated. This rule allows the CBO to whistle past the graveyard and score tax cuts in a way that makes them appear more affordable.

Another reason I can think of is even less noble: expiring tax provisions are a bonanza for lobbyists and congressional fund raisers. The threat of an impending tax increase or an expiring tax loophole can mobilize clients and raise more funds. This is the vicious circle of lobbying. Companies hire hoards of lobbyists to obtain special treatment. While the lobbyists desire a reputation for success, they do not want to be so successful that they are no longer needed. It would be in the interest of lobbyists to create a dependence, which expiring tax provisions do very nicely. For this reason, tax rules should not only be simple but also permanent.

SIMPLE AND EQUAL

The best way to ensure that rules are simple and effective is to apply them to Congress, where they originate. Seems like common sense? Until February 2012, members of Congress were not bound by the same insider-trading restrictions that applied to corporate insiders. After several suspicious trades by top members of Congress were documented in a book, this anomaly has been quickly rectified, at least on paper.[17] It remains to be seen how aggressive would be the Securities and Exchange Commission to go after Senators and Congress people. But the problem goes well beyond insider trading.

The US Congress lives by rules that are very different from those imposed on ordinary businesses. If the corporate executive of a publicly traded company lies during a conference call with analysts or in an annual report, he can be sued. Politicians, on the other hand, lie regularly during electoral campaigns and while in office, with no consequences. Wouldn't it be nice if we could sue a lying politician?

If the US government had been held to the same accounting rules as the private sector, it would have been forced to consolidate Fannie Mae and Freddie Mac and to report all contingent liabilities at market value.

Not only would such a rule make government officials appreciate the costs of the constraints they put on others, but it would greatly improve government's accountability. One of the reasons why credit subsidies are so appealing is that they are not immediately accounted for, so they are invisible to most of the electorate. The cost of the implicit support provided to Fannie Mae and Freddie Mac did not appear on the government books for many years. This made it easier for the government to continue supporting them.

The same is true for the support provided to large banks and to students. In principle, this distortion could be partially eliminated by reforming the way the cost is accounted for (or not accounted for). Yet any cost that is uncertain and will occur in the future permits some accounting discretion. There is enormous pressure to hide these costs, and the temptation to fudge the rules is very large. The only way to rout out dangerous accounting gimmicks when calculating cost to the taxpayers is by ensuring that the government follows all the rules that apply to publicly traded companies, including the personal liability of the Chief Executive Officers and the Chief Financial Officers for the integrity of the accounting numbers.

ENFORCEMENT TO THE PEOPLE

No matter what we do to try to level the playing field, it will remain unbalanced. Businesses will always want to lobby Washington for favors. Even if there were a law against government subsidies to any company or industry, clever lawyers and lobbyists would find ways around it. But suppose we introduced such a law along with an enforcement mechanism based on class-action lawsuits—which, for all their abuses, are very important to American democracy. Such a mechanism would grant any citizen the right to sue the subsidized industry in the name of the state and obtain restitution of the unfair subsidy, retaining a finder's fee—say, 15 or 20 percent—for himself. The system would be modeled after *qui tam* actions, in which a private individual who assists a prosecution can receive a portion of any penalty imposed. It could with equal effect be used against the power of lobbies.

A reward system for whistleblowers who help expose corruption can also be an effective way to replace ineffective government agencies. As I explained in Chapter 4, whistleblowers identify corporate fraud more effectively than the SEC does and at a fraction of the cost. And as noted above, a key advantage of a whistleblower-based system is that it is resistant to capture. Any employee can be a whistleblower, and it is too costly for the industry to buy them all off.

CONCLUSIONS

In this chapter, I have argued that to overcome capture we need limited and simple regulation, preferably enforced by a whistleblower reward system. The best way to prevent lobbying is to introduce a law eliminating subsidies to industry, supported by giving citizens the right to sue to recover the cost of subsides paid unfairly. But would these measures reduce the power of government to the extent that it becomes completely ineffective? No. As I will argue in the next chapter, everything that can be done with subsidies can be done with taxes as well. In fact, it can be done better, because the political economy of taxes is more favorable to ordinary citizens.

13

GOOD AND BAD TAXES

It is not very unreasonable that the rich should contribute to the public expense, not only in proportion to their revenue, but something more than in that proportion.

—Adam Smith

MANY PEOPLE WHO SHARE MY CONCERNS ABOUT growing income inequality advocate a massive redistribution of wealth through taxation. I disagree. Redistribution reduces incentives to work, to invest, to excel. It also reduces incentives to come to the United States. European countries like Sweden and France show lower levels of income inequality not merely because they redistribute wealth but because their rich citizens flee to Switzerland, Monaco, or other places that allow them to keep their money. As the international competition for talent increases, the United States cannot lose out by imposing unattractive marginal tax rates.

I further oppose redistribution on moral grounds. When the state starts taking fifty cents of every dollar people make, it transforms people into slaves; confiscatory tax rates thus transcend economic arguments and become a matter of freedom. People who reject all of these arguments may be persuaded by a more strategic one: where socialism and redistribution have ruled, crony capitalism eventually grows, as we see from Italy to Latin America and from Indonesia to Russia.

If it wants to succeed, a promarket agenda should not promote redistribution. It should stand for a better, freer-market system in which merit is rewarded, not penalized. But what role *does* fiscal policy play in a promarket agenda?

WHY TAXES?

Taxes have three potential functions: to raise revenues, to modify incentives, and to redistribute income. The first function is accepted by everyone. Even libertarians agree that the state must perform minimal functions, such as national defense, police protection, and maintaining a court system. To pay for them, the government needs tax revenue. The big question, of course, is how much revenue should be collected and from whom.

The second function of taxes, often ignored, is to shape incentives. Usually this is an unwanted side effect of the first function: for example, as just noted, taxing income discourages people from working. Sometimes, however, modifying incentives is the goal of the tax and collecting revenue is merely a side effect. Most libertarians object to this kind of tax because it represents a not-so-subtle form of state coercion. Historically, for instance, Muslim countries allowed non-Muslims to practice their religion so long as they paid a tribute.[1] Still, that was a kinder form of coercion than the one Christian countries sometimes practiced: executing infidels. My opinion is that incentive-shaping taxes are legitimate if the alternative is some worse form of coercion such as restrictions or prohibition.

The third function of taxation, redistribution, is very controversial. While most people accept a minimal amount of redistribution (there is little support for a tax that is the same for everybody), the extent of redistribution is the subject of debate. It is useful to distinguish between two forms of redistribution. The first is an unequal allocation of fiscal burden that occurs in connection with a plan whose purpose is not redistributive—for example, the wealthy happening to pay a disproportionate share of the costs of police protection or national defense. This milder form of redistribution was apparently endorsed even by Adam Smith, who wrote, "It is not very unreasonable that the rich should contribute to the public expense, not only in proportion to their revenue, but something more than in that proportion."[2] The second form is what I call Robin Hood redistribution, whose actual purpose is to redistribute money from the rich to the poor.

As the role of government grows, taxes increase. Thus the first step toward reducing the tax burden is restricting the number of tasks that government performs. Eliminating subsidies, obviously, is one way to do this. Still, taxes are a necessary evil, since government, most people today agree, should provide a social safety net and fund primary and secondary education. How should these functions be financed?

THE MORAL BASIS OF TAXATION

During the 2008 presidential campaign, a colleague of mine was watching the Democratic convention with his nine-year-old son. At first, the youngster supported Barack Obama's idea of taxing the rich to help the poor. Then his father asked him what category he belonged to. When he realized that he belonged to the "rich," his support for the Democratic candidate vanished. As this example illustrates, our view of the optimal degree of redistribution tends to correspond to where we are in the income distribution. Many people are delighted to tax the rich—but only as long as the rich are those who make more than they do.

One important insight of economics is that taxes should fall most heavily on people whose behavior is least affected by them.[3] Suppose that houses are taxed on the basis of the number of windows they have. Homeowners will start to brick up windows to avoid the tax, even though doing so decreases their satisfaction with their houses—their *utility,* an economist would say. While each homeowner has an incentive to brick up windows and lower his tax bill, collectively homeowners would be worse off doing that. If the tax doesn't generate the necessary revenue, each taxpayer will be forced to pay roughly the same amount in some other form of taxation, except he will be living in a dark house.

Now imagine a different kind of tax, one that people cannot avoid by modifying their behavior—a tax on height, for example. Such a tax is preferable, an economist would say, because it cannot encourage taxpayers to distort their behavior and lose utility.

As we saw at the beginning of this book, people's view of taxation is heavily influenced by their perception of how income is obtained. When they perceive unequal income distribution as the result of luck, they are more likely to accept redistribution. In this sense, the fight against crony capitalism will help relieve pressure for redistribution.

BAD TAXES

Most taxes designed to raise revenue have a distorting effect on incentives, especially on people's willingness to work. Just as a tax on cigarettes reduces the amount of smoking, an income tax reduces the amount of work people do in the formal sector. My next-door neighbor chose not to work, and instead to stay home and take care of his kids, because his wife's income put him in a high income bracket. Had he worked and hired a baby-sitter, he would have had to pay taxes on his income and on the baby-sitter's income. By staying at home, he enjoyed tax-free baby-sitting.

Harvard economist Martin Feldstein, using the 1986 tax reform, estimated that when marginal tax rates on the top income bracket dropped from 50 percent to 28 percent, reported taxable income increased by 44 percent.[4] This didn't fully make up for the reduction in revenues caused by the reduction in the tax rates, but it did pay for half of it and exposed the inefficiency of high taxation.

Many economists have challenged or qualified Feldstein's results. The main qualification is that much of the sensitivity of reported income to taxes is due to tax elusion and evasion, not to people's working harder.[5] But the ability to dodge taxes is a function of the legal code, one that we can reduce and possibly eliminate by getting rid of preferential treatment and loopholes, as I recommended in the previous chapter.

If we exclude tax dodging, taxable income doesn't respond to lower marginal tax rates quite as quickly as in Feldstein's study, but the effect is still there for earners who make more than $100,000 a year.[6] As for outright millionaires, there are so few of them that conducting a large study is difficult. Still, it is legitimate to ask how much superstars—major-league athletes, movie stars, top lawyers and financiers, and so forth—are affected by the marginal tax rates. Would Tiger Woods skip the Masters Tournament if his tax rate went up? Probably not.

However, if Tiger Woods's tax rate went up significantly, he *could* easily move to another country. A study of European soccer stars shows that they move disproportionately to lower-tax countries.[7] Sweden finds itself unable to attract many foreign players and has lost several superstars. This correlation could be spurious, but Spain offered a kind of natural experiment in 2004 by introducing preferential tax treatment for foreign players. Sure enough, the number of foreign stars in Spain increased. Interestingly, the higher a European country's highest marginal tax rate, the worse its club teams in the European Championship League tend to perform. If entrepreneurs behaved like soccer players, the cost of a high marginal tax rate would be very high indeed.

If the government incurred no expenses or had other sources of revenue (like Kuwait's oil revenue), we could get rid of taxes altogether. Unfortunately, in most countries, including the United States, that is not possible. Yet we can reduce the burden by raising revenues through good taxes.

GOOD TAXES

"Good tax" may sound like the ultimate oxymoron at first. But there are certain cases in which taxes may correct distorted economic incentives, doing free markets a favor. Let's begin by recognizing, as even the libertarian tradition acknowledges, that individual freedom has limits: one person's actions may not interfere with another person's freedom. A musician's freedom to play his saxophone at night interferes with his neighbors' freedom to sleep. For this reason we impose limits on behavior, such as making excessive noise at night.

Absolute prohibitions, however, tend to be very inefficient. For instance, if the musician's only neighbor is deaf, then an absolute prohibition on excessive noise at night reduces the musician's utility without increasing the utility of his neighbor. The prohibition becomes much more efficient if it is not absolute. If the damage the musician causes with his playing is less than the benefits that he receives from playing, he can offer a side payment to his neighbor, maybe a promise to water his garden when he travels, in exchange for his tolerance for late rehearsals. Such a contract will leave both of them better off. In the absence of any prohibition at all—this would be a laissez-faire approach—the outcome would again be efficient, though a change would take place in who pays whom: the neighbor who wants to sleep would compensate the musician for not playing, rather than the other way around.

Most electric power plants release pollutants. If we were to prohibit pollution absolutely, most power plants would have to be shut down. But if we take the laissez-faire approach and permit a plant to pollute without reservation, how can its neighbors combat excessive emissions? They cannot easily pay it to curb its emissions (the equivalent of the neighbor's paying the saxophonist to be quiet). You might answer that the Environmental Protection Agency is supposed to intercede in such a case, by allowing the power plant to operate only when the cost of pollution to the neighbors is lower than the benefit of energy production. Unfortunately, as noted throughout this book, government agencies tend to be captured and represent the interests of industry, so there would be no guarantee such regulation would work.

In this case, a tax is an effective alternative. A tax equal to the negative impact that elevated emissions have on the local community will force the producer to factor that cost into his decision-making. When market prices fail to incorporate part of the cost that an activity generates, as is often the case with pollution, such a tax will be beneficial, regardless of the revenue it generates.

But is the tax-setting process less likely to be captured than the regulatory process? It is reasonable to assume so, since the tax-setting process is less demanding of information than the regulatory one is. When the need for information is smaller, lobbies have less power. When the discussion is simpler, democratic control is greater. A vote in Congress on taxing pollution has a better chance of not being captured than an obscure regulatory decision made by a captured agency. Even if the agreed-upon tax is too low, at least we face only the cost of pollution, not the cost of pollution plus the waste of taxpayers' money represented by the cost of the government agency plus the cost of all the distortions to entry that the agency will introduce in the industry in the interest of the incumbents.

The goal of this type of tax (named *Pigouvian* after Arthur Pigou, the British economist who invented it) is to correct distorted incentives, not to raise revenue. If it does generate revenue, however, we have a double benefit: we improve efficiency and we save the need to impose distortionary taxes to pay for government expenses. The tax on tobacco is an example of a Pigouvian tax, if we consider the cost of Medicare and Medicaid to be a cost imposed on the rest of society.

TWO USEFUL PIGOUVIAN TAXES

A Pigouvian tax that has been proposed but not implemented is one on short-term debt held by financial institutions. One of the lessons of the 2008 financial crisis is that an excessive amount of short-term debt financing by financial institutions can easily transform a relatively small loss into a major crisis. When subprime losses hit financial intermediaries in 2007–2008, short-term lenders, fearing bankruptcy, refused to renew lending. This withdrawal of funds forced the intermediaries to sell assets, depressing prices further. It was similar to a traditional bank run, except initiated by short-term lenders.

So why did the financial intermediaries, which could have anticipated this risk, choose to borrow so much in the short term? Because it allowed them to borrow more and borrow more cheaply, increasing profits. The short-term lenders, meanwhile, felt confident that they could get out of troubled companies in time. But while the exit option is available to each lender individually, it is not available to all lenders together. When all short-term lenders try to leave, they precipitate a crisis. In other words, the incentives to borrow short-term exceed what is optimal from a social point of view.

Some have argued that the best way to solve the problem is to eliminate the debt deduction. However, the real problem is not all debt but short-term debt. In an environment of close-to-zero interest rates, eliminating the debt deduction would have the perverse incentive of *favoring* short-term debt (on which the lack of deductibility would have almost no impact) over long-term debt.

A better solution is a tax on short-term debt, especially that held by financial institutions. By taxing the use of short-term debt (with maturity of less than a year, for example), we can discourage both excessive leverage and short-term leverage, preventing a crisis. Also, a 1 percent tax on outstanding short-term debt would raise $21.5 billion annually just among the top nine institutions. This is equal to the total amount of taxes raised from the 65 million households making less than $30,000 a year. So this tax could exempt 65 million households from paying taxes, while stabilizing the financial system and preventing a new crisis.

The ultimate Pigouvian tax is a progressive tax on corporate lobbying. Lobbying per se is not bad, but the imbalance in lobbying is. Larger companies lobby disproportionately more and consequently obtain disproportionately greater benefits. Heavily taxing lobbying, and redistributing the proceeds to support the arguments of the more diffused interests, would help level the playing field. It would also reduce the incentive to lobby—both because it would act as a disincentive on the activity being taxed and because each lobbying firm would know that part of its money was being used to support the opposing side. Finally, a heavy tax on lobbying would reduce shareholders' incentives to pressure their managers to lobby.

THE POLITICS OF TAX AND SUBSIDIES

In principle, government intervention should aim to alter prices in order to achieve some social benefit.[8] The goal of the intervention is to change incentives, and income redistribution is just a side effect, which, at least in principle, could be eliminated. Our current housing policy, for instance, makes owning relatively cheaper than renting, on the theory that homeownership enhances social stability. Federal student loans reduce the cost of college, on the theory that a highly educated workforce is desirable.

When it comes to nudging people to change their behavior, relative not absolute prices matter. A tax on sugar is equivalent to a subsidy to corn syrup: they both have the effect of increasing corn syrup consumption and reducing that of sugar. From a political point of view, however, this equivalence does not hold. Think about the above subsidies and how they would sell politically if we recast them as taxes. The popular home owner subsidy would become an unpopular tax on home rental; the progressive college subsidy would become a regressive tax on people who do not go to college.

Any careful reader would be quick to point out that there is a big difference between a subsidy to home ownership and a tax on home rental: in the first the government is giving money to people, in the other it is taking it away. Yet, the government is us: it does not create wealth, it simply redistributes it, destroying some of it in the process. Thus a proper comparison between these two policies should keep constant the overall government budget. If the policy is a subsidy, it should be considered in tandem with some other tax that raises the necessary revenues.

In the political debate this compensation never occurs. Ethanol subsidies enrich ethanol producers and gasoline taxes make gasoline consumers poorer. As a result, income redistribution becomes not just a side effect but the goal of the policy intervention. The change in incentives is just the fig leaf that gives some intellectual justification to an otherwise unappealing redistribution. When ethanol producers lobby for a subsidy to ethanol, they are trying to redistribute income in their favor: the benefit to the environment is just a good excuse. They use the social argument to make it appealing. Ideas are very powerful instruments of lobbying, and the most devastating effects of lobbying have occurred when the ideas are most appealing.

This design naturally leads to massive lobbying incentives. The benefit of subsidies is concentrated, while the cost is distributed among taxpayers. Thus lobbying in favor of subsidies will be much stronger than lobbying against it.

INVERTING THE PERVERSE POLITICS OF SUBSIDIES

The political dynamics of Pigouvian taxes is exactly the opposite. The burden of taxation falls on a concentrated and politically powerful

group, while the benefit is enjoyed by a dispersed and politically nonin-
fluential one: taxpayers. Politically, it is preferable to raise general tax
revenues. Since the burden of general taxation falls on a large number
of dispersed voters, raising income taxes slightly is easier than imposing
a tax on a specific product, such as pollution—even though the former
tax is distortionary, inducing people to work less, while the latter eliminates a distortion. This is the reason Pigouvian taxes are so rare.

But this is also precisely why I propose that we ban any form of subsidy and restrict government policy to Pigouvian taxes: these would be
few and really needed.

CONCLUSIONS

Taxes can be used to improve the system and raise revenue. Pigouvian
taxes in particular can provide a solution to the problem of regulatory
capture. They can be used to penalize excessive lobbying, and they can
also be used as a substitute for regulation. Because it reduces the information needed to regulate and is comparatively transparent, a system
based on Pigouvian taxes is less captured by vested interests—though
like any system of taxes, it is not perfect.

14

REFORMING FINANCE

The rules of finance are much too serious to be entrusted to bankers.

—Luigi Zingales (with apologies to
Georges Clemenceau)

T HE STRUCTURE OF FINANCIAL REGULATION IN THE
United States resembles sedimentary rock: each layer is the
legacy of a crisis, but there is nothing binding the layers together. The Federal Reserve was created in 1913 to address
the liquidity problems that occurred during the panic of 1907. The Federal Deposit Insurance Corporation (FDIC) was instituted in 1933 to
prevent the kind of bank runs that had forced more than 5,000 banks to
close in the early 1930s. The Securities and Exchange Commission (SEC)
came into being in 1934 to prevent the stock market manipulations that
had prevailed during the 1920s. The Office of Thrift Supervision was
created in 1989, following the savings and loan crisis of the late 1980s.
And the 2010 Dodd-Frank Wall Street Reform and Consumer Protection Act, which brought us the Financial Stability Oversight Council,
was, of course, the result of the most recent financial crisis.

So it's not surprising, when you consider their origins, that these agencies have been stepping on one another's toes. Transparency and investor protection, for example, have been pursued not just by the SEC (its proper role) but also by the Commodity Futures Trading Commission (CFTC) and the Fed. Similarly, the Fed, the FDIC, and the SEC have all been trying to help stabilize the financial system since the crisis began.

The current regulatory system runs into problems with coordination and the communication of information. Lack of coordination across different agencies can tempt industry to avoid regulation entirely. For example, state insurance regulators never oversaw credit default swaps, even though they were essentially insurance products, because they were called "swaps," which made them sound like standard derivatives. As for communication of information, remember the Bear Stearns crisis. Because the Fed didn't regulate investment banks—that was the SEC's job—it was late learning about the extent of Bear's poor financial condition or the risks that Bear's failure would pose to the entire banking system. Consequently, it had no time to plan a possible intervention. Or consider what happened after Bear's demise, when two separate teams of regulators, one from the Fed and the other from the SEC, planted themselves in the headquarters of Lehman Brothers. It wasn't until ten days before Lehman's bankruptcy that they started to pool their information.[1]

How to fix these problems? One common suggestion is centralization, in which all regulatory functions are rolled up into one organization, as Britain does with its Financial Service Authority (FSA). In practice, however, the FSA represents only a partial centralization, because some key monetary policy functions remain with the Bank of England. And during the Northern Rock crisis, Britain's supposedly centralized system failed at the very job for which it was created: effective coordination.

Another possibility is the so-called functional approach to regulation, in which regulators oversee entities according to the kind of function that those entities perform. So, for instance, the same regulator would oversee money-market funds and banks, since they perform the same function—providing short-term liquidity to individuals and firms. But the functional approach maximizes the risk of capture: the more specific a regulator's human capital, the more likely the regulator is to be captured by the regulated entity.

Further, the functional approach does nothing to eliminate two more problems with our current regulatory system. The first is trade-offs among different objectives. At the risk of oversimplification, I would say that government intervention in the financial system has three main goals: price stability; protecting investors and borrowers against fraud and abuses; and financial-system stability. At present, the various regulatory agencies have to make troubling trade-offs among these three objectives. For example, when the Fed extended a loan to Citigroup's ring-fenced toxic assets to help prop up the bank, it traded price stability for financial stability. If those assets turned out to be worth much less than expected, the Fed would find it impossible to re-coup the liquidity it injected, which would risk causing an increase in inflation, because it would have pumped money into the economy backed by nothing. Having such trade-offs made within agencies, and thus nontransparently, poses serious risks.

The second problem with our current system is that when responsi-bilities overlap, it's hard to hold any one agency or individual account-able for any outcome. Whose fault was it that Bear Stearns was forced into a shotgun merger with JPMorgan? Was it the SEC's for failing to oversee the risk of investment banks, or the Fed's for failing to provide liquidity, or was it a lack of coordination between the two or all of the above? As long as fundamental goals are divided in this way, the blame game will prevent anyone from taking responsibility for the results.

Hence the need to rethink regulatory architecture along clear lines of responsibility and goals. We should allocate financial regulation and supervision to three different agencies, each responsible for only one of the three principal goals of financial-system regulation. One agency would be in charge of price stability, more or less conducting the tradi-tional monetary policy that the Fed currently conducts. A second agency would focus on protecting the little guys, whether they're in-vesting in stock, depositing funds at a bank, borrowing from a bank, or buying an annuity or other insurance product. Finally, a third agency would be tasked with systemic considerations, absorbing some of the extraordinary roles that the Fed has taken on during the current crisis, together with other solvency issues (often overseen by state insurance regulators).

The beauty of such a system is that each of the three agencies would have a simple and easily measurable goal. The price-stability agency would have to control inflation. Its effectiveness could easily be measured by the inflation expectations embedded in the difference between standard Treasury bonds and Treasury inflation-protected securities (TIPS). The investor-protection agency's success could be measured through surveys of the trust that people feel in the stock market and other financial institutions. The system-stability agency's goal would be minimizing the risk of a systemic collapse. Its accomplishments could be measured by the price of credit default swaps on the major financial institutions, which captures the probability that these institutions might fail. Major trade-offs among these goals—which, as we've seen, present serious difficulties in the existing setup—would have to occur across agencies, not within them, and thus be conducted in a more transparent fashion.

The main challenge of such a design would be striking these compromises across agencies and communicating crucial information among them. A new board could be set up consisting of the heads of the three agencies, together with a small number of other Senate-appointed representatives. Just as with the Fed board, the minutes of this new board would be publicly released (possibly with a delay), so that the trade-off decisions were transparent and the responsibility for them clearly allocated.

In a sense, this board would not be that different from the Financial Stability Oversight Council, with the main difference being that it would have fewer than ten members instead of twenty-seven. Overly staffed committees do not work. Either the legislators who create them are fools or they do so in bad faith, intending them to fail. I favor the second interpretation.

MONETARY POLICY

Let's examine the three goals of financial regulation one by one, starting with price stability. The relevant agency here is the Federal Reserve, which is charged with making the monetary policy that keeps prices stable. The Fed was wisely designed to be an independent agency, run by experts rather than career politicians. The reason is that when an election is approaching, an elected official could be tempted to increase the money supply to stimulate the economy, even if this would lead to higher inflation down the line.

During the 2008 financial crisis and its aftermath, however, the Fed overstepped its boundaries by acting to ensure the stability of the financial system. This amounted to engaging in *fiscal* policy—and in a country founded on the principle of no taxation without representation, fiscal authority assumed by an unelected agency is rightly viewed with suspicion. So the Fed has been under severe attack by Congress, which would like to limit its discretion.

Congress is correct, although the Fed's missteps are the fault not of its governors but of bad institutional design. By dividing the three major responsibilities of financial regulation among three separate agencies, my proposed architecture allows for having a fully independent monetary authority board *and* a politically accountable financial-stability board.

CONSUMER PROTECTION AND FINANCIAL INNOVATION

Economic theory has a lot to say about which securities should and should not exist but little to say about which new kinds of securities should be created. In other words, it is not good at explaining financial innovation.

One reason for financial innovation is the need to increase the extent to which risk is shared. As companies grew larger in the nineteenth century, the risk of owning them became too big for a single individual to bear. Tradable stock was an innovation that shared risk among many small investors, allowing industry to grow. Another kind of risk is fluctuating home values. Suppose that your job requires you to move to Las Vegas. You do not want to live there the rest of your life, but finding an apartment big enough to accommodate your family is difficult, so you consider buying a house. That step, though, means taking an enormous risk. If you had moved to Las Vegas in 2000 and departed in 2005, the value of your house would have soared 115 percent. If you had moved to Las Vegas in 2005 and departed in 2010, the value of your house would have dropped by 54 percent.[2] To allow people to share the risk they bear in their house investments, Yale economist Robert Shiller has tried to jump-start a futures contract linked to the price of houses in different markets, with mixed results.

Another reason for financial innovation is the desire to reduce the friction that hampers finance. Automatic teller machines were invented to reduce transaction costs, as were credit cards. Similarly, securities backed by an entire pool of mortgages were invented to reduce the informational asymmetry between the loan underwriter and the buyer. If an underwriter sells individual loans, he can cherry-pick the loans to sell. Anticipating that this cherry-picking will give him the worst loans, the buyer will offer much less for each loan than they might be worth. Selling all the loans issued during a certain period avoids this problem.

In all of those examples, financial innovations created value. Unfortunately, not all financial innovations do so. Some are designed to reduce taxes or elude regulations. Others are designed to dupe or cheat investors. Sometimes these two motives are intermingled. Take, for example, the derivatives sold to local municipalities, which helped those municipalities hide their true fiscal situation from voters. Similarly, the Bush and Obama administrations used financial innovation to hide the subsidies paid to financial institutions. As an assistant Treasury secretary in the Bush administration wrote, "An essential insight of the policies undertaken throughout the fall [of 2008] is that providing insurance through non-recourse financing is economically similar to buying assets—indeed, underpricing insurance is akin to overpaying for assets. But insurance is much less transparent than either asset purchases or capital injections and therefore politically preferable as a means through which to provide subsidies to financial market participants."[3]

It might be tempting to conclude that we should regulate financial innovation—to the extent, say, that we already regulate pharmaceutical innovation. Yet drug regulation has been criticized on the grounds that it restricts competition; regulating financial innovation would be subject to the same criticism.

Rather than restricting innovation, I suggest fixing the problems that might lead innovation astray. Here, one problem is that people can easily be duped by overly sophisticated products. But this is not a reason to ban such products; it is a reason to restrict who can have access to them. Fixed-rate long-term mortgages and index funds are products that less sophisticated investors can understand and use. Adjustable-rate mortgages, specialized exchange-traded funds, and individual stocks are intermediate products, suitable for moderately sophisticated investors. And only the most sophisticated investors should use products like double short exchange-traded funds and negative amortization mortgages. To ensure that the appropriate type of investor uses each product, it is enough to assign the burden of proof to the seller. Thus, in case of litigation, the bank that sold a negative amortization loan to an investor must prove that the borrower was sophisticated enough to understand the product.

Another potential problem with financial innovations is that CEOs may use them to "manage" earnings. The solution, again, is not to prohibit these innovations outright but to forbid managers from using sophisticated products unless explicitly authorized by the shareholders. With provisions like these, we can enjoy the benefits of financial innovation without bearing its costs and the cost of regulation.

SAVING MARKETS

Many free-market economists think that well-functioning markets arise naturally in a laissez-faire economy.[4] Unfortunately, this is not the case. A free market's infrastructure and *liquidity*—the presence of many buyers and sellers at the same time—are the ultimate public good: everybody benefits with no cost. Yet individual market participants, especially powerful ones, can benefit from trying to restrict competition and hollow out liquidity. Here lies a fundamental challenge for libertarians. Unrestricted freedom of contract can lock in potential traders in a way that dries up liquidity and prevents market development. If companies could lock in workers at a young age, for instance, the labor market for managerial talent would be constricted. The more comprehensive contracts can be, the shallower the market. This is one of the reasons for prohibiting indentured servitude (in which a person sells his future labor services). The same applies to securities markets. As powerful banks try to exchange securities over the counter, markets become less liquid. For this reason, separating investment and commercial banking, as required by the Glass-Steagall Act, was essential to jump-starting the development of a liquid securities market in the United States.

As I explained earlier, securities markets need to be regulated because in anonymous markets, reputation cannot restrain fraud and abusive practices. The backbone of US securities law was designed in the 1930s to protect small investors against the abuses perpetrated in the 1920s. At that time, individuals owned 90 percent of publicly traded equity.[5] By 2007, that figure had dropped to less than 30 percent.[6] Most of this share is represented by management and insiders, who collectively own 24 percent of the equity in a typical company. At the same time, the percentage of US equity owned by institutions has risen from less than 10 percent to more than 60 percent. Since institutions account for more than a proportional share of trading, we can assert that institutions do almost all daily trading of US stock. On the one hand, this change in stock ownership has made the need to protect unsophisticated investors less urgent. On the other hand, this dispersion of ownership heightens the need to reform corporate governance, empowering institutional investors and making corporate managers more accountable.

The past thirty years have seen over-the-counter (OTC) markets expand at the expense of organized exchanges. The notional values of derivatives contracts traded OTC went from less than $100 trillion in 1998 to almost $700 trillion in 2007.[7] Similarly, funds raised in the private equity market (that is, equity not traded in an organized exchange and not sold to small investors) rose from less than $5 billion in 1980 to more than $250 billion in 2006.[8] This migration from public to private markets suggests that the regulatory gap between the two is excessive. To narrow it, we should deregulate public markets and introduce some disclosure standards into the private one. In public markets, empowering institutional investors, as I have recommended elsewhere, would make it possible to transform some mandatory regulations into optional rules, following the British comply-or-explain system. On the private front, there are compelling reasons to mandate a delayed-disclosure provision in which hedge funds, private equity funds, and even companies' private equity funds report information and performance with a one- to two-year delay. This delay has the benefit of reducing the competitive cost of disclosure, while at the same time allowing for a serious statistical analysis of this market, which will improve allocation of savings.

To fix the stability problems associated with OTC derivatives, we need to move the bulk of derivative trading onto organized exchanges, where daily collateral requirements would guarantee systemic stability and price transparency would force competition, reduce margins, and increase the market's depth. In the United States, the Dodd-Frank Act moves in this direction, and similar efforts are under way in Europe. Nevertheless, the journey is still a long one. The major investment banks are fully aware that every day they delay appropriate market regulation, they earn millions of dollars for their managers' bonus funds.

CURBING RISK ON WALL STREET

We would like the market to be able to assess the risks of large financial institutions. But it cannot do that if market players know that those institutions will be bailed out in a crunch; that is, the existence of a "too big to fail" policy makes it difficult for the market to measure and analyze risk, as I noted in Chapter 4. One option is simply to outlaw the "too big to fail" policy—but such an inflexible approach might prove very costly one day, preventing Congress from acting as catastrophe loomed.[9]

Fortunately, there may be another solution. As many observers have noted, the government's reason for bailing out large financial institutions actually isn't that they're so *large* that their demise would crush the whole system. Rather, the concern is that they have such extensive *interconnections* with other financial institutions—through their various transactions, obligations, and contracts—that a default might trigger losses among an enormous number of counterparties, producing further defaults that could cascade out of control.

To function properly, the financial system needs to operate under the assumption that certain assets, such as deposits, are worry-free. A depositor with money in, say, checking and savings accounts should not have to monitor counterparty solvency or worry about which banks his own bank has dealings with. This sense of security saves a great deal of anxiety and cost and allows the system to operate more efficiently. But the system can sustain this trust only if people do not question the prompt and full repayment of so-called sensitive or systemically relevant obligations. People need to know that even if their banks collapse, not just bank deposits but also short-term interbank borrowing and the network of derivative contracts are secure enough not to suffer.

Once we understand that the issue addressed by "too big to fail" is the interconnectedness of large financial institutions, and therefore the stability of the larger system, we can make some important distinctions. Not all of the debt issued by large financial institutions and not all of the transactions they engage in are systemically relevant or in need of comprehensive protection. Specifically, long-term debt is not systemically relevant, since it is mostly held not by large financial institutions but within the massive portfolios of mutual and pension funds, which can absorb losses in such debt in the same way they absorb losses in equity investments. A default on long-term debt, therefore, would not trigger a cascade of bank failures the way a default on short-term debt could.

The solution is regulation that protects the systemically relevant obligations of large financial institutions—making sure that these institutions, not the taxpayers, would repay the obligations in case of bankruptcy—but that leaves open the possibility that nonsystemically relevant obligations would not be protected. Under this new system, banks would be required to hold two layers of capital to protect their systemically relevant obligations. The first layer would be basic equity. This requirement is not very different from today's standard capital requirement, except that the amount of equity required would be determined not by an accounting formula but by a market assessment of the risk contained in the second layer.

That second layer would consist of so-called junior long-term debt, which means that the institution would repay it only after making good on its other debt. This junior debt would therefore involve more risk for those who bought it, as well as higher rates of return. It would provide an added layer of protection to basic equity because, in the event the institution defaulted, the junior debt could be paid back only after other, more systemically relevant obligations had been repaid. Perhaps most important, because this layer of debt would be traded without the assumption that it would always be protected by federal bailouts, it would make possible a genuine market assessment of its value and risk—and therefore of the value and risk of the financial institution itself.

This is the crucial innovation of my proposed approach. The second layer of capital would allow for a market-based trigger to signal that a firm's equity cushion was thinning, that its long-term debt was potentially in danger, and therefore that the financial institution was taking on too much risk. If that warning mechanism provided accurate signals and the regulator intervened in time, even the junior long-term debt would be paid in full. If not, the institution might burn through some of the junior debt layer, but its systemically relevant obligations would generally still be secure. The firm could suffer, but the larger financial system would remain safe.

This remedy would work more or less like the margin call system in the stock market. When an investor buys stocks on margin, he puts down only part of the cost; as a result, he must show that he has enough collateral to cover the risk his broker is taking in lending him the money to make up the difference. If the stock price drops below an agreed-on level, that risk increases. The broker then issues a margin call, which means that the buyer must either provide additional collateral or sell his stock to pay back the broker in full. The system of financial regulation I am proposing would treat large banks in the same way. They would have to show the regulator that they had enough collateral (in the form of equity) to ensure that all of their debt—not just the systemically relevant part—could be paid in full. And if declines in the value of their underlying assets put the banks' debt at greater risk, they would face a kind of margin call from the regulator, forcing them either to post additional capital or to submit to liquidation. Either way, their debt would be repaid.

The success of this system rests, of course, on the timely intervention of the regulator. If the "margin call" is too slow in coming, the bank's long-term creditors could be at risk (though as long as the delay is not too severe, the systemic obligations would still be shielded). Thus it is essential to have an effective mechanism that assesses risk and triggers a response, warning the regulator and compelling swift action.

In a normal margin account, a broker considers the total value of the investment—which is easily determined, since all assets are traded—and compares the value of the collateral his client has posted with the likely risk of loss. If the collateral is insufficient to cover a plausible decline in the stock's value, he calls for more. But in the system I propose, the value of the financial institution's assets is not as easy to determine, since those assets—commercial loans and home equity lines, for example—are not standardized and not frequently traded, which means that they do not have a clear price. It is therefore difficult to tell when the equity the bank has posted is too thin to protect the existing debt. What, then, would the triggering mechanism be?

Ideally, such a trigger would be market-based—tied to the price of some traded security. The breadth and diversity of the market would shield such a signal from political pressures like those that can be focused on a single credit-rating agency or government regulator. To avoid unnecessary fluctuations and false alarms, the trigger should be a security traded in a market with a lot of liquidity and therefore stability. And its price should be closely linked to the financial event we want information about: whether or not an institution's long-term debt is at risk. Equity prices fail to satisfy this final criterion. As long as there is the possibility of a significant upside, equity prices will stay relatively high even when the company is close to bankruptcy and its debt is at risk of not being paid in full. The price of the junior long-term debt would be a better place to look. When the equity cushion is running thin, that long-term debt becomes endangered and will start trading below par. This option, though, fails to meet another criterion, since the bond market, where such debt might be traded, is highly segmented and illiquid. Bond prices are therefore unreliable signals.

There is one security that is linked to bond prices but remains very liquid—the credit default swap (CDS), essentially an insurance claim that pays off if the underlying entity fails and creditors are not paid in full. The buyer of a CDS for a bank's debt, for instance, makes periodic payments to a third-party seller; if the bank defaults on that debt, the buyer receives a payoff. (A CDS differs from insurance in that the buyer need not actually own the underlying security—here, the bank's debt.)

Since a CDS is basically a bet on the odds of a particular firm's failure, its price reflects the market's assessment of how likely it is that the firm's debt will not be repaid in full. It thus offers exactly the instrument we seek. Under my system, the CDS price for a bank's long-term debt would be used to gauge the risk of the equity cushion's being devoured by losses. If the CDS price were to rise above a critical threshold—thereby flagging imminent danger—the regulator would force the institution in question to issue equity by offering new stock for sale until the CDS price moved back below the threshold. If the price did not fall below that threshold within a predetermined period, the regulator would intervene.

Credit default swaps have developed a bad reputation and are often cited as one cause of the financial crisis. The problem, though, was not with credit default swaps but with the way they were traded: in opaque markets in which companies like AIG could sell the swaps without posting the proper collateral. When traded in an organized exchange with proper collateral, the CDS is a useful instrument for reducing exposure to credit risk. Fortunately, there is a clear trend toward moving credit default swaps onto exchanges, which will naturally require better collateralization to protect exchange members. Thus it seems likely that CDS prices will become increasingly reliable.

Another benefit of this transparent, market-based signal is that it helps address two major risks posed by regulatory intervention in the financial system. One is that a regulator could arbitrarily close down well-functioning financial institutions for political reasons. The other is that a regulator, under intense lobbying by the regulated, might be too soft—a phenomenon known in banking literature as *regulatory forbearance* (and a contributing factor to the 2008 crisis). My mechanism removes most of the regulator's discretion to make either error. The regulator cannot intervene if market prices do not signal distress but would find it difficult to avoid intervening if the market did signal—to everyone—that a firm is in trouble. I would even allow bondholders in a regulated institution to sue the regulator for not responding to a trigger that was clearly set off.

What form should the regulator's intervention take? Here, too, the presence of a market-based trigger for action makes it possible to adopt targeted, prudent measures that avert both overreaction and underresponse. If the trigger were set off by a CDS price that was too high, the regulator would be required to subject the financial institution to a stress test to determine if it was indeed at risk. In a stress test, regulators use sophisticated algorithms to run "what if" scenarios that examine whether a financial institution has sufficient assets to survive serious financial shocks. It would be important for the regulator to apply the stress test before taking any other actions; otherwise, those actions could cause panic that could damage the institution. If, for instance, the regulator allowed rumors to spread about a bank's strength, investors might lose confidence in the bank, start buying credit default swaps as protection, and make the CDS price rise still further.

If the bank passed the test and proved that the CDS price was not accurate, the regulator would then declare the company adequately capitalized. But if the bank failed the test, the debt was found to be at risk, and issuing equity did not improve its situation, then the regulator would replace the institution's CEO with a receiver or trustee. This person would be required to recapitalize and sell the company, guaranteeing in the process that shareholders were wiped out and junior creditors—while not wiped out—received a "haircut," meaning that the value of what they were owed would be reduced by a set percentage. That haircut is crucial to ensuring that the market prices credit default swaps in a way that takes regulator interventions seriously—showing that creditors will pay a price for an institution's failure—and so makes the trigger more reliable.

This regulatory receivership would be similar to a mild form of bankruptcy. But while it would achieve the chief goals of bankruptcy—imposing discipline on investors and management—it would avoid bankruptcy's worst cost—the possibility that one firm's failure could take down the entire financial system.

A potential risk of this proposal is that the news that a regulator is performing a stress test on a bank might scare off the short-term creditors and induce a run on the bank. This problem can easily be fixed by having the regulator guarantee the bank's senior debt for the duration of the stress test. With my early warning system and double layer of protection, the systemic obligations (which, in my mechanism, are all senior debt) will essentially always be paid. So the government is not assuming real risk; it is only defusing the risk of a run. This guarantee can then be lifted when the bank is deemed well capitalized (and more junior debt is issued) or, if the bank is put into receivership, when it emerges from receivership.

CONCLUSIONS

A financial system that helps penniless entrepreneurs transform their dreams into reality is a laudable goal, as is facilitating homeownership. Any laudable goal, however, can be abused when it is used as a fig leaf to cover naked self-interest. The combination of strong vested interests and a powerful ideological justification is irresistible: intellectuals who want money are bought off, and those who are principled are captured by the ideology. To avoid a similar problem, I have tried to design market-friendly financial regulations that begin with identifying the inefficiencies in the marketplace.

15

DATA TO THE PEOPLE

Knowledge is power.

—Francis Bacon, English philosopher,
statesman, and scientist

T HROUGHOUT HUMAN HISTORY, THE TWO MAIN FORMS OF economic interaction have been resource-grabbing and mutual cooperation. Resource-grabbing, which appeals to our selfish side, helps enlarge the slice of the societal pie that a person receives, but it often reduces the size of the pie itself. Mutual cooperation, which appeals to our empathetic and compassionate side, increases the size of the pie but not necessarily of the slice that each person receives.

Adam Smith had the brilliant insight that in competitive markets, mutually beneficial cooperation could be sustained by relying on the self-interested component of human nature. He didn't think that people lack a compassionate side; indeed, he recognized its existence at the beginning of *The Theory of Moral Sentiments*. Nor did he think that people should be selfish. Rather, he thought that if a system of cooperation could function even if people are selfish, it must be robust and resilient.

As Smith correctly pointed out, and as I have emphasized throughout this book, the genius of the free-enterprise system is competition. It is competition—the famous invisible hand—that aligns individual incentives (the selfish desire to have more) with social incentives (the desire to increase the size of the economic pie).

It took economists 150 years to formalize in mathematical models Smith's brilliant intuition in *The Wealth of Nations*. In doing so, they assumed the existence of well-functioning institutions. Yet markets do not arise spontaneously; they are human constructs and depend on a functional legal framework. The design of this framework and its enforcement affect how markets function and how the surpluses they generate are distributed. Besides the broader framework of law, markets also need very specific, smaller-scale rules to operate. Even the most competitive of all markets, the organized exchanges for commodities and securities, are shaped by hundreds of such rules.

From a distance, the rules may not seem that important. But they matter a great deal for the profitability of the parties involved in exchanges and for the efficiency of the market itself. A rule as trivial as the one specifying the number of digits in which securities are quoted has important effects. Securities in the United States were traditionally traded in fractions of eight, a convenient practice in the pre-computer world. In 2001, the Securities and Exchange Commission mandated a move toward the decimalization of quotes. This reduced the bid-ask spreads by 37 percent for securities listed on the New York Stock Exchange and by 50 percent for those traded on NASDAQ. It also reduced the amount of stock a trader was willing to buy or sell at the posted quote by 60 percent.[1] While the first outcome favored the small traders, who saw their transaction costs diminish, the second one potentially penalized the big ones, who saw the market's depth reduced.

The same tension between resource-grabbing and cooperation that exists in the economic sphere is present in the political sphere, where the rules of the game are designed. Does Smith's invisible hand also work here?

The feature necessary for the invisible hand to work in the economic realm is that individuals' decisions influence other individuals only through prices, not directly. Even if everybody else chooses to buy a red tie, I am free to purchase a blue one. The only way decisions by others affect me is through the price of red ties (which will go up). This rule clearly does not apply in the political arena. When politicians pass a law requiring securities to be traded in dollars and cents, rather than in fractions of eight, they have a direct impact on my ability to trade them.

The invisible hand can, however, shape the design of rules if the institutions designing the rules compete among themselves. For example, US states compete with one another for business and population, which could lead them to design the most efficient laws—not necessarily the most advantageous ones for powerful incumbents. Similarly, to the extent that rules and regulations affect the quality and price of traded goods and services, international free trade creates pressure toward more efficient rules and regulation and away from crony capitalism, a point Raghuram Rajan and I made in our book *Saving Capitalism from the Capitalists.*[2]

The problem is that most established institutions wield market power. The competition among organized exchanges is far from perfect, for example, and that among countries is even farther. While some rules (such as a restriction on capital movement) have direct and immediate negative effects on international competitiveness, other rules take time, sometimes decades, to make their damage manifest; in the meantime, incumbents can profit from market distortions. Further, pressure from foreign competition disciplines small countries far more effectively than it disciplines a large, influential country like the United States. There is no guarantee, therefore, that the political process will generate rules for the economy that increase the size of the pie instead of benefiting politically powerful groups. This is where the free-enterprise system can degenerate into crony capitalism.

Most free-market supporters think that the best way to prevent the rules being designed to favor powerful incumbents is pure laissez-faire. But pure laissez-faire is not lack of government intervention; it is active intervention to protect the status quo. (French philosopher Jean-Paul

Sartre illuminated the fact that we cannot avoid choices: not choosing is itself a choice.) If the interests of incumbents coincide with market development, as has occurred several times in history, laissez-faire does indeed lead to competition and free markets. Yet if it does not, pure laissez-faire can breed crony capitalism. Meanwhile, massive government intervention, as we have seen throughout this book, is plagued with problems and leads to worse forms of cronyism. So what is the solution?

In my view, government intervention in the economy should be so limited and so simple that voters can understand it, monitor it, and, if necessary, oppose it. What ultimately makes a capitalism for the people possible is a government by the people. Democracy is as essential to free markets as free markets are essential to democracy. Without free markets, freedom of speech and of the press becomes empty. Without democracy, the possibility of having truly free and competitive markets vanishes.

While democratic control of the rules of the economic game is essential, it is not without its own problems. As political scientist Anthony Downs explained more than fifty years ago, it is in voters' interest to remain ignorant. Yet if they do remain ignorant, they can't recognize policies that promote competitive markets—and politicians then have no incentive to make those markets more competitive.

Downs's argument is basically sound, but it goes too far. It is neither feasible nor desirable for all citizens to become informed on all issues. Nevertheless, most people have some interest in public affairs and spend resources to cast informed votes. Some are willing to spend time and money to buy and read books like this one. While I tried to make this book as entertaining as its complex subject (and my ability) allowed, reading it requires time and effort. It offers no advice on how to make money, nor does it provide any self-help tips. Your reading it to the end is proof that you are concerned about public affairs and are willing to make an effort to improve our institutions. The question is how to leverage a limited amount of similar effort by many people as an effective way to contain cronyism.

Earlier, we saw how muckraking journalists helped improve American capitalism by exposing corruption in business and government. At the dawn of the twenty-first century, corruption is more subtle but no less dangerous. To identify and expose it, we need data and people—not muckrakers alone—to analyze those data rigorously.

THE POWER OF DATA

While there is some truth in Mark Twain's celebrated statement that "there are three kinds of lies: lies, damned lies, and statistics," it reflects an excessive mistrust of numbers. Certainly statistics can be used to lie or mislead. Liars, however, will lie with or without statistics. The more relevant question is whether data analysis makes it easier or harder to lie or, more broadly, to create unfounded arguments to support vested interests.

I believe that data, when subjected to rigorous cross-checking, make it more difficult to support unfounded arguments. Part of this conviction comes from two decades spent at the University of Chicago. The school boasts a strong tradition of empirical research and an even stronger tradition of lively (read: brutal) seminar discussions. At most universities, a speaker is accorded respect, especially when he is an established member of the profession. At Chicago, status elicits no such respect. Our new dean, recruited from Stanford University, decided to start by giving a seminar in his area (operations research). A young assistant professor attacked him, saying that it was "unfortunate" that he made certain assumptions. What in most other places would be considered lack of respect is at Chicago an expression of collegiality. The system isn't always easy. Even after twenty years—I have to admit—I dread giving a seminar there. But I know that my work benefits tremendously from the sometimes painful experience. For this reason, we arrogantly say that a colleague loses twenty IQ points when he leaves Chicago: he misses the salubrious experience of the seminar. Over the years, I have come to compare this seminar with a colonoscopy: it is unpleasant but good for you.

The essence of rigorous data analysis is threefold: good data, smart people competing to find flaws in the analysis, and a level playing field where ideas matter and status doesn't. This combination can produce amazing results. Bill Christie and Paul Schultz, the two researchers who identified the "collusive" quotes on NASDAQ, were PhDs from Chicago.[3] So were the authors who identified the abnormal returns of mutual fund managers when they trade stocks of companies whose CEOs are college mates, a finding so sensitive that they had to avoid using any company names to escape being sued.[4] More recently, one of my students at Chicago, using Russian bank transaction data, was able to estimate that 60 percent of Russian firms employ schemes to evade taxes by at least 40 percent.[5] His findings were so detailed and explosive that I feared for his life, given Russia's lawlessness. His seminar at the Russian Central Bank had to be canceled when the vice governor who invited him was assassinated. Using Illinois transaction data, another Chicago PhD student, working before the financial crisis began, found that 16 percent of the highly leveraged house purchases inflated the transaction price.[6] For this to happen, both the lender and the borrower had to be complicit in the deception. I still remember the sense of disbelief that filled the room at the school when he tried to defend his ideas. Eventually he was vindicated. These researchers don't see themselves as heroes dedicated to cleaning up the corporate world. They simply are pursuing their self-interest: to publish and to get tenure. Nevertheless, in the proper competitive environment their work helps identify dodges and swindles. Indeed, to limit crony capitalism, we need good data and powerful incentives to analyze them.

DATA TO THE PEOPLE

When I was a young assistant professor I worked with confidential data at the Bank of Italy. For supervisory purposes, the Bank of Italy collects all the information (including the amount and rate charged) on all loans above a minimum threshold made by banks to Italian clients. While each bank can observe the amounts other banks lend, the rates remain hidden; only the Bank of Italy can see them. These data are so confidential that I had to work with a bank employee and I could observe only summary statistics, not individual data points.

The first paper I wrote was fairly innocuous; I examined whether banks lower the rate they charge when a firm goes public. Grasping the power of these data, I became more ambitious and asked permission to use them for a different project: to test whether industrialists sitting on a bank's board were getting a sweetheart deal from that bank. It is a simple question that could be answered with those data. It is also a question that the Bank of Italy, as supervisor and regulator of the Italian banking sector, should have found interesting. If the industrialists were getting sweetheart deals, it could weaken the bank and possibly jeopardize the stability of the banking sector. In spite of the potential regulatory implications and the brilliance of the idea (or so I thought), I was stonewalled. In my naïveté, I could not understand why bank officials seemed uninterested in finding out the truth. Now that I am older and more cynical, I think that the bank had no desire to confront reality. Its officials doubtless suspected the truth but wished to keep it hidden.

Data are a major challenge to power. All dictatorial regimes—including, notoriously, the Chinese government today—tightly control data and often manipulate them to prevent people from seeing the regimes' shortcomings. Sometimes the regimes get so involved in the manipulation game that the dictators themselves end up being manipulated. Italy entered World War II partly because Mussolini thought that his army was in better shape than it actually was. And he thought so because he was a victim of his own regime's propaganda.

Dictators are not the only ones who hide or manipulate data. CEOs try to do it all the time. Even honest ones have been known to use data to "beautify" results and hide their true performance. Democratically elected governments do it all the time, too. This effort to spin or control data is an indication of the disruptive power of information.

American banking regulators, for example, produce a confidential rating on bank solvency known as a CAMELS rating (for capital adequacy, asset quality, management and administration, earnings, liquidity, and sensitivity to market risk). The higher the CAMELS rating, the weaker a bank is considered. While there may be (debatable) reasons to keep these ratings confidential for a period of time (e.g., preventing a run on a weak bank), there is no persuasive reason to prevent their distribution after, say, a few years. Interestingly, though, the regulators aren't keen to see the data circulate, since they also reveal the regulators' own performance. A colleague of mine has tried to shed some light on the performance of bank regulators by teaming up with Fed employees with access to the data.[7] Yet the Fed will ultimately decide what data can be released. So much for freedom of inquiry!

In the past, data collection, storage, and analysis were extremely costly. This cost provided a justification for the people in power to refuse to collect data and analyze them. Today, this justification is gone; in a digital world, data are collected automatically and are easy to store and analyze. To protect the analysis of data from bias, however, access to them and the release of whatever they show should not be conditioned on the findings. This is one of the most important and often ignored benefits of mandatory disclosure. "Publicity," wrote Justice Louis Brandeis, "is justly commended as a remedy for social and industrial diseases."[8]

In part, the greater availability of data is a side effect of the evolution of the Internet. Much has been written about the role of social networks in igniting the 2011 Arab Spring protests. Less has been said about the Internet's role in making corporate data easily accessible. I have heard John R. Emshwiller, the *Wall Street Journal* reporter who uncovered the Enron scandal, credit his reporting to data available on the Internet. While waiting for an interview with Enron's then-CEO Ken Lay, he looked up the company's annual report online and noticed a strange footnote about special purpose vehicles, which can be ways firms hide debt off their books, away from investors' eyes. Lay's evasive answers on the subject led Emshwiller to dig deeper. The easy accessibility of the information proved crucial to exposing Enron's deception. The amount of business information available on the Internet is amazing. I have even found circulating online "secret" internal memos of companies for which I serve as a board member.

Dictatorial regimes, like China, have tried to muzzle the Internet through the use of filters. Yet the design of the Internet makes this hard. Historically, the media have been dominated by means of communications that diffused information from a center to a periphery, from few to many. Books, radio, and TV fit this description. Information spread in this way is easy to control and manipulate. This is not true for the Internet.

Arpanet, the direct precursor of the Internet, was funded by the Pentagon. While Bob Taylor, the official in charge at the time, denies that Arpanet had a military purpose, its decentralized structure resem-

bles a technology developed by a researcher at the RAND Corporation
to permit long-distance communication in case of nuclear attack. The
weakest point in any communication system is the coordinating center.
If it goes down, the entire system fails. By contrast, the decentralized
nature of the Internet makes it resilient to attacks. It is precisely this
feature, whatever its origin, that makes filtering information difficult
and allows communication from many to many.

Yet relying on the Internet alone to make business data available is
not enough. From over-the-counter markets to private equity markets,
from government regulators to corporations, there are plenty of data
that can shed light on mistakes, inefficiency, corruption, and unethical
behavior. While industrial secrets and privacy should be protected,
there is no justification for restricting access to old data, such as old
hedge fund trades or CAMELS ratings.

After the space shuttle *Challenger* disaster, the best minds of the
time—including Nobel laureate physicist Richard Feynman—were employed in an investigation in which no stone was left unturned. Ultimately, the culprit was identified as a defective O-ring that became too
stiff at low temperatures and caused a leak. To convince the public,
Feynman demonstrated that conclusion with a televised experiment.

A serious act of data omission was committed by the Financial Crisis
Inquiry Commission (FCIC), charged with finding the cause of the
2008 financial crisis. Economics might not be as precise a science as
physics, but this cannot justify the failure of the commission, which in-
vestigated the financial crisis. With sufficient data, economists do have
methods to identify the likely causes of an economic phenomenon. We
are even better at refuting potential explanations. The availability of
data might impose a limit on our ability, but not our methodologies. In
the case of the financial crisis, the data were not made available to economists, because the interested parties were (and remain) afraid to share
those data.

Unfortunately, the FCIC—composed mostly of elected officials,
rather than experts—wasted its time in political squabbles. Its members could not agree even on how to define subprime mortgages and
calculate how many such mortgages there were in the United States at
the time of the crisis. A subsequent investigation into the work of the

commission was more thorough than the commission's actual investigation of the crisis. Details in the commission's e-mails led the authors of a congressional report to find that the commission's work was guided by politics rather than by facts. After all, the "fixes" to the crisis had already been decided and approved, before any fact was found, and the commission's focus was on supporting or discrediting (depending on individual commissioners' political party affiliation) the Dodd-Frank legislation rather than on establishing the truth. It was a great opportunity lost.

With its subpoena power, the commission could have collected and released the data needed to answer many crucial questions about the crisis. Did companies that compensated their traders (and not just their CEOs) more highly take more risk? Did financial institutions assume excessive risk out of incompetence or stupidity, or were they responding rationally to the implicit guarantee of bailouts offered by the government? Did the market see the spread of lax lending standards and price the relevant pools of loans accordingly, or was it fooled? Who were the ultimate buyers of toxic financial products, and why did they buy them? How important was the role played by fraud? These questions are likely to remain unanswered without disclosure of data. If we don't answer them, there is a risk that we won't find out what really caused the financial crisis until the next one occurs.

PEOPLE TO THE DATA

All the data in the world are useless, however, if researchers fail to analyze them thoroughly. A noted macroeconomist once declared that the real world exists to provide data input for his models. This was a joke, of course, but it contained an element of truth. All too often in seminars I have seen economists reject data in favor of their preferred theories, the opposite of the proper scientific method, which is to correct or reject theories in the light of new data. This reflects an ivory-tower attitude, in which the means justify the ends. Our discipline should serve the economy, not the other way around.

At the beginning of the twentieth century, American writers broke with the European tradition of literary journalism and created investigative journalism. Making this important change possible were a competitive newspaper industry and a vast market of educated voters who made investigative journalism profitable. This revolution would not have occurred, however, if writing for the masses had retained its reputation as a lowbrow activity, as it is still considered in many academic circles. At the beginning of the twenty-first century, we need a new kind of investigator—academic muckrakers. The conditions are ripe. The American academic market is the most competitive in the world and demand is not lacking. However, we need to overcome the (bad) academic social norm that frowns on academics writing for a wider audience.

CONCLUSIONS

Economists like to think about inefficiency in terms of missing markets. Markets provide an effective way to harness individual self-interest to produce the common good. Consequently, when such harnessing fails, we believe that a market must be missing. Pollution, for instance, can be seen as the effect of the absence of a market for pollution rights. Not surprisingly, economists have tried to address the pollution problem by creating the market deemed to be missing (i.e., a market for emissions permits).

I believe that the ultimate missing market is for the right to design the rules of the market itself. Society as a whole benefits from a competitive market, but nobody is willing to pay the cost of creating it. In principle, political competition should provide the missing incentive. After all, if the public benefits from a competitive market, the politicians defending this principle should triumph at the polls. Unfortunately, the political market is distorted by asymmetries in power and by voters' ignorance on economic matters. If voters aren't informed on what policies truly promote competition, it won't pay for politicians to promote those policies. The distorted political market allows crony capitalism to triumph. We have seen that social norms can help us address market failures. I hope that this book helps create awareness of the need to accord social prestige to any effort to promote competition and resist crony capitalism. Academia can play a big role in this respect. If it fails to do so, it must be considered part of the problem.

16

PRO MARKET,
NOT PRO BUSINESS

WHAT DO PEOPLE WANT MOST FROM LIFE? MATERIAL well-being? That's important, but freedom is at least as important, and the two are intrinsically related. As I have argued in this book, intellectual freedom cannot exist without economic freedom; nor can economic freedom exist without intellectual freedom. In turn, both the economic system and the political system need values that legitimize them.

After the fall of the Berlin Wall, capitalist democracy was triumphant. It was the model that made the West prosperous, propelled the Asian tigers into the developed world, became the ideal of the former communist countries of Eastern Europe, and won the Cold War. The twenty years that followed witnessed the seemingly complete ideological triumph of the capitalist model. There seemed to be no alternative.

The intellectual hegemony of capitalism, however, led to complacency and extremism: complacency toward the degeneration of the system, extremism in the application of its ideological premises. Money—regardless of the way it was obtained—ensured not only financial success but social prestige as well. "Greed is good" became the norm rather than the frowned-upon exception. Capitalism lost its moral higher ground.

The 2007–2008 financial crisis and the Great Recession that ensued reopened the debate about economic models. The critics of capitalism suddenly felt vindicated. The crisis, they believed, proved what they had long been repeating: not only are markets unstable, but their wide fluctuations are costly to society. Suddenly this once-minority position started to go mainstream. From Occupy Wall Street to Occupy Davos, angry crowds gathered to protest against inequality, against banks, against the rich—against everything. Yet what they were protesting *for* was never clear. When some proposals emerged, they were the old ones: massive government intervention in the economy and income redistribution. These alternatives have been tried before, and, as we've seen, they do not work. In fact, the crisis itself can be blamed, at least in part, on government policies such as an accommodating monetary policy and the political desire to promote homeownership, which helped inflate a dangerous housing bubble.

The crisis, however, did not shake some free-market thinkers from their lethargy. In an attempt to return to the past, they shifted the entire burden of responsibility away from the private sector and toward the government. They blamed the crisis exclusively on Fannie and Freddie and government housing policy in general. Even if the government had been totally to blame for the crisis—and I do not think it was—these policies were not the result of its intervention *against* the financial industry. They were the outcome of intensive lobbying *by* the financial industry.

THE REAL TENSION

Trying to pit business and government against each other is increasingly a sideshow left over from twentieth-century ideological debates. Consider again the idea of a corporation so large that it faces little competition in the product market and has great sway over the political process.

Would an economy based on a few such companies, to continue the thought experiment, more closely resemble a capitalist system or a socialist one? In both cases, the coercive power of the government would be used to suppress freedom of entry. In both cases, the interests of producers would trump the interests of consumers. In both cases, concentrated economic and political power would lead to a suppression of intellectual freedom, though perhaps to different degrees: experts and opinion makers would be pressured to become cogs in a factory of consensus, with the dissidents deported to the gulag of irrelevance.

When there is no competition and a few exercise total political power, we have socialism. If there are a few corporations instead of a single large one—the state—the situation is better, true, but only by degree. Economic theory teaches us that unless many corporations exist and compete, a few big companies will prefer to collude against the public.

Fortunately, the United States remains far from this dystopia. Unfortunately, it is beginning to drift in that direction. As we have seen, there are many causes for this, but a major one is the intellectual confusion between a promarket system and a probusiness one. While the two agendas often coincide, blurring them encourages crony capitalism.

These are the real contrasts that face us: between meritocracy and inherited privilege, between accountability and discretion, between freedom and power, and between free markets and crony capitalism.

THE GENIUS OF COMPETITION

The true genius of the capitalist system is not private property, not the profit motive, but competition. Private property without competition leads to abusive monopolies, while competition can work wonders to maximize welfare even when private property is less than secure. The more *political* competition there is, the better the outcome in terms of policy and freedom. And as Adam Smith taught us (and as the two-hundred-year history of economics has confirmed), competition is the ultimate reason why free markets bring such abundant economic benefits.

For competition to work its wonders, though, we need rules. University of Chicago MBA students distorted the results of course bidding to exploit a loophole; likewise, businesses operating under bad rules produce distorted results. But where do we look for good rules? If we believe in the danger of regulatory, political, and intellectual capture, it is difficult to see how we can use the state's might to limit the political use of economic power. The cure might be worse than the disease.

The numerous proposals I have offered in this book try to resolve this conundrum. They aim cumulatively at reducing government intervention in the economy only in those cases in which doing so is likely to generate better outcomes. For example, a complete ban on government subsidies would invert the political dynamic in a way that fights cronyism. Industry would then lobby to keep taxes in check instead of to win government aid. When an issue becomes sufficiently important, such as the role that banks played in the financial crisis, a popular demand for government intervention will still arise. Yet did the intervention require the 2,300 pages of the Dodd-Frank Bill and sixty-seven follow-up studies? What if the problem had been stated to the public simply as "Should we tax banks' short-term funding or not?" Such a straightforward policy, were it approved, would have eliminated the employment opportunities of an army of lawyers and political consultants hired to navigate the new law.

Similarly, if Congress stuck to setting tax rates but refused to approve preferential tax treatment, this would minimize the risk of political distortions to the economy. My presumption, based on historical evidence, is that democratic governance works best when it does not demand too much of the citizenry. The only congressional votes that receive any scrutiny by the vast majority of voters involve simple issues that are controversial enough to demand a final roll call. The public pressure on these votes can overwhelm the influence of lobbyists.

ACCOUNTABILITY

Accountability based on access to government and business data is also crucial to protecting free markets. Most of these data are proprietary and those who control them will fight aggressively to protect them:

information is valuable and data dissemination could be a form of illegitimate expropriation. But there is an easy way out. Delayed disclosure of data could hardly hurt anyone and would shed light on suspicious patterns and cronyism. What also would help minimize cronyism is not a plethora of new government regulators (they are the first to be captured) but a village of potential whistleblowers. Whistleblowers benefit society but—on average—lose out personally: they find themselves fired and often ostracized. Finding ways to compensate whistleblowers for the valuable information they provide in fighting fraud would encourage more of them to come forward.

The best way to limit crony capitalism is to level the lobbyists' playing field. While it will never be perfectly level, data disclosure, whistleblower statutes, and class action suits certainly would help rectify its current tilt.

A MARKET-BASED ETHIC

Another important element of the agenda that this book advances is a rediscovery and renewal of the moral foundation of capitalism. Part of what supported the system in its early days was the widespread conviction that competition allows the best to emerge. This conviction provided moral legitimacy to the capitalist system as well as a social norm that helped support the functioning of capitalism itself. Money was a manifestation of success but not the sole purpose of economic life. Those who succeeded by breaking the rules were not rewarded with social prestige.

For capitalism to work this way, however, those who believe in free markets need to promote essential social norms. Despite certain excesses, political correctness has greatly contributed to tremendous improvements in America. Various groups' struggles for equality wouldn't have progressed so quickly if it weren't for the fact that discriminatory attitudes were not only prosecuted by the law but socially sanctioned as well. The same is true for smoking. Notwithstanding the active disinformation campaign of the tobacco industry, the scientific truth prevailed: smoking is now actively stigmatized. This social sanction has worked far better than prohibition would have. A similar battle needs to be fought in the economic arena. Opportunistic actions that are detrimental to society at large should be condemned and the people engaging in them shunned. Society scorns athletes who take performance enhancers. But what about businesses that lobby to extract subsidies from the government, a much more pernicious form of performance enhancer? Business schools—the institutions with the greatest interest in the long-term survival of capitalism—could lead this campaign to apply market-based norms to business.

Last but not least, this book highlights the important role that academia can play in such a battle. Intellectual competition fosters rigorous analysis and forces accountability. If this book spurs a debate on the role that academic economists can play as a watchdog for free markets, it will have achieved its goal of helping to recapture the genius of American prosperity—a capitalism for the people.

ACKNOWLEDGMENTS

WHILE MY NAME ALONE IS ON THE BOOK'S COVER, this work owes a debt to many people. First of all, my thanks go to my wife, Jill, who supported me morally and physically during this writing. I used to tease her that she never made it past page 10 of my previous book. She has more than redeemed herself in reading multiple drafts of this manuscript and giving me great encouragement and advice. It is not an overstatement to say that the book wouldn't have been written without her help.

This book owes a lot to the many wonderful co-authors who collaborated with me in the academic papers the book is based on. My profession's greatest benefit is that I not only get to work with very smart people but also get to pick who I work with, so I can be sure to work with the nicest people. I took full advantage of this benefit. Much of my earlier work was with Raghu Rajan, with whom I co-authored the earlier book. I learned a lot from Raghu. All my work on trust and civic capital was done with Luigi Guiso and Paola Sapienza. Our collaboration has turned into a deep friendship. My discussion of the role of media is based on joint work with Alexander Dyck and David Moss, while the one on whistleblowers was joint work with Alexander Dyck and Adair Morse. My work on the effects of the bailout was with Pietro Veronesi, who retaught me how to price contingent claims. The proposal on how to curb risk on Wall Street comes from joint work with Oliver Hart. Oliver was not only co-author on some of my journal articles, my former dissertation adviser, and one of the best living economists but also an example of moral and intellectual integrity. When I have any doubts about what might be right or wrong, I find his intellectual guidance invaluable.

At different times both Brian Anderson and Yuval Levin asked me unexpectedly to write for their magazines (*City Journal* and *National Affairs*, respectively).Their willingness to take a chance on a little-known author is evidence that meritocracy is still alive in this country. Working for them encouraged me to develop some of the arguments contained in this book.

I also owe a great debt to Brian Anderson, Ben Plotinsky, and Bernadette Serton at the Manhattan Institute, who helped edit this book and were very encouraging throughout the writing process. I am thankful, too, to Adrienne Schultz, who edited the first version of the manuscript, and to Conor Dewitt, Peggy Eppink, and Erika Morey, and especially to Cecilia Gamba, who helped with fact checking. I also want to thank the Initiative on Global Markets at the University of Chicago and the Stigler Center at the University of Chicago, which supported these research assistants financially.

I benefited from extremely helpful comments from many patient readers: Kete Cockrell, Harry Davis, Alessandro De Nicola, Darrell Duffie, Steve Haber, Todd Handerson, Oliver Hart, Mario Macis, David Moss, Enrico Piccinin, Eric Posner, Richard Posner, Paola Sapienza, Amit Seru, Francesco Trebbi, and Stefano Visentin. I owe them a great deal.

My deep thanks go to my wonderful agent, Eric Lupfer. And finally, I want to thank my editor, Tim Bartlett. In teaching venture capital I learned that there are two types of venture capitalists: the value adders, who spend time improving a company's chances of success, and the option buyers, who regard their investment in startups as financial options—you do nothing and hope you end up in the money. The same, I have found, is true with editors. Tim is definitely a value adder.

NOTES

FOREWORD TO THE PAPERBACK EDITION

1. Roy P. Basler, ed., Marion Dolores Pratt and Lloyd A. Dunlap, asst. eds., *The Collected Works of Abraham Lincoln* (New Brunswick, NJ: Rutgers University Press, 1955), 528.

2. See http://www.opensecrets.org/lobby/

3.See http://www.opensecrets.org/bigpicture/

4. Committee on Oversight and Government Reform. "How Countrywide Used Its VIP Loan Program to Influence Washington Policymakers," July 5, 2012.

5. Jean Eaglesham, "Who's Counting? Not U.S. on Convictions Tied to 2008–09 Crisis," *Wall Street Journal*, May 13, 2012.

6. Bill Scher, "How Liberals Win," *New York Times,* January 7, 2012.

INTRODUCTION

1. In 2010 the median *household* income was $49,445; in 2000 it was $53,164. See US Census Bureau, http://www.census.gov/hhes/www/income /data/historical/household/, table H-6.

2. In 2010 the median *personal* income for males aged twenty-five to thirty-four years was $31,793; in 1980 (in 2010 dollars) it was $39,250, with a loss of 19 percent. See US Census Bureau, http://www.census.gov/hhes/www /income/data/historical/people/, table P-8.

3. These Pew survey results can be found at http://www.people-press.org/2011/12/15/frustration-with-congress-could-hurt-republican-incumbents/.

4. S. Djankov, R. La Porta, F. Lopez-de-Silanes, and A. Shleifer, "The Regulation of Entry," *Quarterly Journal of Economics* 117 (February 2002): 1–37.

5. L. Guiso, P. Sapienza, and L. Zingales, "People's Opium? Religion and Economic Attitudes," *Journal of Monetary Economics* 50 (2003): 225–282.

6. Jonathan Reuter and Eric Zitzewitz, "Do Ads Influence Editors? Advertising and Bias in the Financial Media," *Quarterly Journal of Economics* 121, no. 1 (2006): 197–227.

7. Richard Smith, "Conflicts of Interest: How Money Clouds Objectivity," *Journal of the Royal Society of Medicine* 99 (June 2006): 292–297.

ONE

1. Rafael Di Tella and Robert MacCulloch, "Why Doesn't Capitalism Flow to Poor Countries?" Economic Studies Program, The Brookings Institution, *Brookings Papers on Economic Activity* 40, no. 1 (2009): 285–332.

2. A. Alesina, E. Glaeser, and B. Sacerdote, "Why Doesn't the US Have a European-Style Welfare State?" Economic Studies Program, The Brookings Institution, *Brookings Papers on Economic Activity* 32, no. 2 (2001): 187–277.

3. Primo Rapporto Luiss, *Generare Classe Dirigente: Un Percorso da Costruire* (Rome: Luiss University Press, 2007).

4. US Office of Management and Budget, http://www.whitehouse.gov/omb/budget/Historicals; see also B. R. Mitchell, *International Historical Statistics: The Americas 1750–1988* (New York: Stockton Press, 1993).

5. See Daron Acemoglu, Simon Johnson, and James Robinson, "Reversal of Fortune: Geography and Institutions in the Making of the Modern World Income Distribution," *Quarterly Journal of Economics*, November 2002, vol. 117, pp. 1231–1294, and Acemoglu, Daron, Simon Johnson, and James Robinson, "The Colonial Origins of Comparative Development: An Empirical Investigation," *American Economic Review*, December 2001, vol. 91, pp. 1369–1401.

6. Adam Hochschild, *King Leopold's Ghost: A Story of Greed, Terror, and Heroism in Colonial Africa* (Boston: Mariner Books, 1999).

7. R. Rajan and L. Zingales, "The Great Reversals: The Politics of Financial Development in the 20th Century," *Journal of Financial Economics* 69 (2003): 5–50.

8. L. Guiso, P. Sapienza, and L. Zingales, "Does Local Financial Development Matter?" *Quarterly Journal of Economics* 119 (2004): 929–969.

9. *Moore v. American Tobacco et al.,* Case No. 94–1429, filed May 23, 1994.

TWO

1. This is the title of a book about the early history of southeastern Pennsylvania. See James T. Lemon, *The Best Poor Man's Country* (Baltimore: Johns Hopkins University Press, 1972).

2. Julia B. Isaacs, "International Comparisons of Economic Mobility," *Economic Mobility Project*: An Initiative of The Pew Charitable Trusts, www.pewtrusts.org.

3. Roger Abravanel, *Meritocrazia* (Milano: Garzanti, 2008).

4. Jodi S. Cohen, "Clout Goes to College," *Chicago Tribune,* May 29, 2009.

5. What we do not easily observe is the vast amount of money that champions make through advertising. The fact that this amount is known to have increased tremendously in the last twenty years makes the evolution of the prize money even more remarkable.

6. Steve Kaplan and Joshua Rauh, "Wall Street and Main Street: What Contributes to the Rise in the Highest Income," *Review of Financial Studies* 23, no. 3 (2010): 1004–1050.

7. See http://en.wikipedia.org/wiki/Claude_Harmon.

8. See http://www.fundinguniverse.com/company-histories/Acushnet -company-company-History.html for the 1948 figure and http://www.golfchannel solutions.com/markets/usa for the 2008 figure.

9. If the surge in the prize money were due to increasing donations by rich golf-loving executives who are now better able to subsidize the prize out of their personal fortunes, this rise in value could simply be an effect of the increased income divide between executives and workers, not a manifestation of its underlying causes. In fact, it is the other way around. The Masters started as a subsidized event and is now a money-making machine, even without donations or exorbitant ticket prices—just international appeal.

10. Clifford Roberts, *The Story of the Augusta National Golf Club* (Garden City, NY: Doubleday, 1976), p. 59.

11. David Westin, "Purse Exceeds $1 Million," *Augusta Chronicle,* April 7, 2001.

12. Bob Harig, "Unlike Most Practice Rounds, the Masters' Brings Plenty of Passion," *ESPN.com,* April 7, 2008.

13. Westin, "Purse Exceeds $1 Million."

14. Tim McDonald, "Is the Masters Really the Most Prestigious Sporting Event in America?" February 25, 2008, http://www.worldgolf.com/column /masters-most-prestigious-sporting-event-in-america-6559.htm.

15. Marianne Bertrand and Antoinette Schoar, "Managing with Style: The Effect of Managers on Corporate Policy," *Quarterly Journal of Economics* 118 (2003): 1169–1208.

16. See http://sportsillustrated.cnn.com/more/specials/fortunate50/2007 /index.html.

17. Pew Economic Mobility Project, "Findings from a National Survey & Focus Groups on Economic Mobility," March 12, 2009. www.economicmobility.org.

18. Economic Policy Institute, *The State of Working America,* http:// www.stateofworkingamerica.org/.

19. OECD, "A Family Affair: Intergenerational Social Mobility Across OECD Countries," *Economic Policy Reforms 2010: Going for Growth* (OECD Publishing, 2010), pp. 181–198.

20. Daniel Aaronson and Bhashkar Mazumder, "Intergenerational Economic Mobility in the United States, 1940 to 2000," *Journal of Human Resources* 43, no. 1 (2008): 139–172.

THREE

1. See http://transition.fcc.gov/Bureaus/Common_Carrier/Reports/FCC -State_Link/SOCC/95socc.pdf.

2. For the price from a landline with a $5-a-month plan, see http://www .att.com/public_affairs/long_distance_news/product_reference_and_pricing _guide/VoiceSection8.4.2.pdf.

3. Technically, this result derives from the fact that the competitive equilibrium is in the core; hence no coalition is made better off by closing off trade with the rest of the economy. I thank Oliver Hart for pointing this out to me.

4. Sandra Black and Philip Strahan, "The Division of Spoils: Rent Sharing and Discrimination in a Regulated Industry," *American Economic Review* 91, no. 4 (September 2001): 814–831. A wage differential is not necessarily evidence of discrimination, since it can reflect unobserved differences. Yet if there is effective discrimination, there will be a wage gap.

5. "'The East India Company: Its History and Results,' by Karl Marx," *New York Daily Tribune,* July 11, 1853.

6. R. Ekelund and R. Tollison, *Politicized Economies: Monarchy, Monopolies, and Mercantilism* (College Station: Texas A&M Press, 1997), p. 196.

7. Ibid., p. 197.

8. Adam Smith, *The Wealth of Nations,* Book V, Chapter I, Article 1d (New York: Bantam Books, 2003), p. 941.

9. Nick Robins, *The Corporation That Changed the World: How the East India Company Shaped the Modern Multinational* (London/Ann Arbor: Pluto Press, 2006), p. 92.

10. *Spectrum Sports, Inc. v. McQuillan,* 506 U.S. 447 (1993).

11. Alan Greenspan, "Antitrust," in Ayn Rand, ed., *Capitalism: The Unknown Ideal* (New York: New American Library, 1967), p. 71.

12. The threat of entry is credible only if new potential entrants do not have to pay a lot to enter. In most situations, however, they do. Consider, for instance, a new cell phone operator trying to enter the US market. It has to build a network and it has to advertise. These costs are not fully recoverable if it is forced to exit; hence the operator's threat of entry is not credible. See William J. Baumol, John C. Panzar, and Robert D. Willig, *Contestable Markets and the Theory of Industry Structure* (New York: Harcourt Brace Jovanovich, 1982).

13. John K. Wilson, "Price-Fixer to the World" (December 21, 2000), http://www.bankrate.com/brm/news/investing/20001221c.asp.

14. See http://www.justice.gov/atr/public/speeches/4489-7.htm.

15. "Oil Production Subsidiaries," *Troika Dialog Research Report,* February 2000.

16. Owen Lamont, "Cash Flow and Investment: Evidence from Internal Capital Markets," *Journal of Finance* 52, no. 1 (1997): 83–109.

17. R. Rajan, H. Servaes, and L. Zingales, "The Cost of Diversity: Diversification Discount and Inefficient Investment," *Journal of Finance* 55 (2000): 35–80.

18. Rui Silva, "The Real Cost of Conglomerates," University of Chicago working paper (2011).

19. James Bovard, "Archer Daniels Midland: A Case Study in Corporate Welfare," *Cato Institute Policy Analysis,* September 26, 1995.

20. Ibid.

21. Michael Fumento, "Some Dare Call Them Robber Barons," *National Review,* March 13, 1987, p. 32.

22. Michael J. Weiss, "The High-Octane Ethanol Lobby," *New York Times,* April 1, 1990.

23. Dan Carney, "Dwayne's World," *Mother Jones,* July/August 1995.

24. Bovard, "Archer Daniels Midland: A Case Study in Corporate Welfare."

25. Fumento, "Some Dare Call Them Robber Barons," p. 32.

26. Wilson, "Price-Fixer to the World."

27. Mitchell Martin, "Citicorp and Travelers Plan to Merge in Record $70 Billion Deal: A New No.1: Financial Giants Unite," *New York Times,* April 7, 1998.

FOUR

1. Condé Nast Portfolio, "The 20 Worst CEOs," *Portfolio.com*, May 2009. http://www.portfolio.com/companies-executives/Portfolio%20List%20of%2020 %20Worst%20CEOs.pdf.

2. See "Executive Incentives," *Wall Street Journal Online*, November 20, 2008, http://online.wsj.com/public/resources/documents/st_ceos_20081111.html.

3. Federal Reserve Bank of Minneapolis, "A History of Central Banking in the United States," http://www.minneapolisfed.org/community_education /student/centralbankhistory/bank.cfm#second.

4. Sidney Ratner, James H. Soltow, and Richard Sylla, *The Evolution of the American Economy: Growth, Welfare, and Decision Making* (New York: MacMillan, 1993).

5. Thomas Hart Benton, *Political Science* (New York: D. Appleton and Company, 1854), p. 372.

6. Randall Kroszner and Raghuram Rajan, "Is the Glass-Steagall Act Justified? Evidence from the U.S. Experience with Universal Banking 1921–1933," *American Economic Review* 84 (1994): 810–832.

7. Randall Kroszner and Philip Strahan, "What Drives Deregulation? Economics and Politics of the Relaxation of Bank Branching Restrictions in the United States," *Quarterly Journal of Economics* 44, no. 4 (November 1999): 1437–1467.

8. Jith Jayaratne and Philip Strahan, "The Finance-Growth Nexus: Evidence from Bank Branch Deregulation," *Quarterly Journal of Economics* 111, no. 3 (1996): 639–670.

9. David A. Skeel, Jr., *Debt's Dominion: A History of Bankruptcy Law in America* (Princeton, NJ: Princeton University Press, 2001).

10. H.R. REP. NO. 55–65, at 43 (1897).

11. The UK personal bankruptcy rate is taken from the "Insolvency Statistics" report published by The Insolvency Service, which is part of the Department for Business Innovation and Skills (http://www.bis.gov.uk/insolvency /About-us/our-performance-statistics/insolvency-statistics). The US personal bankruptcy rate is calculated from bankruptcy filing statistics of the US courts (http://www.uscourts.gov/Statistics/BankruptcyStatistics.aspx) and from US census estimates of people aged eighteen years and over (http://www.census .gov/compendia/statab/cats/population.html).

12. Skeel, Jr., *Debt's Dominion*.

13. Charles Jordan Tabb, "The Top Twenty Issues in the History of Consumer Bankruptcy," *University of Illinois Law Review* 2007 (1): 9-30.

14. William C. Whitford, "A History of the Automobile Lender Provisions of BAPCPA," *University of Illinois Law Review* 143 (2007).

15. Victoria F. Nourse and Jane S. Schacter, "The Politics of Legislative Drafting: A Congressional Case Study," *New York University Law Review* 77 (2002): 575–623 at 612.

16. 145 Cong. Rec. H2723 (daily edition, May 5, 1999), as cited in John A. E. Pottow, "A U.S. Perspective on the Contextual Terrain of Political Economy in Insolvency Reform. In *Canadian Bankruptcy and Insolvency Law: Bill C-55, Statute C.47 and Beyond*, Chapter 15, p. 379.

17. Wenli Li, Michelle J. White, and Ning Zhu, "Did Bankruptcy Reform Cause Mortgage Default to Rise?" NBER Working Paper No. 15968, 2010. John Y. Campbell, Stefano Giglio, and Parag Pathak, "Forced Sales and House Prices," *American Economic Review* 101, no. 5 (2011): 2108–2131.

18. Kimberly Anne Summe, "Lessons Learned from the Lehman Bankruptcy," in Kenneth E. Scott, George P. Shultz, and John B. Taylor, eds., *Ending Government Bailouts as We Know Them* (Stanford: Hoover Institution, Stanford University), ch. 5.

19. See http://dealbook.nytimes.com/2008/10/10/early-results-published -in-lehman-swaps-auction/.

20. Dean Baker and Travis McArthur, "The Value of the 'Too Big to Fail' Big Bank Subsidy." Center for Economic and Policy Research, Issue Brief, September 2009. http://www.cepr.net/documents/publications/too-big-to-fail -2009-09.pdf.

21. A. Dyck, Adair Morse, and Luigi Zingales, "Who Blows the Whistle on Corporate Fraud?" *Journal of Finance* 65, no. 6 (2010): 2213–2253.

22. Stephanie D. Moussalli and O. Ronald Gray, "Illuminating the Limits of Auditor Accountability Through a Historical Review of Internal Control Evaluation" (January 2, 2010), http://ssrn.com/abstract=1760542.

23. Ibid.

24. Dyck, Morse, and Zingales, "Who Blows the Whistle on Corporate Fraud?"

25. Ibid.

26. A. Dyck, Adair Morse, and Luigi Zingales, "How Pervasive Is Corporate Fraud?" University of Chicago working paper (2011).

27. Testimony by Robert E. Rubin before the Financial Crisis Inquiry Commission (April 8, 2010), http://online.wsj.com/public/resources/documents /Rubintestimony408.pdf.

28. Testimony by Alan Greenspan before the House Committee of Government Oversight and Reform (October 23, 2008).

29. This story is based on Rachel Sanderson, Guy Dinmore, and Gillian Tett, "Finance: An Exposed Position," *Financial Times,* March 8, 2010.

30. "Cities in the Casino. A Derivatives Farce Makes Its Way to Court in Milan. Others Are Sure to Follow," *The Economist,* March 18, 2010.

31. Kroszner and Rajan, "Is the Glass-Steagall Act Justified?"

32. L. Guiso, P. Sapienza, and L. Zingales, "Time Varying Risk Aversion," University of Chicago working paper (2012).

33. R. Rajan and L. Zingales, "Banks and Markets: The Changing Character of European Finance," in *The Transformation of the European Financial System,* Vítor Gaspar, Philipp Hartmann, and Olaf Sleijpen, eds. European Central Bank, 2003.

34. R. Rajan and L. Zingales, "Which Capitalism? Lessons from the East Asian Crisis," *Journal of Applied Corporate Finance* 11, no. 3 (Fall 1998): 40–48.

35. R. Rajan and l. Zingales, "The Great Reversals: The Politics of Financial Development in the 20th Century," *Journal of Financial Economics* 69 (2003): 5–50.

36. "Credit Default Swaps and Counterparty Risks," European Central Bank (2010).

37. Michael Gofman, "A Network-Based Analysis of Over-the-Counter Markets," University of Chicago working paper (2011).

38. Thomas Philippon, "The Evolution of the US Financial Industry from 1860 to 2007," New York University working paper (November 2008).

39. When the seller negotiates a lower commission, he must not only bargain with his own real estate agent, but also with the prospective buyer's agent, who holds a big bargaining chip: the power to steer his client away from the property.

40. Chang-Tai Hsieh and Enrico Moretti ("Can Free Entry be Inefficient? Fixed Commissions and Social Waste in the Real Estate Industry," *Journal of Political Economy* 111, no. 5 [October 2003]: 1076–1121) demonstrate this point empirically, using variation in land—instead of house—prices across US cities. If land prices go up, a house does not become any more difficult to sell. Yet, if the agent commission stays fixed, selling a house becomes more lucrative thanks to the land's escalating value. The effect is an increase in the fraction of the labor force working as real estate agents, lower productivity (sales per agent or sales per hour worked) among agents, and real wages that remain flat.

41. Thomas Philippon and Ariell Reshef, "Wages and Human Capital in the U.S. Financial Industry: 1909–2006," New York University working paper (December 2008).

42. Nancy Rose, "The Incidence of Regulatory Rents in the Motor Carrier Industry," *Rand Journal of Economics* 16 (Autumn 1985): 299–318.

43. Nancy Rose, "Labor Rent-Sharing and Regulation: Evidence from the Trucking Industry," *Journal of Political Economy* 95 (December 1987): 1146–1178.

44. Or, to be precise, 1,091,777. My calculation is based on Thomson One Banker data.

45. Elizabeth Gudrais, "Flocking to Finance," *Harvard Magazine*, May–June 2008, pp. 17–18.

46. See Daniel J. Hemel, " '07 Men Make More," *Harvard Crimson*, June 6, 2007, http://www.thecrimson.com/article/2007/6/6/07-men-make-more-male-harvard/.

47. "Yale College Post-Graduation Activities: Report of the Yale College Class of 2010," http://oir.yale.edu/detailed-data.

48. See http://www.thedailybeast.com/newsweek/2010/11/10/the-richest-counties-in-america.all.html

FIVE

1. Quoted in Tom Kenworthy, "Are House Democrats Victims of Their Fund-Raising Success?" *Washington Post,* October 30, 1989.

2. John R. Lott, Jr., "A Simple Explanation for Why Campaign Expenditures Are Increasing: The Government Is Getting Bigger," *Journal of Law and Economics* 43 (2000): 359–393.

3. Chris Edwards, *Downsizing the Federal Government* (Washington, DC: Cato Institute, 2005).

4. See http://www2.census.gov/prod2/statcomp/documents/CT1970p2-12.pdf

5. Chris Edwards and Tad DeHaven, "Corporate Welfare Update," Cato Institute, *Tax and Budget Bulletin* 7 (May 2002).

6. Ibid.

7. John Porretto, "Lott: Cruise Ship Loss May Top $200M," Associated Press, January 12, 2002.

8. See http://www.census.gov/prod/2011pubs/11statab/income.pdf.

9. John Friedman, "The Incidence of the Medicare Prescription Drug Benefit: Using Asset Prices to Assess its Impact on Drug Makers," Harvard University working paper (2009).

10. Lee Drutman, "The Business of America Is Lobbying," mimeo (2010).

11. See http://www.opensecrets.org/bigpicture/index.php.

12. Quoted in Matilde Bombardini and Francesco Trebbi, "Votes or Money? Theory and Evidence from the US Congress," *Journal of Public Economics* 95, nos. 7–8 (2011): 587–611 at 588.

13. Ibid., p. 588.

14. Drutman, "The Business of America Is Lobbying," p. 4.

15. Ibid., p. 5.

16. See http://www.opensecrets.org/lobby/index.php.

17. Drutman, "The Business of America Is Lobbying," p. 5.

18. Ibid.

19. Ibid.

20. Quoted in Tom Finnigan, "All About Pork: The Abuse of Earmarks and the Needed Reforms," *Policy Briefing Series*, Citizens Against Government Waste, 2007.

21. Charles E. Russell, quoted in David G. Phillips, Judson A. Grenier, and George E. Mowry, *The Treason of the Senate* (Chicago: Quadrangle Books, 1964), p. 20.

22. Robert G. Kaiser, *So Damn Much Money* (New York: Vintage, 2009), p. 17.

23. Edwards, *Downsizing the Federal Government*, pp. 8 and 112.

24. Ibid., p. 81.

25. See http://blog.washingtonpost.com/citizen-k-street/chapters/intro duction/. http://www.opensecrets.org/lobby/firmsum.php?id=D000000208 &year=2006.

26. This belief, shared also by former British prime minister Margaret Thatcher, is supported by some recent evidence. People who become owners develop more promarket beliefs, from the conviction that effort is rewarded to the belief that one can make it on his own. See Rafael Di Tella, Sebastian F. Galiani, and Ernesto S. Schargrodsky, "The Formation of Beliefs: Evidence from the Allocation of Land Titles to Squatters," *Quarterly Journal of Economics* 122, no. 1 (February 2007).

27. Congressional Budget Office, "Updated Estimates of the Subsidies to the Housing GSEs" (April 2004).

28. Gretchen Morgenson and Joshua Rosner, *Reckless Endangerment* (New York: Times Books, 2011).

29. Ibid.

30. Quoted in Morgenson and Rosner, *Reckless Endangerment*, p. 76.

31. Congressional Budget Office, "The Budgetary Cost of Fannie Mae and Freddie Mac and Options for the Future Federal Role in the Secondary Mortgage Market," June 2, 2011.

32. For a discussion of industrial companies, see Gregor Andrade and Steve Kaplan, "How Costly Is Financial (Not Economic) Distress? Evidence

from Highly Leveraged Transactions That Became Distressed," *Journal of Finance* 53 (October 1998): 1443–1494; regarding financial institutions, see Pietro Veronesi and Luigi Zingales, "Paulson's Gift," *Journal of Financial Economics* 97, no. 3 (2010): 339–368.

33. Veronesi and Zingales, "Paulson's Gift."

34. Walker F. Todd, "Bailing Out the Creditor Class," *The Nation,* February 13, 1995, p. 193; Jeremy Adelman, "Tequila Hangover: Latin America's Debt Crisis," *Studies in Political Economy* 55 (1998).

35. Alan Greenspan, *The Age of Turbulence* (New York: Penguin Press, 2007), p. 159.

36. Benedetto De Martino, Colin F. Camerer, and Ralph Adolphs, "Amygdala Damage Eliminates Monetary Loss Aversion," *Proceeding of the National Academy of Science* 107, no. 8 (February 23, 2010): 3788–3792.

37. Bong-Chan Kho, Dong Lee, and René M. Stulz, "U.S. Banks, Crises, and Bailouts: From Mexico to LTCM," *American Economic Review* 90, no. 2 (May 2000): 28–31.

38. Mark Lewis, "Rubin Red-Faced over Enron? Not in the *Times,*" Forbes.com, February 11, 2002.

39. "The Politics of Enron: Four Committees in Search of a Scandal," *The Economist,* January 17, 2002.

40. "No Line Responsibilities," *Wall Street Journal,* December 3, 2008.

41. Gérard Gennotte and Hayne Ellis Leland, "Market Liquidity, Hedging, and Crashes," *American Economic Review* (December 1990): 999–1021.

42. Data courtesy of Robert Shiller at http://www.multpl.com.

43. Ben Bernanke and Mark Gertler, "Monetary Policy and Asset Price Volatility," in Federal Reserve Bank of Kansas City, *New Challenges for Monetary Policy* (1999), pp.77–128 at p. 78.

44. David S. Scharfstein and Jeremy Stein, "This Bailout Doesn't Pay Dividends," *New York Times,* October 20, 2008.

45. FOXBusiness, "Yale's Swensen: Pols Missing the Point," January 6, 2009, www.foxbusiness.com/search-results/m/21735678/yale-s-swensen-pols-missing-the-point.htm.

46. For some direct evidence, see L. Guiso, P. Sapienza, and L. Zingales, "Time Varying Risk Aversion," University of Chicago working paper (2012).

47. These losses are calculated *ex ante*, at the time of the intervention; see Veronesi and Zingales, "Paulson's Gift." *Ex post* taxpayers ended up with a small gain, but that was just luck.

SIX

1. Andrew Pierce, "The Queen Asks Why No One Saw the Credit Crunch Coming," *Telegraph,* November 5, 2008.

2. The data are from Robert Shiller's web page at http://www.econ.yale.edu/~shiller/books.htm.

3. C. Himmelberg, Christopher Mayer, and Todd Sinai, "Assessing High House Prices: Bubbles, Fundamentals, and Misperceptions," *Journal of Economic Perspectives* 19 (2005): 67–92.

4. Robert Shiller, *Irrational Exuberance* (New York: Broadway Books/Crown Business, 2nd ed., 2005), p. 13.

5. See http://www.federalreserve.gov/monetarypolicy/files/FOMC20061212 meeting.pdf.

6. Joseph E. Stiglitz, Jonathan M. Orszag, and Peter R. Orszag, "Implications of the New Fannie Mae and Freddie Mac Risk-Based Capital Standard," *Fannie Mae Papers* 1, no. 2 (March 2002): 2.

7. Inasmuch as I gathered this information from the Internet, my estimates likely underestimate the phenomenon.

8. It is important to note that academic economists also benefit from another feature that regulators lack: intense competition. When the industry has captured most of the field and general consensus reigns, there is a natural incentive for academics to be controversial and say the opposite—an incentive that does not exist for regulators.

9. Alexander Ljungqvist, Christopher Malloy, and Felicia Marston, "Rewriting History," *Journal of Finance,* forthcoming.

10. Henry Thomas Stelfox, Grace Chua, Keith O'Rourke, and Allan S. Detsky, "Conflict of Interest in the Debate over Calcium-Channel Antagonists," *New England Journal of Medicine* 338 (January 8, 1998): 101–106.

11. Deborah E. Barnes and Lisa A. Bero, "Why Review Articles on the Health Effects of Passive Smoking Reach Different Conclusions," *Journal of the American Medical Association* 19, no. 19 (1998): 1566–1570.

12. See Robert T. Foley, *German Strategy and the Path to Verdun: Erich von Falkenhayn and the Development of Attrition, 1870–1916* (Cambridge: Cambridge University Press, 2005).

13. Arthur Meier Schlesinger, *A Thousand Days: John F. Kennedy in the White House* (Boston: Houghton Mifflin, 1965), p. 250.

SEVEN

1. Charles Postel, *The Populist Vision* (New York: Oxford University Press, 2007), p. vii.

2. Margaret Canovan, *Populism* (New York/London: Harcourt Brace Jovanovich, 1981), pp. 289, 293, 294.

3. See http://www.census.gov/hhes/socdemo/education/data/cps/1946/p46–5/tables.html and http://nces.ed.gov/pubs91/91660.pdf at p. 363.

4. These data are provided at http://www.census.gov/hhes/www/income/data/historical/people/, table P8.

5. Here I am citing the 1946 regime data from http://www.systemicpeace.org/polity/polity4.htm. Democracy is defined as a polity score of 6 and above. For population figures, see the UN's 1950 data at http://esa.un.org/unpd/wpp/Excel-Data/population.htm.

6. I consider the following to be (or to have been) communist countries: China, North Korea, Albania, the USSR, Bulgaria, the Czechoslovak Republic, East Germany, Hungary, Mongolia, Poland, Romania, Vietnam (DRV), and Yugoslavia. In 1950, when the world population was 2,532,000,000, the total population of these countries was 864,000,000.

7. The world illiteracy figure is quoted from UNESCO, "World Illiteracy at Mid-Century: A Statistical Study" (1957), http://unesdoc.unesco.org/images/0000/000029/002930eo.pdf (accessed February 7, 2012); the US illiteracy figure is quoted from National Center for Education Statistics, "Illiteracy," *120 Years of Literacy,* http://nces.ed.gov/naal/lit_history.asp#illiteracy (accessed February 7, 2012); and the high school data are quoted from Robert J. Barro and Jong-Wha Lee, "A New Data Set of Educational Attainment in the World, 1950–2010," NBER working paper (2010).

8. Angus Maddison, *Dynamic Forces in Capitalist Development: A Long-Run Comparative View* (New York: Oxford University Press), pp. 284–292.

9. "A Game of Catch Up," *The Economist,* September 24, 2011, p. 16.

10. The countries in question are Cuba, Laos, North Korea, and Vietnam. The respective population figures are quoted from the CIA's *World Fact Book.*

11. See http://nces.ed.gov/programs/digest/d10/tables/dt10_420.asp.

12. Edwin G. West, "Are American Schools Working? Disturbing Cost and Quality Trends," *Cato Policy Analysis* 26 (August 9, 1983).

13. Marco Pagano, Ailsa A. Röell, and Josef Zechner, "The Geography of Equity Listing: Why Do Companies List Abroad?" *Journal of Finance* 57, no. 6 (December 2002).

14. David Daniels, "In Dodd-Frank's Shadow: The Declining Competitiveness of U.S. Public Equity Markets," *Harvard Business Law Review* (March 28, 2011).

15. Committee on Capital Markets Regulation, "The Competitive Position of the U.S. Public Equity Market" (December 2007).

16. Ibid.

17. M. Halling, M. Pagano, O. Randl, and J. Zechner, "Where Is the Market? Evidence from Crosslistings in the U.S.," University of Vienna working paper (2006).

18. In the transcript at http://errolmorris.com/film/fow_transcript.html, McNamara is quoted as saying: "Of the top thousand executives at Ford Motor Company, I don't believe there were ten college graduates, and Henry Ford II needed help."

19. Sharon Kay, "Remote Surgery," http://www.pbs.org/wnet/innovation /episode7_essay1.html.

20. "Base Point Early Payment Default: Links to Fraud and Impact on Mortgage Lenders and Investment Banks," BasePoint Analytics LLC working paper (2007).

21. Paola Sapienza and Luigi Zingales, "A Trust Crisis" (2009), www .financialtrustindex.org.

22. See www.financialtrustindex.org.

23. William H. Riker, Liberalism Against Populism (San Francisco: W. H. Freeman, 1982), p. 10.

24. Ronald Formisano, *For the People: American Populist Movements from the Revolution to the 1850s* (Chapel Hill: University of North Carolina Press, 2008), p. 20.

25. Postel, *The Populist Vision,* p. 5.

26. From the *St. Louis Globe-Democrat,* in *Clinton Caucasian,* December 1, 1892. See Postel, *The Populist Vision,* p. 4.

27. Margaret Canovan, "Taking Politics to the People: Populism as the Ideology of Democracy," in Yves Mény and Yves Surel, eds., *Democracies and the Populist Challenge* (New York: Palgrave, 2002), p. 27.

28. Rudiger Dornbusch and Sebastian Edwards, "The Macroeconomics of Populism," in Rudiger Dornbusch and Sebastian Edwards, eds., *The Macroeconomics of Populism in Latin America* (Chicago: University of Chicago Press, 1991).

29. Daron Acemoglu, Georgy Egorov, and Konstantin Sonin, "A Political Theory of Populism," MIT working paper (2010).

30. Sapienza and Zingales, "A Trust Crisis."

EIGHT

1. I thank my colleague Steve Davis for this suggestion.

2. C. Schoen et al., "State Trends in Premiums and Deductibles, 2003–2010: The Need for Action to Address Rising Costs," Commonwealth Fund, November 2011.

3. Susan Fleck, John Glaser, and Shawn Sprague, "The Compensation-Productivity Gap: A Visual Essay," *Monthly Labor Review* (January 2011): 57–69.

4. See http://tinyurl.com/6pc46s3.

5. Theodore Caplow, Louis Hicks, and Ben J. Wattenberg, *The First Measured Century: An Illustrated Guide to Trends in America, 1900–2000* (Washington, DC: American Enterprise Institute Press, 2001).

6. Dennis Cauchon, "Grants More Than Offset Soaring University Tuition," *USA Today,* June 27, 2004.

7. Fleck, Glaser, and Sprague, "The Compensation-Productivity Gap."

8. Frank Geary and Tom Stark, "Examining Ireland's Post-Famine Economic Growth Performance," *Economic Journal* (October 2002): 919–935.

9. D. Raff and L. Summers, "Did Henry Ford Pay Efficiency Wages?" *Journal of Labor Economics* 5, no. 4 (October 1987): pp. S57–S86.

10. C. Shapiro and J. Stiglitz, "Equilibrium Unemployment as a Worker Discipline Device," *American Economic Review* 74, no. 3 (June 1984): pp. 433–444.

11. Sherwin Rosen, "The Economics of Superstars," *American Economic Review* 71, no. 5 (1981): 845–858; R. H. Frank and P. J. Cook, *The Winner-Take-All Society* (New York: Free Press, 1995).

12. Matthew J. Salganik et al., "Cultural Market Experimental Study of Inequality and Unpredictability in an Artificial Cultural Market," *Science* 311, no. 854 (2006).

13. Implicitly, I assumed that the promise is contingent on the realization of profits. One could pay up front in cash to adopt it. There are two problems with this strategy, though. First, it is hard to verify use: people can download the software to receive the bonus and then not use it. Second, this strategy would require very deep pockets, again creating a barrier to entry.

14. See, for example, Sherwin Rosen, "Authority, Control, and the Distribution of Earnings," *Bell Journal of Economics* 13, no. 2 (1982): 311–323.

15. See, for example, Stephen A. Marglin, "What Do Bosses Do? The Origins and Functions of Hierarchy in Capitalist Production," *Review of Radical Political Economics* (July 1974): 60–112.

16. Lucian Bebchuk and Jesse Fried, *Pay Without Performance: The Unfulfilled Promise of Executive Compensation* (Cambridge, MA: Harvard University Press, 2004).

17. Edward P. Lazear, Kathryn L. Shaw, and Christopher T. Stanton, "The Value of Bosses," Stanford University working paper (2011).

18. Kevin J. Murphy, "Executive Compensation," in Orley C. Ashenfelter and David Card, eds., *Handbook of Labor Economics,* vol. 3 (Amsterdam: North Holland, 1999).

19. Bengt Holmstrom, "Moral Hazard and Observability," *Bell Journal of Economics* 10 (1979): 74–91.

20. Marianne Bertrand and Sendhil Mullainathan, "Are CEOs Rewarded for Luck? The Ones Without Principals Are," *Quarterly Journal of Economics* 116, no. 3 (2001): 901–932.

21. Jay Yarow, "Developing Nissan's Electric Car Cost 'Significantly' Above $500 Million," *Business Insider,* July 28, 2009.

22. Edward P. Lazear and Sherwin Rosen, "Rank-Order Tournaments as Optimum Labor Contracts," *Journal of Political Economy* (October 1981): 841–864.

23. V. A. Ramey, "Time Spent in Home Production in the 20th Century United States: New Estimates from Old Data," *Journal of Economic History* 69 (March 2009): 1–47.

24. G. Ramey and V. A. Ramey, "The Rug Rat Race," Brookings Papers on Economic Activity, Spring 2010.

25. John Bound, Brad Hershbein, and Bridget Terry Long, "Playing the Admissions Game: Student Reactions to Increasing College Competition," NBER working paper 15272, August 2009.

26. Alex Williams, "Lost Summer for the College-Bound," *New York Times,* June 4, 2006.

27. Cecilie Rohwedder, "London Parents Scramble for Edge In Preschool Wars," *Wall Street Journal Online,* February 12, 2007, p. A1.

28. In "Estimating the Payoff to Attending a More Selective College: An Application of Selection on Observables and Unobservables," *Quarterly Journal of Economics* 117, no. 4 (2002): 1491–1528, Stacy Berg Dale and Alan B. Krueger find that students of highly selective colleges do not earn more over their lifetime than similar students who go to less selective colleges. Yet, stu-

dents who attend colleges with higher tuitions or spending-per-student (such as Ivy League ones) do.

29. My calculations come from the data of the National Association of Colleges and University Business Officers; see http://tinyurl.com/7fa32vg.

30. Erick Hurst, "Did the Construction Boom During the 2000s Distort the Labor Supply of Low Skilled Men?" University of Chicago working paper (2011).

31. See https://www.eff.org/issues/patents.

32. See http://tinyurl.com/yjd4edy.

33. USDA, Sugar and Sweeteners Outlook, June 2011, http://tinyurl.com 7cb5kxt.

34. For example, Robert Leslie Shapiro (one of O. J. Simpson's attorneys) created Legal Zoom.com, which provides legal services over the Internet, competing with existing law firms. Once legal services are offered online, they can easily be offered from another country, as long as people there study US law. To see how online teaching is changing the world, see http://www.wired .com/magazine/2011/07/ff_khan/all/1.

35. Hurst, "Construction Boom."

36. See http://tinyurl.com/yjd4edy.

37. Michael Barber, Chinezi Chijioke, and Mona Mourshed, *How the World's Best-Performing School Systems Come Out on Top* (McKinsey & Company, 2007). http://ssomckinsey.darbyfilms.com/reports/EducationBook_A4 %20SINGLES_DEC%202.pdf.

38. W. L. Sanders and J. C. Rivers, "Cumulative and Residual Effects of Teachers on Future Student Academic Achievement," in *Research Progress Report* (Knoxville: University of Tennessee Value-Added Research and Assessment Center, 1996).

39. Eric A. Hanushek, "The Trade-off Between Child Quantity and Quality," *Journal of Political Economy* 100, no. 1 (1992): 84–117.

40. Eric A. Hanushek and Steven G. Rivkin, "How to Improve the Supply of High Quality Teachers," in Diane Ravitch, ed., *Brookings Papers on Education Policy 2004* (Washington, DC: Brookings Institution Press, 2004), pp. 7–25.

41. Eric A. Hanushek, "The Economic Value of Higher Teacher Quality," NBER working paper 16,606, 2010.

42. Barber, Chijioke, and Mourshed, *World's Best-Performing School Systems*.

43. Eric A. Hanushek, "Teacher Deselection," in Dan Goldhaber and Jane Hannaway, eds., *Creating a New Teaching Profession* (Washington, DC: Urban Institute Press, 2009), 165–180.

44. Eric A. Hanushek and Ludger Woessmann, *The High Cost of Low Educational Performance: The Long-Run Impact of Improving PISA Outcomes* (Paris: Organization for Economic Cooperation and Development, 2010).

45. Hanushek, "The Economic Value of Higher Teacher Quality."

46. See, for example, Erin Richards and Amy Hetzner, "Choice Schools Not Outperforming MPS," *Journal Sentinel,* March 29, 2011, http://tinyurl .com/7sgja22.

47. Cecilia Elena Rouse, "Private School Vouchers and Student Achievement: An Evaluation of the Milwaukee Parental Choice Program," *Quarterly Journal of Economics* (May 1998): 553–602.

48. Cecilia Elena Rouse and Lisa Barrow, "School Vouchers and Student Achievement: Recent Evidence, Remaining Questions," Princeton University working paper (2008).

49. Chang-Tai Hsieh and Miguel Urquiola, "The Effects of Generalized School Choice on Achievement and Stratification: Evidence from Chile's Voucher Program," *Journal of Public Economics* 90 (2006): 1477–1503.

50. Justine S. Hastings and Jeffrey M. Weinstein, "Information, School Choice, and Academic Achievement: Evidence from Two Experiments," NBER working paper 13623 (2007), p. 4.

51. Raghuram Rajan and Luigi Zingales, *Saving Capitalism from the Capitalists* (New York: Random House, 2003).

52. Congressional Budget Office, "Trends in the Distribution of Household Income Between 1979 and 2007," October 2011.

NINE

1. Richard P. Chait and Zachary First, "Bullish on Private Colleges," *Harvard Magazine,* November–December 2011.

2. See http://tinyurl.com/y5nsu7h.

3. Congressional Budget Office, "Costs and Policy Options for Federal Student Loan Programs," March 2010.

4. College Board, *Trends in Student Aid 2010* (Washington, DC: College Board, 2010), p. 10.

5. Dennis Cauchon, "Student Loans Outstanding Will Exceed $1 Trillion This Year," *USA Today,* October 25, 2011.

6. Clayton M. Christensen and Michael Horn, *Disrupting Class: How Disruptive Innovation Will Change the Way the World Learns* (New York: McGraw-Hill, 2008).

7. David I. Auerbach and Arthur L. Kellermann, "A Decade of Health Care Cost Growth Has Wiped Out Real Income Gains for an Average US Family," *Health Affairs* 30, no. 9 (2011): 1630–1636.

8. Michael F. Cannon, "A Better Way to Generate and Use Comparative-Effectiveness Research," *Cato Institute Policy Analysis,* February 6, 2009.

9. Katherine Baicker and Amitabh Chandra, "Medicare Spending, the Physician Workforce, and Beneficiaries' Quality of Care," *Health Affairs* web exclusive (April 7, 2004): 184–197.

10. W. G. Manning et al., *Health Insurance and the Demand for Medical Care: Evidence from a Randomized Experiment* (Santa Monica, CA: RAND Corporation, 1988).

11. Cory Gusland et al., "Consumer-Driven Health Plan Effectiveness: Case Study: State of Indiana," Mercer Global, May 20, 2010.

12. For a quick introduction, see, for example, Dan Ariely, *Predictably Irrational: The Hidden Forces That Shape Our Decisions* (New York: HarperCollins, 2008), and Richard H. Thaler and Cass R. Sunstein, *Nudge: Improving Decisions About Health, Wealth, and Happiness* (New York: Penguin, 2009).

13. Xavier Gabaix and David Laibson, "Shrouded Attributes, Consumer Myopia, and Information Suppression in Competitive Markets," *Quarterly Journal of Economics* 121, no. 2 (2006): 505–540.

14. Christina Binkley, "Lucky Numbers Casino Chain Mines Data on Its Gamblers, and Strikes Pay Dirt," *Wall Street Journal,* May 4, 2000.

15. Sumit Agarwal et al., "Inconsistent Regulators: Evidence from Banking," University of Chicago working paper (2011).

16. Eugene F. Fama, "Agency Problems and the Theory of the Firm," *Journal of Political Economy* 88 (1980): 288–307; Eugene F. Fama and Michael Jensen, 1983, "Separation of Ownership and Control," *Journal of Law & Economics* 26 (1983): 301–325.

17. "Top 10 Crooked CEOs: Dennis Kozlowski," *Time,* June 9, 2009.

TEN

1. Edward Banfield, *The Moral Basis of a Backward Society* (Glencoe, IL: The Free Press, 1958).

2. Kenneth Arrow, "Philosophy & Public Affairs," Vol. 1, No. 4 (Summer 1972), p. 357.

3. World Value Survey, QuestionV23, http://tinyurl.com/89sy2hj.

4. Luigi Guiso et al., "Cultural Biases in Economic Exchange?" *Quarterly Journal of Economics* 124, no. 3 (2009): 1095–1131.

5. Luigi Guiso, Paola Sapienza, and Luigi Zingales, "Does Culture Affect Economic Outcomes?" *Journal of Economic Perspectives* (2006) 20: 23–48; Eric M. Uslaner, "Where You Stand Depends Upon Where Your Grandparents Sat: The Inheritability of Generalized Trust," mimeo, University of Maryland–College Park, 2007.

6. Luigi Guiso et al., "Cultural Biases in Economic Exchange."

7. The factual account is quoted from the PBS documentary *Triumph of the Nerds: The Rise of Accidental Empires.* The transcript can be found at www.pbs.org/nerds. And the economic interpretation is based on Luca Anderlini and Leonardo Felli, "Transaction Costs and the Robustness of the Coase Theorem," *Economic Journal* 116 (2006): 223–245.

8. L. Guiso, P. Sapienza, and L. Zingales, "Civic Capital as the Missing Link," NBER working paper 15845, March 2010; Jess Benhabib, Alberto Bisin, and Matthew O. Jackson, eds., *Handbook of Social Economics,* vol. 1A (San Diego/Amsterdam: North-Holland, 2011).

9. Ray Fisman and Edward Miguel, "Corruption, Norms, and Legal Enforcement: Evidence from Diplomatic Parking Tickets," *Journal of Political Economy* 115, no. 6 (2007): 1020–1048.

10. Ibid.

11. Orazio Attanasio, Luca Pellerano, and Sandra Polanía Reyes, "Building Trust? Conditional Cash Transfer Programmes and Social Capital," *Fiscal Studies* 30, no. 2 (2009): 139–177.

12. Robert D. Putnam, *Making Democracy Work* (Princeton, NJ: Princeton University Press, 1993).

13. Luigi Guiso, Paola Sapienza, and Luigi Zingales, "Long-Term Persistence," NBER working paper W14278 (2008).

14. Nathan Nunn and Leonard Wantchekon, "The Slave Trade and the Origins of Mistrust in Africa," *American Economic Review* 101, no. 7 (2011): 3221–3252.

15. Paola Sapienza and Luigi Zingales, "Blame Silvio's Antics for Italy's Bond Market Fall," *Financial Times,* July 14, 2011.

16. Yann Algan, Pierre Cahuc, and Andrei Shleifer, "Teaching Practices and Social Capital," Harvard University working paper (2011).

17. Luigi Guiso, Paola Sapienza, and Luigi Zingales, "The Determinants of Strategic Default on Mortgages," *Journal of Finance,* forthcoming.

18. Robert H. Frank, Thomas Gilovich, and Dennis T. Regan. "Does Studying Economics Inhibit Cooperation?" *Journal of Economic Perspectives* 7, no. 2 (1993): 159–171.

19. Gary Becker, "Crime and Punishment: An Economic Approach," *Journal of Political Economy* 76 (1968): 169–217.

20. L. Guiso, P. Sapienza, and L. Zingales, "People's Opium? Religion and Economic Attitudes," *Journal of Monetary Economics* 50 (2003): 225–282.

21. L. Guiso, P. Sapienza, and L. Zingales, "The Values of Corporate Values," University of Chicago working paper (2011).

22. Lauren Cohen, Andrea Frazzini, and Christopher Malloy, "The Small World of Investing: Board Connections and Mutual Fund Returns," *Journal of Political Economy* 116 (2008): 951–979.

ELEVEN

1. John F. Kennedy, "To Keep the Lobbyist Within Bounds," *New York Times Magazine,* February 19, 1956; *Congressional Record* (March 2, 1956): 3802–3803.

2. Rajeev Syal and Jeevan Vasagar, "Anthony Giddens' Trip to See Gaddafi Vetted by Libyan Intelligence Chief," *The Guardian,* March 4, 2011.

3. Benjamin Pauker, "Understanding Libya's Michael Corleone," *Foreign Policy,* March 7, 2011.

4. See www.alldc.org/ethicscode.cfm.

5. Marianne Bertrand, Matilde Bombardini, and Francesco Trebbi, *Is It Whom You Know or What You Know? An Empirical Assessment of the Lobbying Process.* University of Chicago working paper, 2011.

6. See http://rules.senate.gov/public/index.cfm?p=RuleXXXV.

7. Vidal Blanesi, Mirko Draca Jordi, and Christian Fons-Rosen, "Revolving Door Lobbyists," London School of Economics working paper (2010).

8. Bertrand, Bombardini, and Trebbi, *Is It Whom You Know?*

9. John Boehner, "For a Majority That Matters," January 9, 2006. Cited in Bertrand, Bombardini, and Trebbi, "Is It Whom You Know," p. 14.

10. Atif Mian, Amir Sufi, and Francesco Trebbi, "The Political Economy of the U.S. Mortgage Default Crisis, 2010," *American Economic Review* 100 (December 2010): 1967–1998.

11. See www.ilpalio.org/palioenglish3.htm.

12. G. Becker, "A Theory of Competition Among Pressure Groups

for Political Influence," *Quarterly Journal of Economics* 98, no. 3 (1983): 371–400.

13. Robert J. Barro, *Getting It Right: Markets and Choices in a Free Society* (Cambridge, MA: MIT Press, 1996), p. 169.

14. R. H. Coase, "The Coase Theorem and the Empty Core: A Comment," *Journal of Law, Economics, and Policy* 24, no. 1 (1981): 183–187.

15. Eric Lichtblau, "Obama Backers Tied to Lobbies Raise Millions," *New York Times*, October 27, 2011.

16. R. La Porta, F. Lopez-de-Silanes, and A. Shleifer, "The Economic Consequences of Legal Origins," *Journal of Economic Literature* 46 (June 2008): 285–332.

17. See http://profiles.nlm.nih.gov/ps/retrieve/Narrative/NN/p-nid/60.

18. Michael Jensen, "Some Anomalous Evidence Regarding Market Efficiency," *Journal of Financial Economics* 6, nos. 2–3 (1978): 95–101 at 95.

19. This section and the next draw heavily from A. Dyck, D. Moss, and L. Zingales, "Media vs. Special Interests," NBER working paper #14360 (2008).

20. Marie Brenner, "The Man Who Knew Too Much," *Vanity Fair,* May 1996.

21. Dyck, Moss, and Zingales, "Media vs. Special Interests"; David Strömberg, "Mass Media Competition, Political Competition, and Public Policy," *Review of Economic Studies* 71 (2004): 265–284.

22. Brenner, "The Man Who Knew Too Much."

23. Jonathan Reuter and Eric Zitzewitz, "Do Ads Influence Editors? Advertising and Bias in the Financial Media," *Quarterly Journal of Economics* 121, no. 1 (2006): 197–227.

24. David Graham Phillips, "The Treason of the Senate," *Cosmopolitan,* April 1906, p. 488.

25. This and the following information comes from Forest Reinhardt and Richard Vietor, *Starkist (A) and Starkist (B),* Harvard Business School cases 794–128 and 794–139 (Cambridge, MA: Harvard Business School Press, 1994).

26. Reinhardt and Vietor, *Starkist (A) and Starkist (B),* p. 3.

27. Richard Vietor, *Allied Signal: Managing the Hazardous Waste Liability Risk,* Harvard Business School case 793–044 (Cambridge, MA: Harvard Business School Press, 1993).

28. Ibid., p. 3.

29. Ibid.

30. A. Dyck and L. Zingales, "The Corporate Governance Role of the

Media," in R. Islam, *The Right to Tell: The Role of the Media in Development* (Washington, DC: World Bank, 2002).

31. See, for example, the Center for Responsive Politics, www.opensecrets .org, and the Sunlight Foundation, http://reporting.sunlightfoundation.com /about/#.

32. Edward Glaeser, Jose Scheinkman, and Andrei Shleifer, "The Injustice of Inequality," *Journal of Monetary Economics,* Carnegie-Rochester Series on Public Policy (January 2003); Edward Glaeser and Andrei Shleifer, "The Rise of the Regulatory State," *Journal of Economic Literature* XLI (June 2003): 401–425.

33. Louis Brandeis, "Opportunity in the Law," address delivered May 4, 1905, before the Harvard Ethical Society.

TWELVE

1. Lawrence Lessig, *Republic, Lost: How Money Corrupts Congress—and a Plan to Stop It* (New York: Twelve, 2011).

2. Elaine Buckberg, Jonathan Macey, and James Overdahl, "Will Court Short-Circuit Dodd-Frank?" *Politico.com,* August 15, 2011.

3. William Sanjour, "Designed to Fail: Why Regulatory Agencies Don't Work," August 26, 2010, http://tinyurl.com/7pvyyh2.

4. See http://tinyurl.com/6sus4kx.

5. See http://tinyurl.com/7wvfbhf.

6. See, for instance, P. Milgrom and J. Roberts, "Bargaining Costs, Influence Costs, and the Organization of Economic Activity," in J. E. Alt and K. A. Shepsle, eds., *Perspectives on Positive Political Economy* (Cambridge: University of Cambridge Press, 1990), pp. 57–89; and E. Glaeser and A. Shleifer, "A Reason for Quantity Regulation," *American Economic Review Papers and Proceedings* (May 2001).

7. Sanjour, "Designed to Fail."

8. Author's calculations, based on Internal Revenue Service data.

9. GAO Report to Congressional Requesters, "Comparison of the Reported Tax Liabilities of Foreign- and U.S.-Controlled Corporations, 1998–2005" (July 2008), p. 8.

10. Author's calculations, based on data from *The Economic Report of the President: 2011.*

11. Nanette Byrnes, "What U.S. Companies Really Pay in Taxes," *Bloomberg BusinessWeek,* April 23, 2009.

12. Jack Abramoff, *Capitol Punishment: The Hard Truth About Washington Corruption from America's Most Notorious Lobbyist* (New York: WND Books, 2011), p. 243.

13. Raquel Meyer Alexander, Stephen W. Mazza, and Susan Scholz, "Measuring Rates of Return for Lobbying Expenditures: An Empirical Analysis Under the American Jobs Creation Act," University of Kansas working paper (2009).

14. Of course, this provision would have to deal with nontaxable entities like foundation and university endowment. Today, the profits distributed to these entities as dividends are subject to the 35 percent corporate tax rate, while they avoid any personal tax. With the proposed reform, they will see the tax burden on these profits decrease without having a correspondingly higher personal tax burden. So a compensating tax would have to be studied for these entities.

15. G. Stuart Mendenhall, "Death and Taxes," *Annals of Internal Medicine* 149, no. 11 (December 2, 2008): 822–824.

16. Technically, it is a discounted number of expirations in the following ten years, where the annual discount rate is set at 100 percent per year. See Scott R. Baker, Nicholas Bloom, and Steven J. Davis, "Measuring Economic Policy Uncertainty," University of Chicago Working paper (2012).

17. Peter Schweizer, *Throw Them All Out* (Boston: Houghton Mifflin Harcourt Trade, 2011).

THIRTEEN

1. Bernard Lewis, *The Jews of Islam* (Princeton, NJ: Princeton University Press, 1984).

2. Adam Smith, *An Inquiry into the Nature and Causes of the Wealth of Nations,* Book 5, Chapter 2, Article 1 (1776).

3. Frank Ramsey, "A Contribution to the Theory of Taxation," *Economic Journal* 37 (1927): 47–61.

4. Martin Feldstein, "The Effect of Marginal Tax Rates on Taxable Income: A Panel Study of the 1986 Tax Reform Act," *Journal of Political Economy* 103, no. 3 (1995).

5. Thomas Piketty, Emmanuel Saez, and Stefanie Stantcheva, "Optimal Taxation of Top Labor Incomes: A Tale of Three Elasticities," NBER working paper 17616 (2011).

6. Jon Gruber and Emmanuel Saez, "The Elasticity of Taxable Income: Evidence and Implications," *Journal of Public Economics* 84 (2002): 1–32.

7. Henrik Kleven, Camille Landais, and Emmanuel Saez, "Taxation and International Migration of Superstars: Evidence from the European Football Market," NBER working paper 16545 (2010).

8. Another possible justification is that the government ameliorates some inefficiency in the financial market that prevents people from financing their investments with future returns. For instance, the government may be better at enforcing contracts than the private sector is (see my example in Chapter 8). If this is the case, the government should help the private sector enforce those contracts and not substitute for it. In practice, many policies targeted to reduce alleged credit inefficiencies are disguised income transfers.

FOURTEEN

1. Anton R. Valukas, "Examiner's Record," U.S. Bankruptcy Court, Southern District of New York, 2010, http://jenner.com/lehman/ (accessed February 10, 2012).

2. Author's calculation from the S&P/Case-Shiller Home Price Index.

3. Phillip Swagel, "The Financial Crisis: An Inside View," Brookings paper on economic activity, Spring 2009.

4. See Luigi Zingales, "The Future of Securities Regulation," *Journal of Accounting Research* 47, no. 2 (2009): 391–425.

5. J. P. Hawley and A. T. Williams, *The Rise of Fiduciary Capitalism: How Institutional Investors Can Make Corporate America More Democratic* (Philadelphia: University of Pennsylvania Press, 2000).

6. Zingales, "The Future of Securities Regulation."

7. International Monetary Fund, *Global Financial Stability Report: Meeting New Challenges to Stability and Building a Safer System,* World Economic and Financial Surveys, April 2010; Bank for International Settlements, *Triennial and Semiannual Surveys: Positions in Global Over-the-Counter (OTC) Derivatives Markets at End-June 2010,* Monetary and Economic Department, November 2010.

8. Zingales, "The Future of Securities Regulation."

9. This proposal is based on my joint work with Oliver Hart. See Oliver Hart and Luigi Zingales, "Curbing Risk on Wall Street," *National Affairs* no. 3 (2010): 20–34; and "A New Capital Regulation for Large Financial Institutions," *American Law and Economic Association Review* 13 no. 2 (2011): 453–490.

FIFTEEN

1. Laura S. Unger, "Testimony Concerning the Effects of Decimalization on the Securities Markets," U.S. Securities and Exchange Commission, http://tinyurl.com/6teffw5.

2. Raghuram G. Rajan and Luigi Zingales, *Saving Capitalism from the Capitalists: Unleashing the Power of Financial Markets to Create Wealth and Spread Opportunity* (New York: Crown Business, 2003).

3. William G. Christie and Paul H. Schultz, "Why Do NASDAQ Market Makers Avoid Odd-Eighth Quotes?" *Journal of Finance* 49, no. 5 (1994).

4. Lauren Cohen, Andrea Frazzini, and Christopher Malloy, "The Small World of Investing: Board Connections and Mutual Fund Returns," *Journal of Political Economy* 116 (2008): 951–979.

5. Maxim Mironov, *Economics of Spacemen: Estimation of Tax Evasion in Russia* (Chicago: University of Chicago Press, 2006).

6. Itzhak Ben-David, "Financial Constraints and Inflated Home Prices During the Real-Estate Boom," *American Economic Journal: Applied Economics* 3 (2011): 55–78.

7. Sumit Agarwal et al., "Inconsistent Regulators: Evidence from Banking," University of Chicago working paper (2011).

8. Louis Brandeis, *Other People's Money, and How Bankers Use It* (New York: Frederick A. Stokes,), p. 92.

INDEX